EX J. J.
LIBRIS Douglas

THE
DEVELOPERS

THE
DEVELOPERS

James Lorimer

James Lorimer & Company, Publishers
Toronto, 1978

ISBN 0-88862-219-8 cloth

Design: Don Fernley

6   5   4   3   2   1   78   79   80   81   82   83

Canadian Cataloguing in Publication Data

Lorimer, James, 1942-
  The developers

ISBN 0-88862-219-8

1. Land use, Urban — Canada.   2. Real estate business — Canada.
I. Title.

HD 316.L67   333.3'8'0971   C78-001444-8

James Lorimer & Company, Publishers
Egerton Ryerson Memorial Building
35 Britain Street
Toronto

Printed and bound in Canada

CONTENTS

For Carolyn

ACKNOWLEDGEMENTS

This book has been far more the product of a group effort than it might appear. I have had invaluable assistance particularly from Donald Gutstein and also from Valerie Wyatt and Jeff House in gathering research material. Travelling across the country for this book, both Donald and I received tremendous help from planners, citizen activists, administrators, politicians and librarians in every city we worked in. The newspaper clipping files and collections of documents kept by public libraries in these cities — Charlottetown, Halifax, Montreal, Ottawa, Toronto, London, Thunder Bay, Winnipeg, Saskatoon, Edmonton, Calgary, Vancouver, and Victoria — were essential to our research.

The book relies on a combination of primary and secondary source material. Of the secondary material, the rapidly growing Canadian literature on urban studies has been useful in some areas, but the most important source has been the work of journalists writing for the business pages and the local news pages of the country's newspapers. Time after time, a reporter's eye for a telling fact or a revealing quotation has been vital to making a point in the text. Where the information is recorded I have tried to acknowledge these sources.

In a text so full of names, dates, figures, and quotations, many from primary sources but many too from secondary sources, minor errors and confusions are bound to arise. In some instances I may have inadvertently reproduced errors from printed sources. No doubt this book will be read closely for all such flaws. Responsibility for them is mine, and I will of course correct all that are brought to my attention in subsequent editions of this book.

There were many people who played a part in turning this from an idea into a project. Among them were Graham Fraser, Peter Spurr (or at least his report), Robert Bryce and his one-sided Royal Commission on Corporate Concentration, John Aitkin and the editors of *Weekend Magazine* who sent me across the country to find out why suburban house prices were so high in February 1976, John Sewell, and my fellow editors of *City Magazine*. The people at the publishing company, particularly Evelyn Ross, Catherine Keachie and Linda Sheppard, who have gone through the long period it has taken to get this project finished, have been very generous and tolerant of the disruptions it has caused them. And it was a stroke of luck to find Seigfried and Heidi Haase's quiet and sunny suburban house in Herring Cove for two summers running to put the manuscript together. The comments and suggestions of George Baird, Kent Gerecke, Donald Gutstein and Grant Sinclair were especially useful in the revisions of early drafts of the manuscript.

The Canada Council's Explorations Program financed the cross-Canada research and travel which were essential to permitting me to write about the developers across the country. Osgoode Hall Law School and its former dean, Harry Arthurs, also provided some summer research assistance.

J.L.

PREFACE

I have finished this book with quite a different attitude towards Canada's urban land developers than I had three years ago when I began work on this project.

My interest in the land development industry came originally from my involvement in city politics. In the late 1960s and early 1970s I was active in several citizen groups that opposed controversial public and private development projects, and as a journalist I wrote about other groups in similar battles. I was startled to discover that city politicians at that time seemed ready and willing to do virtually anything the developers asked of them, whatever the arguments or strength of citizen opposition. I naturally wanted to know more about this industry and the sources of its tremendous influence at city hall.

I did some research on the industry in the early 1970s, not enough to understand it fully but sufficient to give me a healthy respect for the profits the developers were earning from their controversial projects. Other researchers and journalists also took up the subject, and a small number of books and articles began to accumulate that dealt with various aspects of the business.[1]

From my early encounters with developers, I knew that they were inventive, bright, tough political opponents, usually ruthless in pursuing their business interests. Their tactics (and indeed their personal styles) were often more reminiscent of organized crime than anything else, particularly the developers involved in the rough world of high-rise apartments. (Indeed, the connection between the developers and organized crime is more than a superficial one of style, as the report of an Ontario royal commission into violence in residential construction unions and the work of investi-gative journalist John Whitelaw have indicated.)[2] I saw business-men whose crude desire to make a fortune as fast as possible allowed no one and nothing to stand in their way. Fine buildings were routinely knocked down, homeowners harrassed to sell the houses they'd lived in for years, tenants used as hostages, politi-cians and planners paid off when necessary.[3] It was hard to see much that could be admired in an industry where these tactics were, and to a large extent still are, all in a day's work.

What brought me back to the subject of the development indus-try after a lapse of several years was an enormous research report done for the Central Mortgage and Housing Corporation, the fed-eral government's housing agency, which emerged from under wraps in Ottawa in 1975.[4] The report went into considerable detail about the suburban land development business. It indicated the remarkable and little known role of the larger and more respect-able corporations in the suburbs and in the dramatic escalation of house prices between about 1973 and 1975. I decided to undertake a thoroughgoing study of the industry, dealing with every major city in Canada and every major type of land development project.

I soon realized in my work on this book that the dealings be-tween developers and the local political scene create a misleading impression of the industry. Looking at the business side of the development industry provides quite another perspective. Here the developers' achievements are real and in many ways admir-able. They have created a completely new industry in this country in just over thirty years. They have built a new kind of business organization, the land development corporation, and they have in-novated and refined five new types of urban building forms un-known in Canada just three decades ago.

The developers have done their best to build cities that are suc-cessful in financial terms and that provide accommodation people need. Their best, as I argue later in this book, has had some very unsatisfactory consequences for our cities, for urban residents, and also for the economy as a whole. This is in part the developers' responsibility but it is also in part the fault of others. The devel-opers could have done, and many of them would have preferred to do, a far better job of contributing to a productive Canadian econ-omy. They have fallen short not so much as a result of their own greed or their own limitations as of the reluctance of the federal government and the financial institutions to ensure that entrepreneurial energy and Canadian investment capital are used in ways which are in the best interests of the country as a whole.

I have often been critical of the development industry in the past, and this book is certainly no public relations whitewash. Given the analysis I offer of the industry and the criticisms I and others have of its activities, many developers may feel that this book is a flat-out attack on them and everything they have done. Some may well respond in kind, and no doubt there will be those who will find fault with most of the facts, analysis and policy proposals I have to offer. Just before I launch into the controversy which is likely to come with publication of this book, however, I'd like to say clearly that I think the story of the development industry is a success story, though a flawed one. The developers as a group are an impressive example of the ability and energy of Canadian entrepreneurs in action. They deserve a considerable measure of admiration for what they have achieved. That is not to say that their dealings with citizens, customers and city hall are above reproach; rather it is to say that there is much more to the industry's story.

So I have finished this book with a sense of respect for what the developers have done, and a greater appreciation of the ways in which some of the industry's failings are not so much the responsibility of the developers themselves as of government (of whom the industry is already suspicious, though I think in a rather unconsidered way) and of the financial institutions (who are not at all the benefactors of the industry they are portrayed to be). How this effort at industrial innovation in the postwar Canadian economy succeeded, and how the development industry developed the flaws I believe will destroy it, are major themes of this book. It is time that the business side of an industry whose political activities are so well known emerge from the shadows, and that the developers' peculiarly Canadian story be told.

PART I

1

THE ENTREPRENEURS

Robert Keenan does not look much like the millionaire he is. He looks as if he would be a lot more comfortable out on a job site directing a work crew than he is sitting in his office in Thunder Bay. The office is in a modest new building just beyond the old Port Arthur downtown. It would be a good spot for a sheet metal business, and in fact the sign outside identifies this as the location of Keenan's family business, Keenan Sheet Metal. Keenan Sheet Metal, however, is a division of Headway Corporation, Thunder Bay's major land development company.

Just before going to talk to Keenan I met with a city planner to go over maps of who owns what land and what developments in Thunder Bay. Headway's name kept popping up in the conversation, a hotel here, a suburban shopping centre there, a downtown redevelopment project, subdivisions underway, a big land assembly to the south. "Who says Headway owns this town," the planner commented with a laugh at one point.

Thunder Bay is too big and too diverse to be one of those company towns that dot Canada's resources frontier. Right in the middle of the country, four hundred miles east of Winnipeg, nine hundred miles northwest of Toronto, it's a medium-sized city of just over one hundred thousand formed of the forced marriage of Fort William and Port Arthur. It has grown by more than 50 percent since the end of the Second World War. It has neither the air of a boomtown nor a sense of stagnation; it is neither wealthy nor depressed.

Robert Keenan began as a small businessman, and he and his

associate Harry Ganja decided to get into house-building in 1955 when business for small contractors was very good. He's taken up a whole range of opportunities since then, and today Headway is indeed a major presence in Thunder Bay. Keenan is still in the house-building business, producing one hundred or so of the six hundred new houses built in the city every year. He also services raw land and turns it into house lots for his own house-building operation and for other small builders. He has built the 307-unit seven-storey Hudson Heights apartment project, and owns another 1,600 rental units in other cities.[1] Keenan also put up 2,430 housing units in northern Ontario centres for the provincial public housing agency, Ontario Housing Corporation, up to 1972. At that time Headway had contracts for another $16 million in apartment projects, but only a year later the company was out of business, citing "severe losses" as the reason. Keenan owns half of the County Fair shopping centre in Thunder Bay, and 100 percent of the Northwood shopping centre. He was selected by city hall as the developer of a new downtown shopping centre, Keskus, on land expropriated by the city using federal-provincial urban renewal money. He owns a new hotel in town, the Landmark. The only major aspect of the land development business that Robert Keenan is not involved in is office buildings.

As a small house-builder who got bigger first in housing, then in land, and then in rental properties, Robert Keenan is much like many other entrepreneurs who went into the land development business in Canada in the 1950s and early 60s. What makes Headway's presence more noticeable than most is that Keenan and Headway virtually *are* the land development business in Thunder Bay. In most other cities there is more than one entrepreneur active in the local market.

It was, however, quite a long time before Headway expanded its operations to the point that it attracted attention and controversy in Thunder Bay. For its first decade, it was a growing house-building operation. By 1964, Thunder Bay builders were running into a problem that was common in the housing industry: a shortage of serviced lots to build houses on. Keenan and Ganja took up an idea that was also tried in other cities, usually successfully: they organized a builders' co-op, Lakehead Developers Ltd., which pooled the resources of a number of small residential contractors and used the money to assemble raw land, service it with roads, sewers and so on, and then sell the finished lots to the builders who were part of the co-op. Headway owned 40 percent of Lakehead, and Keenan was the company's president. For a time another Thunder Bay builder, Ed Mayotte, was the company's general manager but then an outsider, John Brown, was hired to do this job.

Organizing Lakehead and buying up a suburban land assembly was Keenan's first key move. The second came after the Thunder Bay builders had a few years of experience working closely together. In 1969-70, Keenan took over two major house-building firms that were part of the Lakehead group. Builders J. M. Kauzlarick, W. A. Boyd and T. O. Sohlman sold their companies for Headway shares plus seats on the company's board and a continuing role as senior managers. At the same time the remaining builder-shareholders of Lakehead were bought out, and the land assembly and development company became a wholly owned subsidiary of Headway. The outside builders were given seats on Lakehead's advisory board and a guarantee of a continuing supply of serviced lots. Keenan was now firmly in control of Thunder Bay's only large suburban land assembly. Partly to finance this step, Headway sold shares to the public in 1969-70, though effective control of the company remained with Keenan and Ganja. In the early 1970s, Keenan expanded Headway's activities to begin to build up a larger portfolio of income properties — shopping centres and hotels, in addition to apartments.

It was not long after the reorganization and public sale of shares that Headway began to attract criticism. The company was in the news in Ontario when opposition MPPs queried its remarkably successful record of being the lowest bidder on public housing projects. Then a committee of Thunder Bay's social planning council analyzed Headway's local operations and complained that it effectively dominated the local housing market because it was the only major private developer of suburban house lots.

"There was a lot of bad publicity around 71-72," Keenan recalled several years later. "Most people ignored it. We ignored it. The critics thought better of it, or moved away."

Nevertheless Headway had to expand beyond the Thunder Bay market if it was going to continue to grow. It moved into other kinds of business, cash and carry building supply stores and a chain of gas bars, but these added little to Headway's profits. A more successful strategy was expansion into housing in other cities similar in scale to Thunder Bay: Regina, Timmins and Sault Ste Marie. Headway even did some house-building in Toronto's suburban Mississauga.

Back at home, Keenan did more than wait for the critics to give up or move away. Headway stopped adding acreage to a land bank which CMHC researcher Peter Spurr pegged at 1,170 acres in 1973, enough land to provide all of Thunder Bay's new suburban lots for nine years.[2] It was the only developer assembly Spurr located in the city. Headway continued developing the land it held, and pressed the city to change its official plan so that a 680-acre parcel Headway owned south of the city would be designated for residential development. Keenan said that there were several reasons for Headway's not adding more acreage to its land bank, but allowed that the monopoly charges were on his mind. "That might have something to do with it."* A citizen's group complained to the Royal Commission on Corporate Concentration when it was touring the country in 1976 that there had been only one residential subdivision outside the Headway orbit developed in Thunder Bay in the past ten years.

It was just after the first controversy about Headway's monopoly in Thunder Bay that the price of suburban house lots exploded in most Canadian cities. Headway marked up its prices, but not as fast or as high as developers in other markets where there were only a few suppliers and tremendous consumer demand for new houses. Everyone in the business knew that the going prices in some cities

---

* Headway was not, however, entertaining the idea of getting out of the profitable land development business. There are other methods besides outright purchase of holding suburban land for future development: options to buy at a specified price, for instance, or joint venture agreements with owners. Headway's land bank was not growing, but the company was finding ways of keeping well ahead of its needs for raw land to service. In 1976, it optioned $1.2 million in development land, and in the 1976 annual report Headway assured its shareholders that its land inventories were big enough to "meet the operating requirements of existing divisions of the company into the early 1980s."

of $20,000 to $30,000 for ordinary suburban lots in 1973-75 were far above costs and were yielding enormous profits. Keenan himself suggested that some of the bigger developers in Winnipeg, Calgary, Edmonton and Vancouver were "embarrassed" by the profits they were making on their land development. New suburban houses were in short supply in Thunder Bay as late as 1976, when the market had slumped in many other cities. "The last six houses we had up for sale," Keenan said in February that year, "sold in less than two days."

At about the same time, Headway found itself in competition with another developer in its home market. A 50 percent interest in a local house-building operation, Mayotte Limited, was purchased by Nu-West Development Corporation Ltd. of Calgary, a larger and more profitable development firm run by another builder entrepreneur, Ralph Scurfield, who had the advantage of a much richer local market to operate in. Scurfield had been a long-time business associate of Keenan, and a director of Headway. He resigned from the Headway board only shortly before buying into Mayotte. If Keenan had finally encountered a competitor in the development business in Thunder Bay, at least it was someone he was well acquainted with.

Nu-West's move into Thunder Bay came not long before Robert Keenan would no doubt be thinking of retiring from the business. Several entrepreneurs like Keenan who got their start in the 1950s have sold their companies to the owners of the larger development firms, usually run not by their owners but by professional managers. Most of the industry is being swept up into half a dozen giant firms surrounded by another dozen or so medium-sized ones. A company like Headway is a likely takeover prospect. It has prospered modestly through the 1970s, going from before-tax profits of $1.8 million in 1972 to $2.8 million in 1973, $3.0 million in 1974, down a bit in 1975 and $3.0 million again in 1976. Keenan's own shares in the company were worth about $3 million on the basis of the 1978 stock market price, and would probably be worth more than that to a large corporate developer looking to take over Headway.

The new industry. The remarkable fact is that there was no such thing as the land development industry in Canada thirty or so years ago. Of course there were real estate speculators, property investors, landlords, builders and many other people who were used to making some money out of urban real estate, but there were no companies like Headway that combined elements of all of these activities.

Since the Second World War, the development industry has quickly grown to become a major presence in Canadian business. The thirty-five leading companies in the industry whose shares are sold on the stock exchanges had total assets, mainly land and buildings, of $6.7 billion at book value in 1976.[3] Two or three of the larger privately held developers for which published figures are not available would easily add another $2 billion to the total. These figures do not represent what the properties owned by the developers are worth today; rather they record what the developers paid for them. At current market values, the developers control something like $14 to $18 billion in urban real estate. That amount is only a fraction of the total of urban land and buildings in Canadian cities, but it represents an enormous concentration of wealth by a relatively small number of people in a short period of time.

The development industry has quickly passed through several major stages in its history. When it started after the war, there were literally hundreds of small entrepreneurs who saw the opportunities that were being created particularly in apartment and suburban house construction. Often, like Robert Keenan, they were already involved in a related field. Sometimes they were professionals working for other entrepreneurs already in the business. William Teron, for instance, was a draftsman working for a builder who decided that he could build houses too and make money. He built one, sold it for a profit, built a second, and went on eventually to develop a large land assembly he named Kanata on Ottawa's western edge. In 1973 Teron was given the job of running the federal government's housing agency, Central Mortgage and Housing Corporation, and later he became both head of CMHC and deputy minister of the federal government's urban affairs ministry.

Not all the entrepreneurs were as successful as Keenan or Teron, but most fared modestly well. Every city had its own crop of local developers by the late 1950s and early 1960s. They are a fascinating and diverse lot, but what they have in common is a strong sense of independence, aggressiveness, rough edges and self-centredness. They pushed ahead, they were willing to take risks, and their self-confidence increased as they witnessed their own, often amazing, success.

Bruce McLaughlin. Bruce McLaughlin's career demonstrates how successful a land developer in Canada can be, and how the very qualities which are strengths in the business can also lead to serious problems. McLaughlin has been involved in a wide variety of projects: he put together an enormously profitable suburban land assembly in Toronto, he bought up Grouse Mountain ski lift (with land assembly attached) in Vancouver, speculated on the success of the federal government's Mirabel airport (whose official symbol is now a white elephant, drawn as charmingly as the PR people can manage), and built the world's largest Holiday Inn for visitors to the Montreal Olympics in 1976 — except that the hotel was still incomplete in 1978. McLaughlin's company, S. B. McLaughlin Associates Limited, for a time looked like one of the most remarkable success stories in the land development business. A couple of years later, it was hard to believe that McLaughlin would survive the mess he got into, yet he emerged from his difficult period with control of the company apparently intact, projects underway again, and a land assembly which if it were sold today would yield his company a cool $300 million — at least — in profits.

McLaughlin started building when he was fifteen, in 1941. After the war he was a contractor for several years, building cottages in the summer north of Toronto and houses in the winter in Port Credit, then a small town fourteen miles west of Toronto on the shores of Lake Ontario. In 1953 he retired temporarily from business to go to university, first to the University of Toronto and then to Osgoode Hall Law School. McLaughlin got back into land development in the late 1950s with a strategy in mind. As he explained once to an interviewer, he was very conscious of the pressure of economic growth that was rapidly filling up hundreds of acres of land around Toronto with suburban housing and industry. That growth seemed to be headed west, partly because of the Toronto airport northwest of the city, partly because American investment in manufacturing was concentrating itself in the corridor between Windsor and Toronto. McLaughlin looked at Highway 10, which runs straight north from Port Credit to the town of Brampton, and realized that as Toronto sprawled westward Highway 10 would be another Yonge Street. So he began to buy up as much undeveloped land as he could on both sides of Highway 10.[4] There already was a small town at the crossroads of Highway 10 and Dundas Street. McLaughlin decided that if there was to be a new urban metropolis adjoining Toronto on the west, its centre would be at that intersection or close to it, so he bought land just north of it. When McLaughlin started buying, he was offering local farmers pretty fancy prices for land that would have been worth only $200 or $300 an acre in agricultural use. He was mindful of the need to obtain as much land as possible with his limited cash resources and tried to get people to sell for a little money down and a lot of money later.*

By the mid-1960s it was clear that McLaughlin had been right about the direction and scale of Toronto's growth. The provincial government was supporting suburban growth west and north of Metro Toronto where several large land assemblies had been put together in the 1950s and 1960s. Expensive trunk sewage services and expressway construction and expansion set the stage for large-scale residential construction in Bramalea, next door to Brampton; Erin Mills, an eight-thousand-acre assembly northwest of McLaughlin's lands; and Meadowvale. In 1967 the provincial government combined McLaughlin's old home base of Port Credit with Streetsville and the old Toronto Township, and called the result the Town of Mississauga. McLaughlin started developing the three thousand acres of Mississauga land he owned. In November 1968 McLaughlin and the town reached an agreement for the basis on which McLaughlin would develop his lands.** In 1970, McLaughlin

---

* McLaughlin's first major purchase in this key land assembly area was the 100-acre Fenn farm adjoining Highway 10 on the east side in 1959. He paid $4,000 an acre, $12,000 down, and $388,000 later. McLaughlin continued through the early 1960s buying directly from farmers who had lived on their land for years, paying $2,000, $3,000 and $5,000 an acre. Later in the 1960s McLaughlin was buying from small speculators and the price was up to $25,000 and $30,000 an acre for some parcels. (Title search, February 1976)

** With development about to start, McLaughlin as usual found himself short of cash. In 1969 he made a novel deal to get his hands on

received planning approval for 720 acres of residential land on which about eight thousand housing units from high-rise apartments to condominiums, row houses and single-family homes were built.[5]

McLaughlin's intentions for his land assembly were much more ambitious than just another Toronto bedroom suburb. If Mississauga was to be a city, and McLaughlin thought that's what it should become, he wanted to own and build its city centre. In 1970 he put up his first office building, a five-storey headquarters for his development company, where he thought the city centre should go. He then scored a crucial tactical victory by persuading the new town of Mississauga's council to trade in its old town hall (located on seven acres at the crossroads of Highway 10 and Dundas Street) for a fine new building in what McLaughlin had by now named his City Centre. In the early 1970s McLaughlin added an enormous regional shopping centre, named Square One, to the City Centre site. Square One totalled 1.5 million square feet, and boasted three department stores, a giant supermarket, and 170 other shops. McLaughlin tried to overshadow with sheer size the other nearby regional shopping centres, particularly the Sherway Gardens project, which he had tried and failed to stop at Ontario's planning appeal board, the Ontario Municipal Board.

While servicing and construction were going ahead on the Mississauga farmland, McLaughlin was expanding his land assembly activities. He added 1,047 acres in Georgetown, farther to the northwest and conveniently located at the end of a rail commuter service later instituted by the provincial government. He took over another development company that owned three thousand acres in Caledon, even farther from Toronto, in 1972. The wave of Toronto-area acquisitions climaxed in 1973 when, for $50,000 down and another $1.3 million in shares and promissory notes, McLaughlin bought the Chinguacousy Country Club, where he

---

$5 to $10 million to help finance his first major subdivision, Mississauga Valleys. The money was a loan from Imperial Oil Limited. As well as paying normal interest rates for the money, McLaughlin agreed to install Esso oil furnaces and hot water heaters in all the houses in the project, and that only Esso service stations would be built on the highways running along the perimeter of the subdivision. (*Globe and Mail* 20 December 1969)

liked to go riding. The purchase, however, was no rich man's indulgence: soon country club land was being developed for exurban estates.

By the early 1970s McLaughlin's company had reached the financial big time. Its revenues from sales of land and houses had been a few million dollars a year after it went public in 1968, and bottomed at $1.6 million in 1970, yielding a gross margin over costs of just $695,000 that year. Sales in 1971 were up dramatically to $20.5 million, yielding a gross margin of $7.8 million; in 1972 $28.3 million, yielding $9.7 million; and in 1973 $14.6 million, yielding $7.4 million.

Increased activity, higher sales and bigger profit margins do not mean the end of a developer's cash shortages. By 1971, McLaughlin's land assembly had cost the company a total of $72 million, of which about $31 million was cash and $41 million mortgages. But the price that land would sell for on the open market in 1971 was estimated, by an independent appraisal, at $135 million.[6] McLaughlin would have made a profit of $62 million on his land assembly if he'd closed up shop in 1971 and sold off his holdings at market value. Most of that profit, $54 million of it, was from his 3,500 Mississauga acres which had cost about $13,000 an acre and were now worth $28,000 an acre.

In order to turn some of that profit into cash so that the company could continue its development activities, McLaughlin came up with a scheme in 1973 to sell a 50 percent interest in all his undeveloped Mississauga lands to a consortium of Canadian financial institutions, the Royal Bank, the Toronto Dominion Bank, Canada Trust, T-D Realty Investments, and Canadian General Electric Credit Ltd. The price was to be $38 million, much of which would have been profit to McLaughlin. At the last minute, however, the deal fell through.

In the end, McLaughlin found another route to greater financial stability for his company. In 1974 he sold a sizeable minority interest in his personal holding company that controlled 45 percent of S. B. McLaughlin Associates shares. The purchaser was a company controlled by Edward and Peter Bronfman, one branch of the influential Bronfman family of Montreal, which is involved in other parts of the development industry as we will see in the next chapter.

The collapse of the 1973 land sale was only the beginning of McLaughlin's difficulties. In December 1973 there was an unexpected and potentially cataclysmic change in McLaughlin's world: the pro-development Mississauga town council was voted out; the old mayor defeated by a young reform candidate, Murray Dobkin; and a sudden shift in attitudes towards growth occurred at city hall. McLaughlin and other major Mississauga developers found that there were no more approvals readily forthcoming for development. Questions were being asked about whether Mississauga should favour intense commercial development on McLaughlin lands, or on the old crossroads centre of the community at Highway 10 and Dundas Street.[7]

McLaughlin's company was far too big to have all its activities depend on the shifting politics of one municipal council. Diversification outside Mississauga, and perhaps outside land development, was urgent. It happened speedily. In January 1974 McLaughlin got into the peat moss business by buying a company with peat operations (and large land holdings) in Manitoba, New Brunswick and B.C. In May 1974 McLaughlin took over Grouse Mountain Resorts Ltd., a chair lift and skiing operation in North Vancouver. McLaughlin saw Grouse Mountain through the eyes of a land developer, however, and realized that today's ski hill might be tomorrow's suburban land development. By 1978 McLaughlin was proceeding with development of land at Grouse Mountain's base.

It was expansion into Quebec that got McLaughlin into serious trouble. A purchase of 2,500 acres of land twelve miles from Mirabel did not seem like such a good idea after the airport got into operation and proved to be nothing like the magnet for industrial activity that had been expected. More serious, a first venture by McLaughlin into the hotel business, an 889-room building in downtown Montreal, ran into terrible construction difficulties. For a long time work was halted while the project was incomplete. McLaughlin's original hotel partner withdrew, and there were unsuccessful discussions with several hotel chains. McLaughlin took a loss in 1976 of $30 million on the hotel project, not a large amount in comparison with the company's huge potential earnings on its suburban land assemblies but substantial compared with pretax profits in 1976 of $8.3 million before the loss. "The trauma of the hotel would literally finish most land developers,'' commented financial analyst Ira Gluskin. "But McLaughlin has geographically prime land, and a president who knows the land development business and has good financial connections.''[8]

Adding insult to injury, McLaughlin invested in major capital improvements at Grouse Mountain for the skiing season of 1976-77. But there was almost no snow at all that winter.

In 1977, however, McLaughlin's company seemed to get underway again. Mississauga reform mayor Murray Dobkin was defeated in the 1976 municipal elections, and things were back to normal at city hall. The city was approving a plan for the City Centre area which gave McLaughlin the rights to build the lion's share of an enormous projected amount of offices, retail space, hotel rooms plus almost half the housing units. A controversial high-rise apartment project that had been bitterly opposed by a majority of the local council in Toronto's suburb of Etobicoke was finally approved by the Ontario provincial cabinet. McLaughlin made a deal with London, Ontario, housebuilders Matthews Group to sell a half-interest in 385 acres of Mississauga land for about $70,000 an acre, giving him a profit on the deal of an estimated $25 million and the prospect of another $25 million when the land was finally developed and sold. The Mississauga acreage, which to date had cost McLaughlin an average of about $15,000 an acre in purchase price, taxes and carrying costs, was now worth about $140,000. Construction was expected to begin in 1978.[9] In 1978 a deal was finally arrived at with the Sheraton chain to get the Montreal hotel back on the rails.

There was a loss of $11.1 million in 1976, and a tiny profit of $1.9 million in 1977. McLaughlin still held a land bank that now totalled 8,500 acres, including a sizeable portion of the original Mississauga assembly. Sold at its market value, that land bank would generate McLaughlin a profit of $300 million or more over its costs.[10]*

---

*This pendulum swing of tremendous success alternating with amazing disaster has deeply affected Bruce McLaughlin. At the peak of his early success in 1973, McLaughlin published a book entitled *100 Million Canadians*, in which he set out his views about a whole wide range of issues dealing with Canada's economic and social future,

There's no doubt now that McLaughlin was right when he looked north up Highway 10 from Port Credit and saw a pot of gold. There are no more than a dozen individuals in the country who have made as much money in real estate development as McLaughlin with his key 3,500-acre Mississauga assembly. But it's also obvious that for McLaughlin there is a lot more at stake than just money. He has constantly looked for new fields to conquer, and ways of going beyond the conventional achievements of other developers. His Mississauga City Centre scheme is far more ambitious than most people realize, a leap beyond the "new town" idea which (as we will see in a later chapter) started the postwar development industry off in Canada when E. P. Taylor demonstrated its potential in Toronto's suburban Don Mills. While shopping centre developers have been faltering because they have gone as far as they can on the basis of retailing facilities, McLaughlin is successfully combining retail space with offices, civic facilities, and industry on a massive scale. When the suburbs are obviously in trouble because of their reliance on cars as virtually the only mode of transportation, McLaughlin's shopping centre already has 3.5 million people coming to it by bus every year, in addition to the 4.2 million cars entering its parking lots as of 1977.

McLaughlin once explained his attitude to his business to an interviewer: "Being a developer is like being a hockey player...Everyone who plays hockey appreciates the sheer joy of gliding on the ice, but it's the goals that keep us going.

"It's a good feeling, all right, when you score a goal. But it doesn't last. You have to keep trying for another or you lose interest in the game."[11] McLaughlin has certainly kept on trying. And, after a bad period, he seems to be scoring again.

Government creates an industry. Like Robert Keenan, Bruce McLaughlin prospered because he recognized opportunities in

---

and argued that to be an independent and wealthy country we need a development strategy that would increase our population, largely through immigration, to 100 million by 2025. The book is not at all like the smooth, self-serving statements generated by anonymous public relations writers for senior corporate businessmen. It is the inspired statement of a free-wheeling entrepreneurial mind.

land development and house-building and seized them. These opportunities were not, however, unexpected and unplanned. They came about as a deliberate result of government economic policy, one goal of which was to see the emergence of a new kind of building industry in the postwar period.

It was Ottawa which took the lead in promoting this new industry in the early 1940s when the shape of the postwar economy was being planned. It was clear that there would be an enormous pent-up demand for new housing as soon as the war was over, and that there was a need to create a building industry almost from scratch. The federal government decided that it wanted more than just house-builders and houses; it wanted to see a new kind of building industry, with large corporations each capable of producing a sizeable quantity of urban accommodation. The field was no longer to be the exclusive preserve of small-scale independent businessmen as it had been up to the war.[12]

This policy arose from an unlikely but powerful coalition of interests in the 1940s. Supporting it were the spokesmen for corporate business in the federal cabinet, starting with C. D. Howe; left-oriented social policy thinkers whose roots were with the League for Social Reconstruction of the 1930s and the CCF, which was scoring major electoral successes in the early 1940s; and powerful senior Department of Finance mandarins whose job it was to manage the postwar economy so as to ensure full employment and avoid any recurrence of the Depression of the 1930s.

Housing had been a major problem during the war, particularly because rapid industrialization to produce war goods had created an urgent demand for urban accommodation for the new factory workers. There had been relatively little house-building in Canada since the 1920s, because of the impact of the Depression. One of the many aggressive and successful Crown corporations set up during the war by the minister in charge of war production, C. D. Howe, was Wartime Housing Limited. This government-owned, pioneering, large-scale house builder produced nineteen thousand new rental houses between 1941 and 1945. When the housing shortage continued after the war, Wartime Housing built another twenty-seven thousand units. This operation demonstrated that large-scale corporate enterprise could function as efficiently in house-building as in many other fields.

A preference for large corporations was the constant between federal economic policy in war and in peace. As the war came to an end, corporate business spokesmen in Ottawa did all they could to ensure that the publicly owned businesses set up during the war were dismantled or sold to private interests. The principle of private ownership was applied rigorously to housing. Said Howe at a federal-provincial conference on postwar economic planning in 1945, "It is the policy to ensure that as large a portion as possible of housing be built by private initiative."[13]

A related concern behind federal postwar housing policy was the desire to encourage home ownership. The political unrest of the thirties and the impact of the newly organized CCF made the Liberals look for social policy measures that they thought would moderate potential radicalism. Before the war, home ownership had been a minority phenomenon in Canadian cities, and was on the decline. In 1931 only 37 percent of all households in Canada's twelve largest cities were owner-occupiers, and by 1941 the figure was down to 34 percent.[14] The federal government resisted postwar pressures to stay in the house-building field and instead sought to encourage home ownership. In 1949 a decision was made to sell the Wartime Housing Ltd. units to their occupants. A new Crown corporation, Central Mortgage and Housing Corporation, was set up in 1946 to deal with housing policy and to lend support to the creation of a private house building industry.

The preference of corporate business representatives like C. D. Howe for large privately owned house builders was shared by intellectuals and planners interested in social policy and housing. The most distinguished of this group, Humphrey Carver, spelled out the argument in an influential 1948 book, *Houses for Canadians*, in which he complained about "the small speculative builder" who "undertakes the erection of only a few houses at a time," and urged the case for corporate-scale house builders:

> Fundamental changes in the [house-building] process can only be brought about through the entry of large-scale producers into the housing industry, and they could only enter upon such a business if they could anticipate a continuing market which would justify the necessary capitalization. Since the expectation of such market conditions has never yet

seemed justified, the organization of the residential building industry has stagnated. . . . It is only when large-scale projects are planned that there are opportunities to introduce important features of industrial organization aimed to reduce the high labour costs in the building process.[15]

A very wide range of programs to support, encourage, finance and subsidize the building industry was developed in Ottawa in the 1940s and 1950s. Two things were provided. First, a ready supply of investment capital to finance new urban construction was generated, so that potential homeowners could get mortgage money to enable them to buy new suburban houses even though their savings were modest and developers could obtain mortgage funds to build rental properties. Second, Ottawa arranged that most or all of the profits earned by companies in the land development business could be retained to increase their effective profit levels and provide them with cash to support rapid expansion and growth. It was a low-tax approach to the industry.

In the early years, Ottawa directly provided investment capital for new residential construction both to would-be home buyers and to apartment builders. Measures were devised to reduce or eliminate the risks of builders and developers, and of lenders in the urban real estate field. Gradually Ottawa phased out the bulk of its own direct mortgage lending as the financial institutions, the life insurance companies, the trust and loan companies and later the chartered banks were persuaded to undertake federally guaranteed low-risk mortgage lending. Many other policy measures were required from federal, provincial and municipal governments to create and support this new industry. The range of programs which were developed emerges later in this book as we look in detail at how the land development business works. The original justification for all these steps was the need to create almost from scratch the capacity to build the housing and other forms of urban accommodation urgently needed in postwar Canadian cities. But this had to be done in a way that conformed to the ideology and interests of the federal Liberals, and their preference for large corporate enterprise over both small business and any form of public or non-profit involvement in land and construction. The policy was a great success, on its own terms. Ottawa still looks with great favour on its own creation. Said John-Robert Gauthier, parliamentary secretary to the urban affairs minister, in a speech to the industry in 1976, "The federal government has had a good relationship with all segments of the housing industry for the past thirty years or so. . . . It's a good arrangement, and the best part of it is that the Canadian people are the direct beneficiaries."[16]

Yet the industry which has emerged is as dependent on measures of government support and subsidy as it was in its infant stage. Noted builder-developer Keith Morley of Richard Costain (Canada) Ltd. regarding government housing policies in 1976: "If subsidies were stopped today, the level of housing starts would probably drop more than 50 percent."[17] Even more important than subsidies are less visible structural supports provided to housing and other forms of land development through government regulation of mortgage lending and tax legislation.

It is also worth noting that what Ottawa set out to obtain is not in fact what it created. Federal policies were aimed at creating a *building* industry. What they have produced is a *land development* industry. A building industry, dominated by a few large, rational, vertically and horizontally integrated corporations would make its money out of construction. The land development industry, however, makes most of its money not out of new buildings but rather out of urban land. Bruce McLaughlin's fortune is based not on the volume of construction his company performs, but rather on the profits he makes out of the land he owns and develops. The same is true for the rest of the development industry.

Ottawa's Robert Campeau. No developer in Canada better illustrates the continuing and close relationship between government and the industry than Robert Campeau. Campeau is Ottawa's preeminent developer, the closest equivalent to Thunder Bay's Robert Keenan. Campeau has been involved in every aspect of land development: offices, shopping centres, hotels, high-rise apartments, industrial land, and suburban housing. His company has expanded its operations to Toronto, Montreal, Calgary and many other Canadian cities, but its base and the key to its strength is still Campeau's home town, Ottawa. As the home of the federal government, Ottawa is the closest thing to a one-industry city this country has, and Campeau has often seemed to be developer by appointment to the federal government.

Like many of the other early entrepreneurs, Campeau got his start in the burgeoning postwar suburbs. He built his first house in 1949 for $6,000, and sold it for $7,000. By 1953, his construction company had assets of $563,000. A little more than two decades later, assets had increased a thousand times, to $545,913,000. Campeau had ninety-seven acres of suburban land in his land assembly in 1953, ten thousand acres in 1975. The company's remarkable record of growth and diversification had not been trouble-free, but Campeau has survived the difficulties with his company intact, and with his control uncompromised.[18]

Robert Campeau is a colourful, highly visible figure in Ottawa. His controversial development projects and long-time running feud with Ottawa's one-time mayor Charlotte Whitton made his local reputation in the 1960s. Campeau is a construction man, interested in the complexities of how high buildings are put together and in ways of making the process faster and more efficient. His company is active in construction, and has diversified into the building materials and lumber business. He runs a dynamic one-man show, a fact which caused a firm of investment analysts writing about the company in 1972 to confess: "We are completely bewildered as to how operating control of this type of situation is effectively maintained..." In spite of outsiders' bewilderment, Campeau has steered his company from success to success. With a board of directors of mainly management types with a few outsiders, often associated with the federal Liberals (Senator Louis Giguere, Quebec Liberal party bagman involved in the Skyshops affair, was a director of Campeau for many years), Campeau has single-handedly built one of the country's largest development corporations.

Campeau's first major step beyond residential construction was the Place de Ville downtown office-hotel project in Ottawa. Built in 1966-67 on a site acquired from the Ottawa Transportation Corporation, Place de Ville included 565,000 square feet of office space rented by the federal government. Its twenty-five-storey and twenty-storey twin towers broke through a height maximum bylaw that had been in effect in Ottawa since 1914. Campeau waxed eloquent about this project; with it, he said, Ottawa "will go from the little league to the big league."[19] Noting that the hotel in the complex had major convention facilities, he said: "Think of what that will do to the downtown area. It will make it live again."

By 1968, Campeau was producing five hundred housing units a year in Ottawa. He had two thousand rental apartments, the city's largest downtown commercial development, and a major shopping centre underway. Campeau's suburban land bank had grown to three thousand acres. The assembly had cost $7.2 million, and an independent appraisal indicated that it was already worth $23 million at market value, giving Campeau a potential profit of $15.8 million.[20] Partly to give the company a needed infusion of cash, Campeau sold 1.6 million shares to the public that year at $10 each. But Campeau himself held 2.5 million shares directly and indirectly.

In 1970, in a surprise move, Campeau sold controlling interest in his company to Power Corporation, the Montreal-based conglomerate controlled by financier Paul Desmarais. Under the takeover deal, Campeau absorbed the real estate assets owned by Power Corp. including twenty-two shopping centres across Canada and three thousand acres of suburban land assembled by William Teron for further expansion of his Kanata project west of Ottawa. Apparently another aspect of the deal was that Campeau would receive additional cash and financing for its operations from Power's financial subsidiaries. When this did not happen, Campeau Corp. in 1972 borrowed $27 million in Swiss francs in Switzerland (no one knows from whom) and bought back the shares Power Corp. held.

During the 1970s Campeau carried on in the suburban housing business, but pressed its diversification into other cities and other types of development. It had taken over a major parcel of downtown waterfront land in Toronto from a small developer in trouble, and it started construction of a luxury hotel, the Harbour Castle, and an apartment building which was later converted into a condominium.

By 1974, Campeau was himself in trouble. The rising value of the Swiss franc against the Canadian dollar forced the company to take a loss of $13.8 million on its $27 million loan, giving it a loss in 1974 of $8.3 million. The Toronto hotel opened in April 1975 at a time when a number of new luxury hotels were opening, most of them in more accessible locations, and it lost money. The luxury condominiums on the Toronto waterfront were selling slowly, and though Campeau was ready to proceed with construction in 1976 of a second tower, he had to wait until 1978 for sales to justify going ahead.[21]

The continuing strength of the suburban land development and house construction was important in this period, with 1975 sales of $45 million running 60 percent higher than the previous high of 1973 and double the 1974 level. By this time Campeau's suburban land bank totalled ten thousand acres, most of it around Ottawa. There were a few other major owners of suburban development land, but none with anything like Campeau's holdings. Noted *Ottawa Journal* reporter Susan Riley on Campeau's land bank: "Wherever Ottawa-Carleton planners looked over the last few years, they saw Campeau, — sometimes alone, sometimes in partnership with other big builders."[22] Campeau's profit margins on sales of serviced lots from this land bank were high, particularly after the dramatic increases in lot prices that occurred in Ottawa and many other cities in 1973-74.

And just when Campeau seemed surrounded by trouble, two major projects in his home base got going which seemed good enough to keep the company out of difficulty. Already the largest single landlord of office space rented by the federal government, Campeau made a deal to build a massive $180-million downtown redevelopment scheme, Les Terrasses de la Chaudière, in Hull and to lease office space in it to the federal government for $14 million a year for thirty-five years. Part of the project was being built on land Campeau had leased (with no public tender being called) for $1 from the National Capital Commission. Ottawa got an option to purchase the project from Campeau at the end of thirty-five years, but for a price of $50 million. Opposition MPs calculated that Ottawa would pay as much as $508 million for the project which it could have constructed itself for only $140 million.

Equally important to Campeau was his success in winning an important battle he waged with another giant development firm, Cadillac Fairview, for the right to build a major new regional shopping centre in Ottawa south. Both firms had potential sites, and each argued that the area could support only one major project.

The two were in different local municipalities, and the politicians from each lined up behind their respective developers. Ottawa's regional government had the planning power to approve one and disallow the other, and in the end they selected Campeau. Coming in early 1977, it was a victory Campeau needed.

The large development company had by no means come to the end of its difficulties. The Harbour Castle hotel had to be turned over to Hilton to manage. A sagging Ottawa housing market led to a dramatic decision by Campeau in 1978 to close down his Ottawa house construction division and to lay off management employees. Evidently finding himself with more cash on hand than there were attractive development projects to invest in, Campeau undertook a buy-back scheme to purchase shares from shareholders who owned shares originally sold to the public for $10 each in 1968. The company was offering to buy back its shares at $7, less than the original offer price but more than they had been selling for on the stock market.[23] Even at the $7 price, however, the shares owned by Robert Campeau and on behalf of his family were worth $16.3 million. And, ignoring all its other assets, Campeau's land bank in Ottawa was worth at least $500 million more at current market prices than it had cost the company to buy and hold.

At the end of 1977, Campeau ranked fourth among the large public land developers in Canada, with assets having a book value of $625 million and a market value in excess of $1 billion. Robert Campeau's success at building this huge company was the more remarkable given the problems he had encountered and apparently overcome. But it's clear he didn't do it on his own, and he couldn't have done it on his own. Campeau follows the conventional form, and offers tributes in his annual reports to his employees and managers, what he has termed "this most important corporate asset: People!" Even more important, however, have been the many helping hands extended to Campeau by governments at every level. A public body was the source of the land for the Place de Ville project. Another public body was the tenant that made the project viable. The decisions that pushed suburban growth onto Campeau's land assemblies, decisions about expressway locations and trunk sewer and water planning, were made by Ottawa's local and regional governments. Provincial legislation made it possible for Campeau to convert his luxury downtown

Toronto apartment building from rental to condominium units when construction costs threatened to result in rents no one would pay. Just as Campeau was in difficulty elsewhere, the federal government agreed to rent enormous amounts of his office space on the Hull side of the Ottawa River. And the Ottawa-Carleton regional government used its planning power to award Campeau the right to build south Ottawa's new regional shopping centre, without having to face competition from a rival centre owned by a rival developer.

Campeau has seized many opportunities in land development, and has used them to build a huge and very profitable company. But like all other developers, he has had the benefit of a wide range of government policies and practices which together created the circumstances in which the development industry was able to emerge and grow so far and so fast in postwar Canada.

Entrepreneurs across the country. Every Canadian city has a group of entrepreneurs who have built the local development industry. They are usually people much like Robert Campeau, Bruce McLaughlin and Robert Keenan: independent, strong-minded, anxious to run their own show, likely to make big mistakes as well as to score major successes. They are usually figures on the local political scene, partly because their projects are highly visible and political, partly because the developers love being in the public spotlight even when they are being cast in the role of villain. There are occasional exceptions to this: Edmonton's Donald Love, a latter-day manager turned entrepreneur, has built his Oxford Development Group Ltd. into the country's third-largest public developer quietly and unobtrusively. Toronto's Reichmann family, with its private, family-owned Olympia & York Development Ltd., has stuck mainly to downtown commercial-office projects and has assets that rival the largest public companies. The Reichmanns attract little public attention. But most of the entrepreneurs are too strong-willed and self-centred to keep out of public view.

Vancouver. The most visible Vancouver developer of the 1960s was Tom Campbell, who boasted that he was worth millions in real estate and was therefore qualified to be mayor of the city. Everyone in Vancouver could point out Campbell's curved high-rise apartment building as they crossed the Burrard Bridge. Campbell was duly elected (on a platform of opposition to one major development project, Pacific Centre in downtown Vancouver) for two terms. He consigned himself to political and media oblivion one fateful night at a public meeting called to discuss the proposed Third Crossing of the Burrard Inlet which Campbell dearly wanted to build to serve a large project proposed by the CPR on Vancouver's waterfront. The crossing opponents were a wide coalition of Vancouver's citizens and citizen groups. Campbell accused the hall-full of people of being "Maoists, Communists, pinkos, left-wingers and hamburgers."[24] Campbell was retired by his party in favour of a less controversial mayoralty candidate in the next election.*

Edmonton. Edmonton's most diversified developer-entrepreneur is Charles Allard, a medical surgeon who owns Allarco Developments Ltd. At last count, Allarco had 8,800 acres of development land on the outskirts of Edmonton, plus land for development in Mexico, Las Vegas and southern Ontario. Allarco also owned the Oliver's restaurants in Edmonton, Winnipeg and Calgary, two television stations, a trust company, a life insurance company, and an executive jet transportation company. Allard's range of interests and activities is very unusual for the land developers. His most recent project, an enormous petrochemical plant, marks a major step from commerce and financial activities into

---

* Campbell's place as Vancouver's most plain-spoken developer was taken by Jack Poole, who with his entrepreneurial associate Graham Dawson is the controlling shareholder of Daon Development. Daon is a phenomenal financial success, with assets that jumped from $18.8 million in 1969 to $123 million in 1976, and with declared profits going from $1.7 million in 1969 to $15.3 million in 1976. Poole denounces government regulation of the development industry ("Bureaucratic pollution seems to increase almost hourly," he said in 1975) and land speculation ("The present environment on the Lower Mainland is an absolute utopia for the speculator," he said in 1975) and then coolly informs his shareholders every year about how much Daon's own suburban land assemblies and property holdings are worth compared with how much they cost. In 1974, the company would have realized profits of $21 million if it had sold off its holdings at their market value. Three years later, the figure had reached an amazing $126 million. (*Financial Post* 5 April 1975; *Vancouver Province* 2 June 1975; Daon Development Corporation *Annual Reports* 1974-6)

basic industrial development. In a generally right-wing Edmonton business community, Allard is noted for his very conservative views. Noted one business acquaintance: "He makes Ronald Reagan look like a radical."

Calgary. Calgary has seen many of the most aggressive and successful early entrepreneurs in the development business sell their companies to larger, professionally managed corporations. This has left Ralph Scurfield, a house-builder who is the principal shareholder in Nu-West Development Corporation Ltd., the city's leading active entrepreneur. Scurfield's own firm is one of the four major suburban land developers in Calgary, and he is also by far the largest single shareholder in a second major firm in the same business, Carma Developers. Carma started as a co-op of forty Calgary house-builders, but by 1972 Scurfield owned 38 percent of its shares and by 1976 this was up to 47 percent.

Winnipeg. Like other prairie cities, Winnipeg has produced a group of local entrepreneurs who together dominate the suburban land development and house construction business. The most successful of these was certainly the Simkin family, who started out after the war in the used construction equipment business.[25] They soon expanded into fields that used this equipment, particularly road paving and services installation in the suburbs. When business was restricted by the unwillingness of suburban municipalities to take on the debt burden of new services, the Simkins took municipal bonds instead of cash in payment for their work. The bonds were redeemed as the serviced lots were built on. The family company, BACM, began to buy raw land and sell serviced lots to house-builders, extending generous terms to the builders while being careful to regulate the number of lots each one bought to the amount BACM thought that builder could handle. The company expanded across western Canada, entered the heavy construction field, and took over the Calgary-based Engineered Homes Ltd. construction and land development firm in 1967. But in 1968 the Simkins decided to get out, and sold a majority of the shares in BACM to Genstar Ltd., a conglomerate of Belgian parentage. Genstar acquired most of the rest of BACM's shares in 1970, and since then it has used the company as its key operating arm in the land development and house construction business in western Canada. Saul Simkin remains a director of Genstar, but he plays no active role in the company he built which is now run by a group of professional managers.

London. In London, Ontario, two local builders, the Matthews Group Ltd. and Sifton Properties Ltd., between them dominate the suburban land development field. The most colourful local developer, however, is Gordon Jeffery, of the powerful Jeffery family that figures prominently in the city's influential economic elite. Jeffery is distinguished for having got rezoning for a 220-unit apartment building, and then going to the local committee of adjustment to get permission for a minor variation in the plans to add one more unit to the building.[26] The single unit, however, turned out to be four storeys on the top of the building, incorporating living quarters for Jeffery plus a 120-seat concert hall with its own pipe organ. Jeffery is something of a music enthusiast. On the top of his penthouse, there was even to be a helicopter landing pad. The next-door neighbour, a rug-cleaning business, took exception when Jeffery got his "minor" variance, but as they were appealing the decision Jeffery's building was under construction and the excavation undermined one of the walls that adjoined Jeffery's site. This led to a lawsuit, and before the suit got to court contractors managed to drop a load of bricks on the rug cleaner's roof and front awning. Eventually Jeffery bought the property, $1,035,000 for the building, and another $450,000 from Jeffery and his contractors for damages.

Toronto. Toronto's rich real estate market has produced a large crop of developer entrepreneurs, of whom Bruce McLaughlin is only one. The professional managers of both foreign-owned (mainly British) and Canadian-owned corporations played a larger role in suburban land development in Toronto than in many other cities, but many entrepreneurs' fortunes have been made in suburban land. An equally attractive field from the mid-1950s was apartment construction. There are four large high-rise developers in Toronto, and only one of these, Cadillac, chose to go public and diversify aggressively beyond the Toronto market into other land development activities. The office development field alone has been the basis of the billion-dollar privately held Olympia & York firm owned by the Reichmann family.

Montreal. Unlike almost every other Canadian city, Montreal has no large developers whose fortunes are based on suburban land development and house construction. Housing in Montreal is still provided by hundreds of small builder-entrepreneurs, as it was in other cities until the process of corporate concentration got underway starting in the mid-1950s. The difference, as we will see, results not from the lack of potentially successful entrepreneurs in Montreal, but from the government context in which Montreal developers operate. In other development fields, Montreal has its fair share of local entrepreneurs and more than its fair share of foreign investors who have played a very significant role in apartment and office development. Foreign interests have had a major role in land development in most major Canadian cities, but the extent of their participation in Montreal (ably documented by financial journalist Henry Aubin in his book *City for Sale*) is unusual.[27] And no one has ever succeeded in matching the entrepreneurial talent demonstrated in Montreal two decades ago in the late 1950s by the extraordinary American wheeler-dealer developer William Zeckendorf, whose Place Ville Marie project (on land owned by the CNR) is still the textbook example of how to build an immensely profitable downtown office-shopping-hotel complex.

Halifax. In Halifax, the only prominent local entrepreneur in land development is Ralph Medjuck. Medjuck's flamboyant life style is mocked, behind his back, by the city's conservative old-family scions who dominate its social, political and economic life, but then Medjuck has done little to endear himself to the local establishment. In 1966 he opposed a development company put together in an afternoon at the Halifax Club, according to the story, whose shareholders included two of the city's wealthiest families, the Jodreys and the Sobeys.[28] Medjuck and the rival company both sought the right from city hall to build a downtown development project on land expropriated by the city using the federal government's urban renewal program. The establishment firm won with its Scotia Square plan, but ironically this company is one of the least profitable public real estate corporations in Canada. Medjuck has had his own problems in the small and not very lively Halifax real estate market. He has put up almost every kind of development, but he has run into difficulties several times and been bailed out by government, on one major occasion by city hall, on another by CMHC. In the face of a depressed and overbuilt local market, Medjuck decided in 1978 it was time for a change and went to Edmonton to start some projects there. He certainly didn't leave Halifax behind, however; when a group of Halifax aldermen were in Edmonton in summer 1978 attending a conference of city politicians, who should turn up to have breakfast with them at their hotel but Ralph Medjuck.

End of the buccaneers. Owning their own companies, managing them every day, making the major decisions without having to answer to anyone except themselves, seizing opportunities where they saw them, squeezing the most they could out of their limited cash resources, the entrepreneurs got the land development industry going in Canada and built the first successful development corporations. They were not alone in the industry; right from the beginning there were some professionally managed corporations, often the offshoots of British property companies, active in land development in Canada. The entrepreneurs were, however, the industry's powerhouse.

In one way, it was the entrepreneurs' very success which led to the second phase in the development industry's history: a period of takeovers and mergers starting in the mid-1960s, when smaller firms were put together to make larger ones, and the large corporations went on developing as they absorbed even more of the entrepreneurs' companies. Sometimes it was the more successful entrepreneurs taking over the less successful ones, but usually it was the owners of the larger development corporations with far greater access to capital resources that conducted the takeovers. With the takeovers usually came the replacement of the entrepreneurs with professional managers. By the late 1970s, some of the original entrepreneurs were still around, and so were many other small-time operators in every field of land development in every city. But they were now on the fringes of the industry, its inspiration perhaps, not its guts. "The industry," sighed Richard Shiff, president of Bramalea Limited, has "come to the end of the buccaneer era."[29] It was now to be governed by the corporate managers in pursuit of moderate but regular increases in assets, cash flow and profits, without the spectacular swings between success and trouble that characterized the entrepreneurial era.

About the book. This book is the story of this amazing and important new industry. Having looked at the entrepreneurs who founded it in this chapter, in the next chapter we see the corporate managers in operation in three investor-owned development corporations: Cadillac Fairview, Trizec, and Genstar. In the final chapter of this first part of the book, there is an explanation of how the development corporations work, where their money comes from, what they do with it, and how they make their profits.

Though the industry is diverse in the size and ownership of its firms, it is quite uniform in terms of what it actually produces. The development industry builds five major types of development projects, which together have accommodated the needs of urban Canadians for work space, living accommodation, shopping and entertainment. Each of these development types — the corporate suburbs, high-rise apartments, industrial parks, office towers, and shopping centres — is a postwar innovation. Each is a radical departure from the way the same needs were accommodated before the Second World War. Not only was 1945 a watershed because it marked the beginning of the development industry; it also marked the point when the new building forms began to emerge that now provide the bulk of new urban space. The chapters in Part II look in turn at each of the major types of development projects which the developers have built. These chapters examine the physical features of these building types, public attitudes towards them, and their impact on people's lives. They also deal with the intriguing details of how these projects are put together and financed by the developers, how they are subsidized directly and indirectly by government, how profitable they are, and how these profits affect how much people pay for houses, apartments, offices and shopping centres.

The final part of the book considers the consequences of the industry's achievements. The developers have had enormous impact on the lives and daily activities of most urban Canadians. Their financial success has been dramatic enough to affect the distribution of wealth in the country. The industry has also exercised a major influence on the overall pattern of economic activity in Canada. All these effects are examined briefly. The question of whether the industry's current methods of operation are the most satisfactory and acceptable way of providing the urban accommodation the country requires is also assessed. The industry's very success has generated a political movement which has had an impact in many cities, and which has both posed a challenge to its power and generated an alternative to the industry.

The concluding chapter returns to the point where we began, to reconsider the question of how successful the industry's founders have been and how much they have added to the country's growth and prosperity.

2

THE CORPORATE MANAGERS

The entrepreneurs have never had the field of land development entirely to themselves, even in the industry's early days. At the same time as they were learning how to succeed in this new business (and while that leading Canadian entrepreneur, E. P. Taylor, was showing how to do it with his path-breaking suburban housing development in Toronto, Don Mills) the professional managers of investor-owned development corporations were beginning to make their mark in Canada.

The most important manager-run companies in the industry's first years were owned by British property investors. British property firms had experience in land development and ownership, and they saw opportunities to repeat in postwar Canada the successes they already had in Britain. For the British upper class who are often involved in these companies, it was perfectly natural and part of a long tradition to look to invest some of their wealth in property in this part of "the Empire." By the end of the 1950s, many British property companies' subsidiaries were looking for projects in Canada. "Clearly our property groups will colonize on a tremendous international scale," crowed Britain's *Investors' Chronicle* in 1961. "The British property man has no peer."[1]

Canadian investors were considerably more cautious about moving into land development until the entrepreneurs had demonstrated its profitability and long-range potential.* There was an

---

* Land has of course always been closely intertwined with the activities of the largest corporations and wealthiest families in Canada.

occasional exception to this rule, for instance, a group of institutional investors put together by A. E. LePage, a firm of real estate brokers, who formed Markborough Properties, whose principal asset was a land assembly near Bruce McLaughlin's properties west of Toronto. The most prominent early involvement by major Canadian investors in land development was that of both branches of the Montreal Bronfman family. Cemp Investments, set up by Sam Bronfman, got into land development early. Edward and Peter Bronfman have had a smaller but important role in the industry.

In spite of their late start, the investor-owned professionally managed development corporations have now emerged to dominate the industry in Canada. They have two key advantages over the entrepreneurs: money and staying power. The investor-owned corporate developers use their access to cash and to investment capital to buy up the entrepreneurs' companies when their founders are ready to sell. Given how valuable these companies

---

Land policies were used by colonial administrations to promote the kind of society they wanted to see in Canada before 1867. When that original Canadian corporation, the Hudson's Bay Company, sold its vast territories to the Canadian government in 1870 it was careful to hold on to a substantial portion of the best farmland in the west, and also to keep what turned out to be well-located pieces of urban land. The promoters of the CPR were well aware that they were in the land business as much as the railway business, as their decisions about where to run their lines and locate their facilities would dictate the basic shape of urban western Canada. George Stephen, one of the CPR promoters, said that the syndicate "looked for a return of our capital and a legitimate profit entirely to the growth of the country and the development of the property." The Hudson's Bay Company and the CPR's land company, the North West Land Company, together owned fully five-ninths of all the arable land in the west when settlement got underway.

Most large Canadian corporations and wealthy families stood back from land development, however, during the industry's early post-war stages. Later on, after the entrepreneurs had demonstrated the enormous potential and profitability of land development, major corporations and wealthy families like the Woodwards, the Eatons, the Richardsons and the Sobeys began to get directly involved themselves in land development. (Frank Lewinberg, "Towards a political economy of urban land and housing: the Canadian situation," [M.A. thesis, Massachusetts Institute of Technology, 1973] p. 37, p. 50)

are, the investors and their development corporations are really the only potential buyers. Also, the entrepreneurs usually run a one-man show, with no one else having the resources to follow them, so when they are ready to bow out of their companies they are almost certain to be replaced by professional managers.

The managers running land development companies operate very differently from the entrepreneurs. Instead of being independent and answerable mainly to themselves for their mistakes, they are accountable to boards of directors representing their companies' owners who hire and fire them. Instead of the brilliance and self-confidence of the entrepreneurs, the managers follow well-beaten paths and repeat proven formulas.

Discussing the role of the entrepreneurs in land development in 1973, Bruce McLaughlin noted: "My skills are as an entrepreneur, a responsible, creative developer. Without things to develop I'm dead." In the light of McLaughlin's career, it's easy to see what he means. But he went on to say: "Without things to develop, my company is also dead."[2] That, it should be noted, is not quite so. Run by professional managers, McLaughlin's firm could carry on undertaking new development projects. Even if it halted its development work, however, the company would still receive indefinitely an annual flow of income and profits from the portfolio of property assets it has built up. The entrepreneurs live and die, but their companies can go on forever — run by professional managers.

The record of the managers as initiators of development projects, however, is poor compared with that of the entrepreneurs. The growth of the investor-owned development corporations has come not from successful development projects they have undertaken as much as from takeovers of successful entrepreneurs. In the end, the professional managers' strength and control of the development industry comes more from the money they have access to than from their own skills as developers.

In this chapter we look at the three biggest investor-owned development corporations in Canada, Trizec, Cadillac Fairview, and Genstar. The three are a study in contrasts. Trizec was a British-controlled corporation that was once the largest public real estate developer in Canada, but which has had serious problems and lost its pre-eminence. Cadillac Fairview is now number one in the industry, and is the combination of an investor-owned company with a group of early industry entrepreneurs who have effectively permitted their company to be taken over by the Bronfmans while they turn themselves from entrepreneurs into professional managers. Genstar is a company with long roots in European capitalism, and its hard-nosed understanding of the realities of corporate power and monopoly profits means that it will soon emerge as a far more powerful corporation than any of its developer rivals, and one of the dozen richest corporations in Canada.

Trizec. Trizec is the unlikely creation of a U.S. wheeler-dealer developer and two of those "peerless" British property men. Trizec's history as a major Canadian property corporation starts with a rather unlikely deal in the mid-1950s between William Zeckendorf and Donald Gordon, then president of Canadian National Railways.[3] Gordon and Zeckendorf agreed that the CNR would give Zeckendorf a ninety-nine year lease on a Montreal block of land which had previously been part of "the hole" where the CNR's tracks emerged from a tunnel under Mount Royal. The deal was approved by the federal government in 1957, and construction began in 1958 of a project Zeckendorf named Place Ville Marie which today totals 2,929,000 square feet of offices and commercial space.[4] Ironically Prime Minister Louis St. Laurent wanted to prevent the CNR's downtown Montreal land holdings from falling into the hands of foreign interests, and this led to stipulations about the structure of Zeckendorf's development company, intended to ensure that the development be undertaken by a Canadian company.[5] But as it turned out, Place Ville Marie became the key asset of the largest foreign-controlled development corporation in Canada.

Zeckendorf was constantly short of cash, and he made a deal in 1960 with a British property group around the merchant banking firm of Philip Hill to create Trizec, owned 50 percent by Zeckendorf's "Canadian" company and 50 percent by the British firms, Second Covent Garden Property and Eagle Star Insurance.[6] Into Trizec went ownership of Place Ville Marie and several other key Zeckendorf projects in Canada, including the Yorkdale regional shopping centre in Toronto and the Halifax Shopping Centre. More money problems in 1963 led to Zeckendorf's being forced to give up his interest in Trizec, and the British group had to reconcile themselves to hoping that the losses they'd had on other deals with Zeckendorf in the U.S. would eventually be made up by profits on the Canadian properties they now owned through Trizec.[7]*

The British installed Canadian professional managers to run the Montreal-based company. James Soden, described as a hard-driving, plain-talking Montreal lawyer, had been Zeckendorf's lawyer in the Montreal operation of Zeckendorf's company, and he went on to be Trizec's senior full-time manager.[8] "I'm the one who's known for inheriting all the lemons," Soden later told a newspaper reporter, referring to Zeckendorf's Canadian projects owned by Trizec, but in fact there turned out to be nothing sour about Zeckendorf's work.[9] Toronto's Yorkdale shopping centre, where sales are more than $150 million a year, is considered by the industry to be the country's single most profitable regional shopping centre.[10] The Halifax Shopping Centre, an enclosed mall built by Zeckendorf in 1960 with an Eaton's store across the street from Simpsons' long-time suburban location, was successful in capturing shopping dollars from a large number of residents in a city with one of the country's weakest downtowns.[11] And Zeckendorf's Place Ville Marie is held in awe by Canadian developers as the pioneering project which has spawned imitations in the downtowns of all major cities, none of them more successful.[12]

Soden and Trizec's managers saw themselves as pioneering professional property corporation management. "We're seeing a lot of transition in the industry," Soden told the *Financial Post* in 1971. "There's a much higher degree of professionalism now. We now have a Canadian Institute of Public Real Estate Companies — in fact, because I was pressing so hard for it, I wound up as first president. Real estate is much more technically oriented than in the past, and our people have to be increasingly better qualified.

---

* The British interests behind Trizec were later brought together into a single company, Star Holdings, which was in turn an arm of a vast British real estate operation, English Property. English Property had a number of senior officers on Trizec's board and exercised effective control of the company. Later, Canadian directors from companies taken over by Trizec were added to the board but English Property remained firmly in charge of its Canadian subsidiary.

It's not any more the seat-of-your-pants business it was, and this gives me a great deal of satisfaction."[13]

What replaced entrepreneurial ideas and deals were long-term corporate planning and strategy. Trizec's managers didn't talk much about this in public at first, but by the mid-1970s they were stressing the desirability of buying and holding strong commercial properties for profits and capital gains over the long term. Said Trizec president William Hay in 1974, "Our original investors were long-term investors so we're not traders, we're not buyers and sellers."[14] What the company looked for was growth: "Steady and sustained earnings growth rather than one that has big bumps in it," said Hay. In the 1975 annual report, Soden talked about Trizec's long-standing policy of "concentrating its investments in those projects which offer the greatest opportunity for appreciation over the long term."

This strategy of acquiring good developments and holding onto them both for the profits they generate every year and for accrued long-term increases in value has been central to British property investors, and it is not surprising to find it being used by Trizec. How it was implemented by the company's Canadian management, however, is another matter. As they waited for Zeckendorf's fundamentally sound properties to turn profitable and convert annual losses into annual profits, which happened in 1967, Trizec's management concentrated on adding to their properties by buying other companies owned by real estate entrepreneurs. There were some early purchases of individual buildings, and then a Winnipeg-based string of nineteen nursing homes.[15] In 1970, there was a reorganization of Trizec's major British shareholders and Star Holdings chairman Robert Potel arrived in Canada to announce that Star and Trizec together were putting $10 million into a new company that would expand in the U.S. property market.[16] In fact, however, Trizec's biggest step came in 1970-71 when it purchased Cummings Properties Ltd., owned by Calgary's Cummings family, and a few months later Great West International Equities, controlled by the Hashman family of Calgary and Edward and Peter Bronfman of Montreal. Cummings yielded Trizec $100 million in properties: twenty-one office buildings, four shopping centres, seven apartment buildings and some projects under way at the time of the purchase.[17] Great West added more commercial properties, including a string of Hyatt hotels, and yielded Trizec a further spread of its assets across the country instead of the original focus on Quebec which worried stock analysts.[18] The takeovers made Trizec by far the largest Canadian public real estate company in 1972.[19] Rumours of further takeovers circulated in 1973-74, first with British-controlled MEPC and later Cambridge Leaseholds with whom Trizec had got to the point of agreeing on a price before calling the deal off.[20]

Trizec's spectacular growth in assets continued through the 1970s, going from $545 million in 1972 to $896 million in 1976. But profits were still a problem, especially in comparison with the other quickly emerging giant, Cadillac Fairview. In 1975 profits actually went down substantially from 1974, interrupting a regular series of annual increases that (with a slight deviation in 1970) had gone on for the previous decade. In 1975 Trizec was also having difficulties with the federal government's Foreign Investment Review Act, which required that acquisitions by Trizec be subjected to FIRA review.[21]

The first shakedown came in 1975 when Trizec sold off some of its small holdings of apartment buildings. Later in the year, Trizec sold $100 million in properties to another large developer, Bramalea Consolidated Developments Ltd.[22] This included Trizec's interests in two Hyatt hotels, and some shopping centres in western Canada. Soden put the best possible face on the situation by saying that the properties were "programmed for disposal" and explaining that Trizec was holding only "the best" of its developments.[23] "There are," he said, "shopping centres and there are shopping centres."

The second Trizec shakedown came only months later, in a dramatic announcement that Edward and Peter Bronfman were assuming "control" of the company. They had become involved in Trizec originally when they received 9 percent of Trizec's shares in the takeover of Great West International Equities. The deal was a complicated one, and was evidently structured with both eyes firmly fixed on the FIRA and the need to establish that Trizec was Canadian-controlled. The arrangement was that Trizec's British parent would put 2.9 million of its Trizec shares into a new Canadian holding company.[24] Edward and Peter Bronfman also put 1.1 million shares into the holding company. The company was struc-

THE CORPORATE MANAGERS 39

tured to give the Bronfmans 50.01 percent of the voting shares, and 49.99 percent of the equity. English Property was left with 2.1 million Trizec shares which they did *not* put under the control of the Bronfmans. With about eight million Trizec shares outstanding, that ensured that English Property would remain in a powerful position at Trizec, independent of the new holding company that controlled four million shares. To guarantee that the Bronfmans would not run away with Trizec, there were further complications.[25] The Bronfmans agreed that there would be no amendments to the constitutions of the holding company or Trizec, and no change in the nature of the business. Moreover, sales by either group of their shares were subject to complicated restrictions. How much involvement English Property still had in Trizec was illustrated by the fact that the British company continued to include Trizec as one of its subsidiaries in its reports to shareholders, but this apparently made no impression on FIRA, which duly ruled that Trizec would now be considered a Canadian-controlled company.*

Even with the $100 million sale of the properties to Bramalea, 1976 wasn't much better than 1975 for Trizec. Operating profits for the year were actually down and only the extraordinary profit from the Bramalea sale pushed up year-end after-tax profits to $4 million, a small margin for a property company whose assets totalled $896 million, and *less* than the level achieved in 1972 when Trizec was at the top of the heap for a brief period of pre-eminence. And 1977 was not much better, with assets up to $931 million and after-tax profits only slightly up to $4.8 million.

The new set of Trizec managers faced exactly the same problems as the old ones had. The company had some office building

---

* No one was more astonished by this deal than Trizec's professional managers. "We didn't know it was coming," a vice-president said flatly. Chief executive officer Soden said he was "taken by surprise." Someone else, who refused to be quoted by name, told business press writers that Soden in fact was "outraged." A few months later, Soden's name disappeared from Trizec's list of officers and directors. Peter Bronfman became the new chairman of the board and a new manager, Harold Milavsky, was appointed president and chief executive officer. (*Globe and Mail* 27 April 1976 and 9 June 1976)

projects on the Place Ville Marie model underway, but the office space market was soft in every Canadian city except Calgary and Edmonton. A controversial downtown project discussed for seven years in Winnipeg was about to get started, though the downtown office market there was weak.[26] There was little growth opportunity in the shopping centre field.

No doubt by accumulating assets Trizec was building up investments which in the end would make hundreds of millions of dollars in profits for the company's owners. But current operating profits were low, and the company was paying almost all of them out in dividends. It is impossible to tell for sure from the available financial information, but it's quite possible that Trizec's total profits would have been higher more than ten years later if it had added nothing to William Zeckendorf's Canadian projects acquired in 1963. Place Ville Marie, Yorkdale and the others are now very profitable developments. Nothing the professional managers have added to Trizec can come close to matching them. William Zeckendorf's best ideas are still Trizec's main asset.

Cadillac Fairview As Trizec was getting bogged down in the mid-1970s, another firm leapt ahead to become Canada's largest publicly listed real estate corporation. At the end of 1977, Cadillac Fairview Corporation Limited had assets of $1,269,243,000. It owned fifteen thousand rental housing units; it had thirty-five shopping centres across Canada including some of the very largest and most successful; it owned 1.3 million square feet of rental space in industrial parks in Canada and another 2.8 million square feet in the U.S.; it was working on the development of an eight-thousand-acre suburban land assembly in the Toronto area, Erin Mills, which will eventually house 170,000 people; and it owned interests in downtown retail-commercial projects like Vancouver's Pacific Centre and Toronto's Eaton Centre which totalled 2.3 million square feet of retail space and 6.8 million of office space.[27] In its 1977 annual report, Cadillac Fairview boasted that it was satisfying "the public's demands for all types of residential, commercial and industrial accommodation."

Cadillac Fairview's huge scale is a result of a merger in 1974 of three large development corporations. What was unusual about this merger was that the entrepreneurs didn't drop out after they had sold their company to large corporate interests. Instead, they made the transition from independent operators to professional managers, and ended up with a large share of the management power in the new corporate giant. Cadillac Fairview brought together Cadillac Development Corporation Ltd., Fairview Corporation and Canada Equity & Development Company Ltd. The entrepreneurs owned the controlling block of shares in Cadillac, which got its start in the high-rise apartment business in Toronto in the 1950s. Fairview was controlled by Cemp Investments, owned by one branch of Montreal's Bronfman family, and had always been run by professional managers. The third company in the merger, Canadian Equity and Development Company Ltd., was E. P. Taylor's vehicle for big-time real estate projects in the 1950s. Cadillac and Fairview had joined together to control it in the late 1960s. In the new Cadillac Fairview giant the Cadillac entrepreneurs strengthened their position in the short term enabling them to obtain the heavy financing they needed to undertake large-scale projects. Cemp and the Bronfmans gained the accumulated portfolio of Cadillac projects and the expertise of the Cadillac entrepreneurs functioning as managers. For the moment at least, Cadillac Fairview seems to have the best of both worlds: of the entrepreneurs, and of the professionally managed corporations.

Cadillac Development began as a small apartment developer in Toronto in 1953.[28] The founders were two engineers, A. E. Diamond and Joe Berman. Their earliest projects (still owned by Cadillac Fairview) were small rental projects: Ainsley Court with 56 apartments in 1958, Woodview Court with 59 in the same year, Ivordale Maisonettes with 60 units, Craigton Court with 125. In 1961 two more professionals were brought into Cadillac as owners: Jack Daniels, an architect, and Gerald Shear, a chartered accountant. Cadillac was getting involved in large high-rise projects by the mid-1960s, and by 1970 it owned 10,462 apartments, all in the Toronto area, many in high-rise buildings. In 1971, when 1.8 million Cadillac shares were offered to the public at $6.25 each, the four principals owned seven million shares between them valued at $44 million.

From about 1970 on, Cadillac worked vigorously to diversify its activities. Foreseeing that the high-rise rental apartment boom would not continue indefinitely, it moved into suburban land development, office building construction and shopping centres. By 1974, Cadillac had added another three thousand apartments including two buildings in Ottawa and one in Hamilton, but it was also very active in building residential properties for sale. It had accumulated a suburban land bank of several hundred acres, it built six shopping centres with another six underway, and constructed four office towers.*

Like Cadillac, Fairview launched its real estate development activities in the 1950s. The company was a vehicle for real estate investment for Cemp Investments, a trust fund set up by Sam Bronfman for his four children Charles (C), Edgar (E), Minda (M) and Phyllis (P) and his grandchildren. The initial guiding force was Leo Kolber, a law school classmate of Charles. Kolber did his first development project while he was still in law school, building six houses in the Town of Mount Royal.[29] Charles first benefited from Kolber's skills in 1953, when Charles lent Kolber the money

---

* Like the other major Toronto high-rise developers, Cadillac often ran afoul of citizen groups who opposed their land assemblies and their redevelopment plans. The worst blow to Cadillac's corporate reputation came in 1971 when Cadillac was pushing (along with its partner in this project, Greenwin Developments) for city hall approval of a high-rise scheme in the Quebec-Gothic area of Toronto. The local ward alderman, Ben Grys, had given strong support to the rezoning at the city's planning board and was also promoting it at city hall. Another Toronto alderman, John Sewell, revealed that Grys's wife had owned two houses in the redevelopment area which had been sold to Cadillac and Greenwin. The sale had been for a combination of cash and mortgages. While Grys was fighting for the rezoning at city hall, his wife held mortgages totalling $125,000 which might well never have been collected if the rezoning had not gone through. While a majority of Toronto aldermen rallied behind Grys and argued he'd done nothing wrong, Sewell and another reform alderman, Karl Jaffary, went to court and got a decision confirming that Grys's actions were improper. Still Grys refused to resign, a majority at city hall refused to censure him, and it was only at the next election that he finally lost his seat. Looking back on the affair two years later, Cadillac president A. E. Diamond made a lame excuse for Grys: "Unfortunately," said Diamond, "Mr. Grys forgot he had a conflict of interest." (John Sewell, *Up Against City Hall* [Toronto: James Lorimer, 1972] pp. 118ff.)

for a successful deal in Westmount. It was in 1957 when Sam Bronfman reached out and brought Kolber in as a professional manager to run Cemp. Fairview's real estate activites took off in December 1958 when, in a fascinating deal with an intriguing early real estate investment company, Principal Investments Ltd., Fairview acquired sixteen land assemblies and two shopping centres under construction.[30] The deal gave Fairview several suburban shopping centres around Toronto, the sites for the Bonnie Doon shopping centre in Edmonton and North Hill in Calgary, and several others across the country. By 1974 Fairview had seventeen shopping centres altogether, including Polo Park in Winnipeg (completed in 1959), Fairview in Saint John (1960), Cedarbrae in Toronto (1960), Les Galeries d'Anjou in Montreal (1968), and the Georgian Mall in Barrie (1973).[31]

Even more impressive than its shopping centre operation was Fairview's ability to mimic the prototype provided by Place Ville Marie and to produce successful major downtown redevelopment projects in other large cities. The first of these was Toronto's Toronto-Dominion Centre, built between 1967 and 1974 with 2,781,000 square feet of offices and 174,000 square feet of shopping space. Ownership is shared 50-50 by Cadillac Fairview and the Toronto-Dominion Bank. The T-D Centre was followed by a repeat performance with Vancouver's Pacific Centre, similar black bank office towers and a shopping mall that included an Eaton's store. Ownership here was split one-third each between Fairview, Eaton's, and the T-D Bank. By 1974 Fairview was diversifying its activities, not just geographically (the company had already spread out its investments across Canada) but by type, getting involved in a small way in the residential business.

Indirectly, Fairview already had a substantial interest in housing through a 30 percent interest (Cadillac had 41 percent) in Canadian Equity and Development Company Ltd., purchased in 1968. Canadian Equity was set up in 1953 by E. P. Taylor and it carried out Taylor's path-breaking suburban development in Toronto's Don Mills. The obvious success of Don Mills led Taylor in the mid-1950s to put together a seven-thousand-acre land assembly, Erin Mills, on the west edge of Toronto.[32] Development was begun here only after 1970. Canadian Equity also owned two large shopping centres in Don Mills, constructed in 1955 and 1960, a small plaza called York Mills shopping centre, built in Toronto in 1953, and a centre in Hamilton.[33]

In 1965, Canadian Equity went public and in 1968 most of its shares were bought by Cemp-Fairview, Cadillac, and a third company, Canadian General Securities Ltd. This third company later dropped out, leaving Canadian Equity controlled by Cadillac and Cemp-Fairview. Canadian Equity was not the only contact between Cadillac and Fairview. Before 1974, Cadillac had undertaken construction projects on behalf of other developers, and in this capacity it had built a number of Fairview's shopping malls.[34]

In October 1973 Cadillac and Fairview announced that they were discussing a possible merger. Details of the deal were released in February 1974. It seemed like a logical move, combining companies with different development strengths and putting the Cadillac entrepreneurs in a position to take advantage of the financial strength represented by Cemp and the Bronfmans. Under the terms of the merger, Cadillac's controlling directors received nine of the seats on the new eighteen-person board of directors. Cemp had the other nine. Cadillac's leading light, A. E. Diamond, became chairman of the new company. Second in command and president of the new company was Neil Wood, formerly the senior manager of Fairview. The three other Cadillac principals carried on as vice-presidents of the new company.

The financial community and stock analysts were impressed with the merger. The only unhappy voices came from minority shareholders in Canadian Equity.[35]* They argued that Canadian

---

* Instead of owning about 30 percent of a company about to commence large-scale and highly profitable development of a single large land bank, Canadian Equity minority shareholders were going to find themselves owning a small percentage of the shares of a much larger company. The potential profits on Erin Mills land development would have made a big impact on the financial statements of a small company like Canadian Equity, but in a giant firm like the merged Cadillac Fairview they would have far less effect. Dissident shareholders estimated that Canadian Equity would make profits of at least $500 million developing Erin Mills's seven thousand acres. That figure is not unreasonable. They argued that Canadian Equity stock prices had been depressed only because the stock market had discounted the possibility of the development being successfully

Equity was only about to start realizing the enormous potential profits in its land bank assembled almost twenty years earlier. These profits would be greatly diluted if Canadian Equity were merged into the much larger Cadillac and Fairview operations. Cadillac and Fairview saw this issue from a different point of view. They knew the profits were coming, and they wanted to avoid paying any corporate tax on them. The merger would make that possible. Analyst Ira Gluskin, author of a study on Cadillac Fairview for the Royal Commission on Corporate Concentration, thinks that this was "an important but probably not the crucial factor" in the decision.[36] Whatever the interpretation, no one disagrees that Erin Mills began to generate enormous profits at about this time, and that the merger enabled Cadillac Fairview to pay virtually no tax on them.

A few months after the merger was completed, Cadillac Fairview produced financial statements showing total assets for the new company at $921 million, compared with $782 million the previous year.[37] In 1976 the total was up to $1,045 million, in 1977 to $1,269 million and in 1978 $1,405,020,000. Toronto's Eaton Centre, third in the company's huge downtown redevelopment projects, was completed early in 1977 and after only a few months — to the general astonishment of the Toronto financial community, who didn't think there would been enough time to establish

---

completed. And they claimed that fair terms would be something like four Cadillac Fairview shares for each Canadian Equity share, instead of the 1.2 offered.

Since Canadian Equity's board of directors was made up completely of nominees of Cadillac and Fairview at the time, it was obvious that they had a conflict of interest in making a decision about whether to approve the proposed merger with Cadillac and Fairview. The conflict was recognized, and instead of the directors making any decision the matter was referred to a special shareholders' meeting. Unattached Canadian Equity shareholders lobbied against the merger with other independent shareholders, and hoped that Cadillac and Fairview would continue to recognize their conflict of interest by not voting their 71 percent interest at the meeting. Cadillac and Fairview did in fact vote in favour of merger, but so did owners of 93 percent of the independently held shares. The final vote in favour: 4,500,000 to 18,000. (*Financial Post* 2 March 1974, 25 May 1974; *Globe and Mail* 31 May 1974, 24 May 1974; *Toronto Star* 23 May 1974, 1 June 1974)

the project's success — Cadillac Fairview announced they were starting work on the second phase of the project.[38]

Meanwhile the company was taking advantage of its enormous financial strength to expand. The first effort was an attempted take-over of another large Canadian development corporation, Abbey Glen, but Cadillac Fairview lost out to another giant, Genstar. By mid-1976 Cadillac Fairview was shopping around for another possibility and had come up with Irvine Co., the owner of an eighty-thousand-acre land assembly forty miles south of Los Angeles.[39] The Irvine Ranch is the largest corporate land development in the U.S., and Cadillac Fairview was bidding against several American competitors. Their offer was $159.8 million in cash and $120 million in notes, totalling $279.8 million. That works out to $3,500 an acre, not a high price to acquire a land assembly which on its own comes close to equalling the hundred thousand acres of suburban land owned by all of Canada's major developers according to a 1973 CMHC survey. While in the end the Irvine Ranch bid was unsuccessful, it seemed to gain the company respect from the Canadian financial community and Cadillac Fairview continued to move slowly into the U.S. market by undertaking development projects in major American cities.

Cadillac Fairview is proud of its record of success. Cadillac's entrepreneurs and Fairview's managers have succeeded in creating a corporation as diverse as the real estate industry itself. Cadillac Fairview will get bigger; it will absorb more small Canadian development corporations; and it will probably expand further in the U.S. It has taken the idea of a land development corporation as far as it can go. For an example of what lies beyond the Cadillac Fairview model, it is necessary to look at a more varied and sophisticated corporation, Genstar Ltd., which understands far better than Cadillac Fairview the underlying principle of the land business: monopoly.

Genstar. When federal planners in 1943-44 were plotting the course of the Canadian postwar economy and looking for the emergence of a "rationalized" housing and construction industry, Genstar Ltd. did not exist. Genstar is now one of Canada's top twenty-five companies. It probably ranks among the most important dozen corporations in the country in terms of the sheer scope of its economic power.

The contrast between a giant like Genstar and one like Cadillac Fairview is remarkable. In spite of its size, Cadillac Fairview looks at the world with a small investor's mentality. It seeks safe investments where it can turn a dollar now, and hope for a big return eventually. Genstar is a corporate giant that aims at oligopoly power in every industry where it is active.

Genstar got its start in Canada in 1951 as a new company sponsored by an old, rather obscure but very powerful Belgian multinational, Société Générale de Belgique.[40] Genstar was first named Sogemines, reflecting the interest of its Belgian parent in getting involved in mining and resource extraction in Canada. Almost from the beginning, however, construction was the field that attracted the company's interest. It started in construction materials (cement, glass) and branched out into other construction supplies, construction equipment, construction firms, and finally land. In fact Genstar has treated urban land and construction in Canada as if they were resources like oil, nickel, or uranium. The pace of Genstar's growth is incredible. In 1958, the company's sales were $13.2 million and its after-tax profits were $1.9 million.[41] In 1976, only eighteen years later, sales were up sixty-seven times to $888 million. Profits in 1976 were $55.7 million.

The company which gave birth to Genstar is itself a remarkable organization. Originally incorporated in 1882 in Brussels, it is a giant in its own country. It functions as a bank, holding 40 percent of all the bank deposits in Belgium, and controls one-fifth of Belgium's industry.[42] It had extensive operations in the Belgian Congo, reportedly controlling two-thirds of the Congolese economy and extracting minerals via its related company Union Minière. In the modest and understated language of multinational corporate business, Genstar said of its founder: "Société Générale ... is a major developer of industry in Europe and other parts of the world and has substantial interests in chemical and cement industries.[43] No one is sure exactly who owns Société Générale. Since the company's founding it has had close links with some of Europe's oldest and wealthiest families, and even now the Belgian royal family is closely associated with it.

Financial writer Henry Aubin reports that at the top there are connections between Société Générale and both the Rothschilds
and the Rockefellers[44] and that the current deputy chairman of
Genstar in Canada, Charles de Bar, is in fact Archduke Charles of
Hapsburg. De Bar divides his time between Montreal, Genstar's
head office, where he serves on the executive committee of Genstar's board of directors, and Brussels where Société Générale's headquarters are located. De Bar appears to be the principal
link between Société Générale and the Genstar operation. The
complete story of Société Générale's ownership is hidden behind bearer shares, whose owners remain unidentified for tax
reasons.

Genstar is reluctant to discuss the exact nature of the relationship between it and Société Générale. In 1970, Genstar told
shareholders of a company it was buying that Société Générale
"may be considered to be a 'parent' of the company within the
meaning of the Securities Act of 1933."[45] In 1975 corporate researcher Donald Gutstein found information showing that Société Générale owned 5 percent of Genstar's shares directly, and
another 4 percent indirectly.[46] But the *Financial Post* reported a 5.8
percent direct holding and a 15.7 percent indirect holding through
companies in which Société Générale had a minority (but
presumably controlling) interest.[47] In 1976, Henry Aubin notes,
Société Générale was sending bulletins to its shareholders de-
scribing Genstar as "one of the companies belonging to the
Société Générale de Belgique group."[48] No doubt the intrica-
cies of these relationships explain why, in a 1976 Genstar prospectus issued in connection with $50 million in debenture funds the
corporation was raising, neither Société Générale nor any of
its related companies appeared on the list of shareholders owning
more than 10 percent of any class of shares in the company.[49] The
one company which did appear on the list was Associated Portland
Cement Manufacturers Limited, a British firm with 10.3 percent of
Genstar's voting shares, which it acquired when Genstar purchased control of its Canadian subsidiary, Ocean Cement.

Genstar got off to a relatively slow start in Canada. It established
Inland Cement in 1954, Iroquois Glass in 1958, and Brockville
Chemicals in 1959. In 1965, Genstar amalgamated with these three

operating subsidiaries and set the stage for a second, more ambitious round of expansion.[50] Independence had come to the Congo in 1960 and, after financing the abortive attempt to sever the mineral-rich Katanga province from the rest of the country, Société Générale was looking for a safer and more welcoming arena for its activities abroad. Apparently Canada fit the bill.

Iroquois Glass was sold in 1967. Three companies involved in manufacturing and marketing fertilizers were taken over in 1967-68 for about $18 million.[51] Genstar added Ocean Cement & Supplies to Inland Cement, paying $2.4 million in cash and $29.9 million in debentures, and making Genstar one of the two cement manufacturers in western Canada with 46 percent of total manufacturing capacity west of Ontario as of 1972.[52] In 1973, Genstar paid $50 million for a large Montreal cement, building materials and construction business, Miron Company Ltd.[53]

Genstar's key move into construction and land development came in 1968 when it acquired the large Winnipeg-based firm, BACM, from the Simkin family and other shareholders. In 1970 Genstar increased its shares in BACM from 54 to 99.9 percent. The total cost of this acquisition was about $40 million.[54] Genstar launched BACM on a series of major takeovers of existing Canadian companies which, according to one analyst, cost another $28 to $30 million. In the Calgary area alone, these takeovers were numerous. Acquired in 1968 were Standard Holdings Ltd. and Jeffries Developments Ltd., which between them held 70 percent of Consolidated Concrete, a ready-mix firm. In 1969 BACM took over Conforce Products Ltd; in 1971 Sun Gold Investments Ltd. and its subsidiaries, Kelwood Corporation Ltd. and Keith Construction Ltd., which were active in land development, house construction and building supplies. In the same year BACM took over Borger Construction Co. Ltd., a residential and municipality utility installation contractor, and Calgary Pipe Ltd., a manufacturer of concrete pipe. Genstar is also active in the resource transportation industry. It owns Island Tug & Barge on the west coast, which it supplemented with Vancouver Tug Boat under the name Vanisle in 1970.[55] Then it took over McAllister Towing and Salvage Ltd., which was added to a group that included Seaspan International and Vancouver Shipyards.

There was a brief pause in the string of takeovers in 1974-75 as Genstar dealt with the difficulties created by the Foreign Investment Review Act. But by 1976 the process was started up again, with the $49 million acquisition of Abbey Glen, at the time Canada's sixth-largest public land development corporation. Since 1965 Genstar has grown from assets of $100 million to $1.2 billion mainly by taking over existing businesses in Canada, many of them Canadian-controlled. Though the company has diverse interests and appears to be expanding in several different directions at once, there is in fact a clear logic to its corporate strategy. The aim is not just profits, but maximum corporate power and control in its field of interest. In each specific industry, maximizing corporate power means first of all becoming one of two or three large firms supplying most or all of the market. In cement manufacturing in western Canada, Genstar is one of two firms. In suburban land development of cities like Edmonton, Calgary and Winnipeg, Genstar is one of three or four corporations supplying most of the new suburban lots. In gypsum wallboard, Genstar is one of four large suppliers in western Canada. In a classic oligopolistic situation, the two or three "competitors" may fight with each other over shares of the market, but generally they respect each other's position and adopt a live-and-let-live attitude.

Genstar has been explicit about its desire to dominate every industry where it is active. "Genstar's policy is to seek 'to become a major factor in each of the industries in which it operates'," the corporation told the federal Royal Commission on Corporate Concentration in 1975.[56] To underline the point Genstar went on to say, "In housing and land development, Genstar has expanded the level of dwellings built by its housing subsidiaries, and has become a relatively major factor in the western Canadian housing market. In addition, an inventory of land for future development has been purchased since 1971."[57] Size is not Genstar's only objective: equally important are lower costs than competitors'. "Genstar furthers the rationalization process in industries where it is striving to attain a significant share of the market and a low-cost position," the brief said.[58] A low-cost position permits Genstar to keep prices down when it so chooses, giving it the potential to drive competitors out of business or into the arms of an acquisition-hungry company like Genstar. As Genstar said in its royal commission presentation: "Genstar's position is that [corporate] concentration *per se* is a legitimate and desirable economic process."[59]

Corporate power and control do not stop at dominance of a single industry, whether it is land development or cement or gypsum wallboard. Genstar is also highly conscious of the supplier relationships that exist between companies. House construction companies need developed suburban lots and construction supplies. Land developers need concrete pipe and ready-mix concrete. Builders need kitchen cabinets, gypsum wallboard, cement blocks, plumbing, heating and electrical supplies. Concrete suppliers need cement, aggregates, and transportation. In its expansion policy Genstar has aggressively pursued companies that complement each other in this way.[60] Transportation comes from Vancouver Shipyards and Seaspan International. Cement is manufactured by Inland Cement and Miron. Concrete products, gravel, aggregates, concrete block and concrete pipe are produced by Consolidated Concrete, Ocean Construction Supplies, Redi-Mix, and Building Products and Concrete Supply. Gypsum wallboard comes from Truroc Gypsum Products. Kitchen cupboards come from Sun Gold. Development land comes from Abbey Glen, BACM and Kelwood. House construction comes from Engineered Homes, Keith Construction and Abbey Glen. Genstar's internal sales in 1976 were $87 million, a hefty portion of the total of its $253 million sales in housing and land.[61]

Using its internal corporate buying power, Genstar gives itself a substantial advantage in its expansion policies. It extends its corporate control and power, since the corporation reduces its buying from outside suppliers and captures business and profits from itself, for itself. Meanwhile, outside suppliers are weakened because they lose their Genstar business to Genstar subsidiaries. This process, termed vertical integration by economists, has been largely ignored by other land development companies while Genstar has pursued it aggressively.

Genstar's corporate policies have landed it in the Canadian courts twice in recent years. In 1973-74, Ocean Cement and the other western Canadian cement manufacturer, Canada Cement Lafarge, were charged — and convicted — of "conspiracy to curb competition by fixing prices and allocating jobs."[62] Asked by the Royal Commission on Corporate Concentration why the two firms were selling at identical prices in 1976, Genstar Western president Ross J. Turner said lamely that if prices were not the same "he would sell all his cement before we would sell ours."[63] Once again that year, both firms tendered substantially identical prices to the City of Winnipeg for its cement supplies. It was the tenth year in a row that the city had received virtually identical bids from the two cement manufacturers.[64]

In 1976, Genstar's gypsum wallboard manufacturer, Truroc, was charged with "conspiring to lessen competition in the production, manufacture, sale or supply of gypsum wallboard" in every province from Manitoba to B.C. from December 1968 to March 1974.[65] Ironically, the charge was laid only months after Genstar officials had explained to the royal commission how their aggressive entry into the wallboard market had kept prices low.[66] Genstar and the other accused pleaded guilty and were convicted in 1978. Genstar was fined $75,000.

The most dramatic testimony to Genstar's success at becoming "the major factor" in industries in which it is active is in the suburban land development business in major western cities. In Edmonton, Calgary and Winnipeg the bulk of all suburban lots are now supplied by three or four major land development corporations. Genstar is one of those. In Edmonton and Calgary, one of BACM's chief competitors was Abbey Glen. When in 1976 Genstar took over Abbey Glen's operation, it greatly increased its dominance of the housing industry in western Canada. Concerned in 1973 about Genstar's activities in house construction in Calgary, the city's chief commissioner arranged for a $78,000 study of the company by two independent analysts, one an accountant and the other a lawyer. The study came to some strong conclusions. Wrote the authors, "Genstar activity levels in the land development, construction, and housing industries could, if they have not already, attain a position where its activities could be deemed capable of unduly preventing or lessening competition or adversely affecting prices in one or more of the said industries to the detriment of the resident of the City of Calgary."[67]

Calgary mayor Rod Sykes was apparently furious that senior officials had ordered this study without his approval.* The report was released to the public after a major controversy in the middle of an election campaign in which Sykes was running for re-election.

---

* When the report arrived on Sykes's desk, he stalled for seven months before doing anything with it because, he claimed, he was waiting for a legal opinion. City lawyer Brian Scott advised that the report should be kept confidential because the city might be sued if it were published. He didn't see much point in forwarding it to Ottawa because federal combines legislation has "no teeth" and corporations found guilty are punished only with small fines.

Somehow, one of Sykes's opponents in the 1974 mayoralty race had learned of the report. Queries from a Calgary alderman drew public admissions of its existence. Still, Sykes and city officials tried to sit on it. Sykes said that the city would be "blown out of the water" by massive lawsuits if the report were released. Simultaneously, however, Sykes said that it contained very little: "It contains less information than a recently published article in the *Financial Post*, and you can get that for 50 cents." Other politicians suspected that the report contained more complete information on the land holdings of Calgary's large developers, and they were correct. As the election neared, the aldermen voted 10-3 to give themselves copies of the report. Then they released it to the public, at $25 a copy.

Genstar's response was first to issue a press release expressing "shock and surprise at the release of the so-called 'secret report'... [which] is loaded with inaccuracies, distortions and unsubstantiated allegations and draws a number of false and erroneous conclusions." Simultaneously, again taking a line already followed by Sykes, Genstar suggested the report contained little that was new, its factual information available from already published documents.

What were the alleged inaccuracies? One of the report's authors, asked that question, muttered and mumbled but in the end refused to say anything about the report or the controversy it had created. Genstar's corporate counsel, James Unsworth, claimed that the report's map of land holdings was inaccurate, and said that Genstar objected to the report's statements that Genstar was big and that it was foreign-owned. Why was the company so anxious to try to get the report off the public record? "We said that we'd sue the city because we meant it. We did it for our employees, for the ten thousand people wondering if they work for some big foreign-owned company that is causing harm to this country." (*Calgary Herald* 1, 4, 5 October 1974; *Calgary Albertan* 1, 4, 8 October 1974, 28 February 1975; telephone interview with James Unsworth)

Genstar responded by claiming that it was inaccurate and distorted, and after the election was safely over with Sykes re-elected Genstar wrote to the city reportedly threatening a seven-figure lawsuit.[68] Neither Genstar nor Calgary would make that Genstar letter public. The upshot was a letter from the City of Calgary to Genstar acknowledging that the report was misleading and inaccurate. Interestingly enough, there was never a proper public statement of exactly what those inaccuracies were. But the City of Calgary statement was on the record, the authors of the report were unable or unwilling to comment on it further, and whenever the Calgary Genstar report was brought up Genstar was able to trot out the Calgary letter as evidence that the report's contents were inaccurate.[69]

The Calgary report did eventually get forwarded to the federal Consumer and Corporate Affairs Department, which is charged with enforcement of the Combines Investigation Act. Almost two years later, the department announced that they had investigated and concluded that no violations of federal legislation had occurred.[70]

In view of its overall corporate strategy, Genstar might have been concerned about the possible changes in federal legislation arising from the federal Royal Commission on Corporate Concentration set up in 1975 to review the question of mergers and takeovers after Power Corp. attempted unsuccessfully to take over Argus Corp. Genstar filed its own lengthy brief, and was the subject of a critical brief by independent corporate researcher Donald Gutstein.[71] There was, however, little reason for Genstar to worry. One of the three commissioners charged with investigating corporate concentration was Pierre Nadeau, himself the president of Petrofina Canada Ltd. and a director of the Royal Bank. A second was R. W. Dickerson, a corporate lawyer from Vancouver. Petrofina's second-largest known shareholder is Genstar's parent Société Générale, and the Royal Bank has been Genstar's main bank since 1951 and has assisted in financing its mergers and takeovers.[72] After the third commissioner, Robert Bryce, dropped out of the inquiry, it was hardly a surprise when the royal commission decided that Genstar was right, and that corporate concentration was a good thing not only for Genstar but for everybody else.

Apart from its convictions for violating federal anti-combines legislation, Genstar has had one major difficulty with Ottawa. This arose in 1974 when the Foreign Investment Review Act was implemented. Genstar's status as a foreign-controlled corporation meant that each of its takeovers would require review and approval by FIRA and the federal minister of industry, trade and commerce. Genstar developed an astonishing strategy to cope with this problem. It decided to Canadianize its board of directors and operating executives, and then to claim that the company was controlled not by Société Générale or any other shareholders but by the board of directors, of whom a majority were Canadian.[73] First some senior positions were switched around. August Franck, a Belgian who up to that time had been chairman of the board and chief executive officer, became chairman of the board only. Charles de Bar, also Belgian and former executive vice-president of the company, was made deputy chairman of the board. Into the post of chief executive officer came not one but two Canadians: Angus A. MacNaughton and Ross J. Turner. Genstar also expanded its board to include a majority of Canadian citizens. None of the new directors, however, had identifiable links to other shareholders with sizeable blocks of Genstar stock. Remaining on the board were both Franck and de Bar along with Max Nokin, one of the Société Générale's senior executives and a fourth director who was an executive of a Société Générale subsidiary. Along with the four Société Générale-linked directors, there were two additional directors connected to Associated Portland Cement Manufacturers, which owns 10.3 percent of Genstar shares. After all these changes, Genstar had each director swear an affidavit for FIRA saying that no one controlled the company, and that it was the board collectively rather than any single shareholder who exercised control. Henry Aubin, who made a detailed study of Genstar's relationship with Société Générale, notes that thirteen of the twenty directors are employees of Genstar, affiliated with Société Générale itself, or executives of foreign-controlled companies in Canada. Estimates are that 60 percent of Genstar shares are owned by foreigners. In addition, Société Générale continues to classify Genstar as one of its group.

FIRA and the minister for industry, trade and commerce accepted Genstar's position and ruled in May 1976 that Genstar would be treated as a Canadian-controlled corporation with no need for FIRA review of its takeovers. This cleared the way for the Abbey Glen takeover in July 1976. Genstar and Cadillac Fairview were both in the bidding, but Cadillac Fairview dropped out. Abbey Glen added enormously to Genstar's market power in housing and land development, particularly in western Canada. It had a suburban land bank of 17,792 acres, of which 50 percent was in western Canada.[74] It also had a large portfolio of income properties.[75] The book value of these assets at the time of the takeover was $127 million, but their actual appraised market value was $213 million.[76] Genstar paid $49 million for the controlling 62 percent block of shares owned by a British property firm. Genstar was very anxious to buy up the rest of the shares from minority shareholders because, as the *Globe and Mail* Report on Business explained laconically, Genstar and Abbey Glen were operating in competition with each other in many markets.[77] If the two companies had to carry on competing, their owners would be faced with constant conflicts of interest. A merger was necessary to eliminate this awkward competition. Abbey Glen minority shareholders duly agreed to sell out to Genstar later in 1976.[78]

In twenty-five short years, from 1951 to 1976, Genstar went from nothing to one of the top three land development corporations in Canada. This growth came not so much from enterprises created in Canada or foreign funds put to work here. Virtually all of its growth came from the takeover of existing companies, most of which were created by Canadian entrepreneurs. Genstar's advantage was its enormous cash resources, much of which was provided by the Royal Bank of Canada, and its ability to foresee high profits generated through the exercise of monopoly power.

The key to Genstar's strategy from the beginning has been that it thinks and acts like a resource development corporation, integrating the process of producing urban accommodation (particularly housing) from the basic cement, wood and land right through to the finished suburban house. Genstar is doing for house construction what Imperial Oil and the other "majors" have done for energy. In a statement filed with the U.S. Securities and Exchange Commission in 1976, Genstar stated that it "encounters vigorous competition in most phases of its business." Genstar has done more to reduce competition in the land development and construction business than any other corporation in Canada. What is left may be what Genstar thinks of as 'vigorous competition', but it is certainly far less vigorous than it would be without Genstar.

In the land development industry in Canada, the largest corporations run by professional managers are quickly absorbing the smaller firms. Both the entrepreneurs and the managers of medium-sized and small development companies are losing ground quickly. The structure which is emerging is one whereby a few giant firms, perhaps a half-dozen at most, will dominate the industry. Cadillac Fairview, Genstar and Trizec are three of these firms. Campeau could be part of this group if Robert Campeau can manage a transfer of ownership and control to interests which do not already control one of the larger firms. A series of mergers has quickly taken Donald Love's Oxford Development to this same scale. Around the giants will be perhaps a dozen middle-sized firms, probably with regional rather than national strength, giving the industry an appearance of competitiveness. Entrepreneur-run firms can be expected only at this level, if at all.

There are literally hundreds of small developers across the country, and it is from this group that the most successful entrepreneurs have emerged. The industry has, however, matured quickly to the point where the same opportunities now no longer exist for small entrepreneurs. The entrepreneurs will continue to survive though they are unlikely to prosper like Robert Campeau, Bruce McLaughlin or even Robert Keenan.

Trizec and Cadillac Fairview represent one version of a mature land development corporation, with the emphasis shifting from development to managing and exploiting a portfolio of property investments as the great British landed estates do. It is Genstar which points up what could easily be the next stage in the industry's development: integration of land development with construction, construction materials and the construction equipment industry creating even larger giant corporations with enormous market power in a very large sector of the economy. Rather than being checked by government legislation, the process of corporate concentration is still being encouraged and applauded by Ottawa. Genstar is showing how to do it, and so far it has no imitators that can match its wealth, connections, or single-minded pursuit of profits and power.

3

MAKE A MILLION, PAY NO TAX:
HOW THE DEVELOPERS
GET RICH

Big or small, Canadian or foreign-owned, local or national, special-
ized or diversified, the developers have one thing in common:
they make money, lots of money. How do they do it?

In the chapters of Part II which follow, we look at each major
type of development project in turn to see how they work financially and what profits they generate. In this chapter, we look at the
overall financial operations of the land development corporations
to see where their money comes from, where it goes, and how
they turn their shareholders' investment plus the investment capital they borrow into property assets and profits.

The key to understanding this aspect of the developers' operations and to seeing how they get rich lies in a few basic principles
and concepts. There are some industry terms that need to be translated into ordinary language. Once you're familiar with these ideas
and terms, seeing how the developers do it is quite straightforward. It's also a useful thing to know because developers always
use the financial necessities of their business as the ultimate justification of the projects they undertake. Planners, city administrators, politicians, and citizens who come up against the industry are
often trying to regulate an industry they don't understand. When
the internal financial operations of the development industry are
widely and commonly understood, proper bargaining and negotiating among the interests involved in its activities are more likely to
occur.

There is, however, an even better reason for understanding how
the developers get rich: it is, in itself, a fascinating story. A variant
on the classic Jack and the Beanstock fairy tale, it illustrates how by

58

starting with a tiny seed you can quickly grow a giant-sized and very valuable company.

The basics. The basic operation of the development business revolves around where the developers get their hands on cash and what they do with it. By watching closely what happens to cash, it's easy to understand the logic of these companies' activities.

Cash. By cash, I mean exactly what everyone else means when they think of cash. Cash is change in your pocket, dollar bills tucked under the bed, and figures in a bank book. Cash for the rest of us is money we've got to spend, and that's just what it is for developers too. Keeping your eye on the cash means watching where a developer's money is coming from, and where it's going. Cash is basic to running a land development business, essential in permitting a developer to make use of his land, his experience, and his political connections.

Equity. Developers have two basic sources of cash. The first is the company's own cash, money that belongs to the company, that it can keep as long as it is in existence, and that effectively costs it nothing. This kind of cash, cash that belongs to the company itself, is termed equity. There are a number of places it can come from. One of these is from the company's owners, the shareholders, who buy the original shares issued by the company and pay the company cash for them. In 1977 Cadillac Fairview had 24,967,804 common shares outstanding and 101,920 preference shares.[1] When those shares were purchased from Cadillac Fairview, the shareholders paid the company a total of $80,431,000 for them. That cash is Cadillac Fairview's. There is no way a shareholder can force Cadillac to refund the money he paid for his shares; the only way for an individual shareholder to get rid of his shares is to sell them to someone else for whatever that other person will pay for them. Nor does Cadillac have to pay any interest on the shareholders' money, at least not on the money paid for common shares. Equity cash from shareholders belongs to the company, to do with what it thinks best.

Besides selling shares, the other way a company can raise equity cash is to earn a profit. Profits are cash in hand, and a company can do one of two things with them: pay the cash out as dividends to the shareholders, so much per share, or keep the cash as retained earnings in the company. Most developers keep most or all of their profits inside the company. Cadillac, on profits of $31.5 million in 1977, paid out $4.3 million in dividends to shareholders and kept the rest as retained earnings in the company. Daon Development Corporation of Vancouver had before-tax profits of $21.5 million in 1977 and paid out dividends of just $1,069,000, keeping the rest in the company as retained earnings.[2] The total equity of a company is the sum of money paid by shareholders for shares plus the profits which have been kept in past years as retained earnings. For Cadillac Fairview, total equity at the end of 1977 was $80.4 million paid by shareholders for stock plus $68.9 million in retained earnings, totalling $149.3 million. For Daon the figure was $5 million in shareholders' payments for capital stock and $30.9 million in retained earnings, totalling $35.9 million.

Corporate borrowings. The second major source of cash for developers is money they borrow from outsiders. There are all kinds of ways that development corporations borrow money, but two are particularly important. One is mortgages. When a developer borrows mortgage money on a property, he gets a percentage, sometimes 75 percent, sometimes 90 percent or 95 percent, of what the finished project is worth. So if the developer owns a building worth $1 million, he can borrow $750,000 or $900,000 or even $950,000 from a mortgage lender. What the developer gets is cash now, and what he agrees to do is pay the mortgage lender 1) interest on the borrowed money and 2) small payments of the loan itself so that over twenty or thirty years (the repayment period) the total amount of the loan has been paid back. Usually the mortgage comes up for renewal every five years; this means that the interest rate gets adjusted to whatever it is at the time of the renewal. From the mortgage lender's point of view, this deal is a very nice one because it is both profitable and secure. Interest rates on mortgages are usually a percentage point or two higher than interest rates on other kinds of corporate borrowings, so the lender is getting more for his money. The loan is secure because a mortgage permits the lender to move in and take over ownership of the mortgaged property if the borrower stops making payments on the mortgage. The lender either gets his money or he gets the mortgaged property. Since the property is always expected to be worth more than the total value of the loan, the lender can be pretty sure that he'll be able to get his money back even if the borrower does get into trouble.

Corporate developers raise most of their new cash through mortgages on their new projects. Mortgage money pays the bulk of the cost of these projects. But they have other ways of borrowing money too. One of these is debentures, which are bonds issued by corporations and work much like Canada Savings Bonds. The corporate developer sells debentures worth $10 million or $50 million, pays interest to the debenture holders for five, ten or twenty years (however long the debentures run), and then pays back the $10 or $50 million. Buyers of debentures exact very complicated guarantees from companies selling them about how the company will function. These are spelled out in legal language in prospectuses which are publicly available any time a public corporation issues a debenture, and which are always full of interesting details on a developer's operation.

Leverage. In most land development projects, developers find the cash needed to pay for the project with a combination of their own cash and borrowed cash, mainly mortgages. Sometimes the developer has to put in one dollar of his own cash for every three dollars he is able to borrow. Sometimes he can borrow ten dollars for every dollar of his own that he puts in. Developers generally try to borrow the maximum number of other people's dollars for every dollar of their own they use in a project. The more they can borrow, obviously, the more and bigger the development projects they can put up. The ratio between their own cash and other people's cash is called *leverage* in the industry. The higher your leverage, the more of other people's money you are able to get for every dollar of your own you invest in a development project.

What developers actually do. The basic activity of every corporate developer in Canada is the same. It is work that can be and often is done by a small number of people working in an administrative office. Developers put together projects: they look for sites to erect a profitable apartment building or shopping centre or suburb, they assemble the site, draw up some kind of plan for the project, get the necessary approvals from governments and public bodies, line up tenants if this is appropriate, line up mortgage lenders to lend them the bulk of the cost of the project once it's built, get the architectural plans for the scheme drawn up, hire the contractors to do the construction, and arrange to sell or rent the building once it's finished.

Most, often all, of the actual work is done by other companies. The development corporation does the organizing, but it need do little or nothing else. Noted a 1973 study of the house-building industry: "60 percent of all HUDAC [the house-builders' trade organization] member firms contracted out more than 75 percent of their work, and subcontracts range from planning, architectural, accounting and engineering tasks to heavy and light construction, and all building trades. The development firm...is an entrepreneurial, owning, organizing and managing entity rather than a physical builder."[3]

Some developers go beyond development itself into construction. Cadillac Fairview has a construction division. So does Daon Development. Genstar has, of course, gone much farther than any other corporate developer in providing all the equipment, supplies and labour that are required to produce new buildings. A developer doesn't need to also be a contractor or builder, however.

Watching the cash flow. All the large development corporations are involved in more than one aspect of the business. Some are fully diversified, producing every major kind of development project. Others are partially diversified, combining say suburban land development with high-rise apartments. There are only a few cases, for instance Carma in Calgary, of firms that are active in just a single field.

This diversification is a result of the way the cash works in the industry. The financial operations of the land developers, and the context of government policy and legislation in which they function, are such that the major types of development projects interlock with each other from the point of view of cash and profits. Developers need to diversify in order to expand as quickly as possible and in order to maximize their real profitability. Vancouver's Daon Development Corporation explains the way they and every other development company work as follows: "We focus on three activities — land development...a source of cash; housing units for resale...a source of cash; income properties for retention...a place to invest our cash and also a means of sheltering other cash from current income taxes."[4]

What this means is that the developers generate substantial cash profits every year by servicing their suburban land banks and selling the lots ("land development...a source of cash") and by constructing houses which are sold to homeowners ("housing units for resale...a source of cash"). As we will see in the next two chapters, the cash profits resulting from house construction are not nearly as substantial as those from land development. Developers who are involved in suburban industrial land development may also sell serviced industrial land in order to generate cash profits.

The cash thus produced is invested by the developers mainly in income properties: high-rise apartments, industrial buildings, office buildings and shopping centres. By borrowing mortgage money from financial institutions, the developers are able to get considerable leverage out of every dollar of their own cash which they put into income properties. The size and scale of the developers' activities in income properties is of course limited by the amount of cash they can generate elsewhere in their operations or borrow. Thus Daon's abbreviated description: "Income properties for retention...a place to invest our cash." Though over the short term of two or three years income properties absorb developers' cash, over the longer term they too generate a flow of cash profits like suburban land development. This cash is added to the total amount available for use in building more income properties for other purposes.

The operating profits yielded by income properties every year are, however, only a small part of their appeal for developers. Consider the implications for the developer of receiving rental income on a high-rise apartment that pays all operating expenses, covers all mortgage interest, provides the cash needed to pay the mortgage principal, and leaves a cash surplus after all these items. What this financial arrangement means is that the tenants of an income property are providing the developer with enough income every year to fully pay for the building. After twenty or twenty-five or thirty years, the period of the developer's mortgage, the developer will own the project outright. All his mortgages on it will be paid off. The tenants of income properties not only provide the developer with an operating profit every year after all expenses, they also provide him with the cash to pay off the mortgage, so he will own outright all his income properties. In 1977, Daon Development held income-producing properties which had cost it a total of $187 million. But Daon didn't actually own these projects outright:

there were mortgages outstanding against these buildings totalling $151.8 million. In twenty or thirty years, however, it will be another story. These buildings will have generated enough cash so that Daon will have paid for them completely out of tenants' rents. Income properties are being bought for the developers by their tenants.

Developers and taxes. In explaining its financial operations, Daon offers two reasons for using cash to invest in income properties. The first, as we've seen, is that they make profitable use of cash generated in other aspects of land development. The second is, at first glance, rather more obscure: "A means of sheltering other cash from current income taxes."

What this innocuous-sounding phrase is actually saying is that *developers who own income properties are able to avoid paying corporate tax on the profits they make in all the various aspects of the land development business.* Following its own prescription, Daon declared profits of $21,558,000 in 1977. It paid no corporate tax at all on these profits. Cadillac Fairview declared profits of $31.5 million in 1977, and paid taxes totalling $1.7 million, an effective rate of tax of about 6 percent. On declared profits of $8.6 million in 1976, Trizec paid a miniscule $130,000 in tax.[5]

Since it was established, the land development business has benefited from an arrangement that means that most developers do not now and never have paid substantial amounts of corporate tax on their profits. The actual rate of tax paid by the industry overall is much less than 10 percent, probably 5 to 6 percent. Most other industries, of course, pay corporate tax on profits in the range of 40 to 50 percent.[6] How is this done? Corporate income tax regulations offer a concession for developers called the "capital cost allowance" (CCA) which enables them to avoid paying most if not all corporate tax. On top of all their legitimate expenses like operating costs and mortgage interests, developers are permitted to add a fictitious expense, the capital cost allowance. The justification for this expense is that it represents the depreciation in value of rented buildings. Ottawa prescribes what that expense can be. A developer can write off 5 percent a year on buildings made of brick, concrete and similar materials and 10 percent on buildings built of wood, until the total cost of the building has been charged as an expense.[7] This expense is fictitious because the buildings owned by developers are not depreciating at anything like 5 percent or 10 percent a year. As long as construction costs are increasing every year, there is a strong argument that the actual market value of a completed building (not the land it is built on) is likely to be going up, because any normal physical deterioration is more than compensated for by the rising cost of constructing an identical building. The developers do not publicly accept that their buildings are not depreciating in value, but they do carefully report every year in their financial statements exactly what their accountants and auditors consider to be a fair and accurate expense for depreciation of their buildings. Daon, for instance, reported that a reasonable expense for depreciation in 1977 on its $185 million income properties was $635,000. Cadillac Fairview's accountants and auditors put the figure at $8.4 million on properties which cost the corporation $748 million. Yet Ottawa's concession for the developers allowed Daon to report on its corporate tax form a depreciation expense not of $635,000 but of about $21.5 million. Cadillac Fairview was permitted to charge not $8.4 million but about $30 million.

The effect of the CCA concession is that the developers show huge paper losses on their income properties business on their corporate tax returns, even though their audited financial statements show that they earned profits on income properties. These huge paper losses offset the profits the developers earn and report in other aspects of their business. The result is that, on their income tax returns, the corporate developers are telling Ottawa that they are break-even or near break-even operations and hence have to pay no tax on profits, since they have little or no profits to tax.*

---

* A valuable lesson in this role of income properties in permitting the developers to avoid payment of corporate tax came in 1975 when Trizec sold $100 million in income properties to Bramalea, a Toronto-area developer mainly involved in suburban land development. The sale left Trizec with sufficient other income properties to "shelter" virtually all its profits from tax. It gave Bramalea enough income properties to do the same thing. Reported the *Globe and Mail*, analyzing reasons for the purchase: "For Bramalea, the advantages are mainly in providing a tax shelter through depreciation allowances from its income generated by developing land and building houses...." The deal worked: in 1977, Bramalea avoided paying $6.7 million in corporate taxes, and actually paid no tax at all that year. (*Globe and Mail* 9 December 1975)

"Deferred" taxes. Every public land development corporation reports in its published financial statements on how much tax it would have paid *if this concession did not exist.* Moreover, these financial statements report every year the total amount of tax that company would have had to pay up to the present if the concession were retroactively abolished. Again, the terminology is deceptively simple and misleading. Taxes which have not been paid but which would have been paid had the concession not existed are usually termed "deferred" income taxes. Tax that is actually paid, if there is any, is termed "current" income tax. On audited financial statements, corporate income tax is always deducted as an expense to produce an after-tax profit figure. Daon, for instance, reports "income before income taxes" of $21.5 million in 1977. Then it shows what is called "provision for income taxes" of $11.0 million. The so-called bottom line figure is termed "net income," and the figure is $10.5 million.

Daon's $10.5 million after-tax profit is not, however, the amount of cash the company had after 1977's operations. That income tax item is not income taxes paid; it is "provision" for income taxes. Daon shows no expense for "current" (i.e., paid) corporate tax. Its total tax expense is a "provision" for tax, "deferred" tax, or in plain language, unpaid corporate tax.

Every year, the accountants and auditors for the developers add on this year's unpaid tax to previous years' unpaid taxes. The total amount is shown as a debt on the companies' balance sheets along with the bank loans and mortgage loans they owe. In Daon's case, the total amount of "deferred" unpaid corporate tax to 1977 was $34 million. For Cadillac Fairview, it was $77 million. For Trizec, $34 million.

For the thirty-five largest public development corporations in Canada, the total amount of corporate tax unpaid because of this concession was an amazing $382 million at the end of 1975.[8] By 1977, the total must have reached at least $450 million. That amount, cash which the developers have been able to keep in their companies because they have not had to pay normal corporate taxes, was very significant in relation to the total amount of equity cash provided by the shareholders to these companies or generated in profits not paid out to shareholders. Total shareholders' equity in the same thirty-five companies at the end of 1975 was $940 million (1977 figures for 22 companies are in an appendix).*

Operating profits. What kind of profits have the developers been making? The question is not as simple to answer as it sounds. It isn't difficult to review the profits the developers say they are making, but the industry is the first to point out that there is more to its profits than the figures that appear as "net income after taxes" on the bottom line of their annual financial statements.

Though audited financial statements are often regarded as hard and fast summaries of a company's actual situation, there is in fact a considerable degree of flexibility in what a company reports as its assets, liabilities, expenses, income and profit. As Robert Rennie, chief executive officer of the large accounting firm of Touche Ross

---

* There is a technical argument the developers often fall back on to explain why these unpaid taxes are not really unpaid, only deferred, and why they will eventually have to be paid. I don't find this technical argument convincing, and I suspect that most developers don't believe it either. It depends on assuming that the developers will cease or severely slow up the rate of construction or acquisition of new income properties, an assumption which is the opposite of their plans. Were the corporate developers to sell off their income properties as buildings, they would have to pay their "deferred" taxes. To avoid this unhappy eventuality, developers don't often sell buildings. They usually sell their company instead. And when property does change hands, there is a last-ditch way of avoiding paying back taxes: demolish the building, and sell only the land. Land is not depreciated; only buildings are. This device is often used by property owners, and is in fact one major reason why it makes tax sense to demolish commercial and rental buildings before their useful life is up.

Even if in twenty years Daon, Cadillac Fairview and the other developers did have to pay the millions in taxes they did not pay in 1977 and previous years, they would have benefited enormously from this loophole. First, they would be paying back dollars they had the use of for twenty years or more, and for which they paid no interest whatsoever. Second, the dollars they would be paying back would—given the rate of inflation—be worth far less then than they were when they went unpaid.

told the 1977 meeting of the Canadian Institute of Chartered Accountants, profit is a "rather flexible" idea, and the final figure for any company depends on a lot of "judgement calls."[9] Investment analyst Ira Gluskin points out that "Real estate accounting is still a bit of an 'art form'."[10] In compiling their financial statements, developers have to keep in mind a number of competing interests: the need to look financially viable, in order to attract investment capital; the need to demonstrate a steadily improving financial record over the years; and the need to produce moderate profit figures, not so high as to attract the attention of tenants, politicians or industry critics who might allege profiteering or suggest that the industry could well afford to pay tax.

A reasonable estimate of the operating profits earned by the developers can be made by adding "deferred" corporate taxes to after-tax profits. The resulting figure I would term "true operating profit." These profits are reasonable to high for the public development corporations, as a rate of return on shareholders' equity. Cadillac Fairview's operating profit in 1977, for instance, was $29.8 million. Shareholder investment in the company in the form of cash paid for shares was $80 million. Retained profits from previous years were $146.1 million, of which $77.2 million was unpaid income tax. The 1977 operating profit as a percentage of shareholder investment plus true operating profits retained from previous years totalling $226.1 million was about 13 percent.

Trizec's true operating profit in 1976 was $8.5 million. Operating profits retained from previous years totalled $51.6 million and shareholder investment was $98 million. The overall rate of return indicated was about 6 percent. For Daon, operating profit in 1977 was $21.5 million. Operating profits retained from previous years totalled $65.1 million, and shareholders' investment was $5 million. The rate of return in terms of operating profit for 1977 was about 30 percent.

Looking at operating profit from another point of view, one can measure the profits now being generated by the shareholders' cash provided to the company when shareholders purchased shares. Cadillac Fairview's shareholders have provided the company over the years with $80 million in cash. With that base, Cadillac Fairview was earning operating profits in 1977 of $29.8 million, a return that year of 37 percent on shareholders' investment. Trizec earned $8.5 million from a base of $98 million, a return of 8.5 percent. But Daon, with just $5 million in shareholders' cash, earned operating profits of $21.5 million in 1977, an incredible 430 percent return, and a performance which only a few of the rapidly growing western developers can parallel.

Appraisal surplus profits. While operating profits for even the large developers are substantial in terms of shareholders' equity, and vary from decent to amazing in terms of shareholders' cash investment in these companies, operating profit is not the only kind of profit the developers are making. Developers earn a second type of profit, appraisal surplus profits.

Cadillac Fairview chairman A. E. Diamond puts it this way: "The real value in real estate lies in holding it for long-term appreciation."[11] What Diamond is talking about is the fact that the land and projects which developers own are increasing steadily in value over the years. Developers record the value of the property they own on their financial statements at the actual historic cost to them of that property. If they purchased an acre of land for $2,000 and have spent another $1,000 on interest and carrying charges since the day the land was bought, it will be recorded on their financial statements as an asset valued at $3,000. In fact, however, its current actual value is likely to be far greater than $3,000, particularly if it is part of a suburban land assembly put together ten years ago and now ready for servicing. The difference between the book value of these assets and their actual market value is termed by the industry "appraisal surplus."

If over the course of a financial year the overall market value of the land and buildings owned by a developer increases, that increase is "appraisal surplus" profit to the developer that year. In addition, the conservative accounting policies followed by developers lead them to reduce modestly every year the book value of their income properties for depreciation. If the actual market value of these buildings is in fact increasing, as it was during the 1970s, this practice also increases the difference between the book value and the market value of the developers' property and adds a further amount to the year's "appraisal surplus" profits.

While operating profits are concrete and represent real cash earned by a developer, appraisal surplus profits may seem more abstract and uncertain. The most direct way for a developer to real-ize the appraisal surplus profits made on a property is to put it up for sale, collect cash from the purchaser, thus creating an operating profit that represents the difference between the selling price and the purchase and carrying costs. The high operating profits earned in suburban land development arise because the developers are realizing the enormous increases in suburban land values between the time they purchased their land banks and the time they sell the land as serviced house lots.*

---

* There are less drastic methods than selling their properties that de-velopers can use to tap their appraisal surplus profits. One frequently used device is remortgaging a property. To do this, a developer who owns land which cost $1 million cash but which is now worth $10 million mortgages the land for, say, 75 percent of its present value. That mortgage produces $7.5 million in cash. It returns the original $1 million which the developer put into the land, and yields a cash surplus of another $6.5 million. And the developer still owns his $10 million in land, though now it is subject to a $7.5 million mortgage, and he has appraisal surplus profits in hand of $6.5 million cash. The same approach of remortgaging on the basis of higher values can be used to realize appraisal surplus profits on income properties.

An imaginative variant on this general principle used by Bruce McLaughlin involves debenture, not mortgage, borrowing with the security for the debenture being effectively the appraisal surplus profits on land owned by the company. In 1975, McLaughlin raised $10 million in cash by selling debentures which were secured by a claim on 220 acres of McLaughlin's Mississauga land assembly. The land had at that time cost McLaughlin $11,940 an acre, $2,625,000 in total. Its appraised market value was $16,286,000. If McLaughlin had sold the land for its market value, he would have realized a total profit of $13,661,000. Instead of selling it and realizing a cash profit that way, McLaughlin turned the potential appraisal surplus profit into cash by borrowing, using that profit as security of the loan. He realized $10 million and not the full $13,661,000, but he got his hands on the cash without having to give up ownership of the land, and without having to compromise the possibility of earning even more appraisal surplus profits on it if its value continued to increase in the future.

In 1978 McLaughlin repeated the procedure, realizing $12 million

There is an ongoing controversy raging in the development industry over whether the developers should report their appraisal surplus profits annually in their financial statements along with their operating profits. Some of the more conservative and established developers argue that these figures should not be collected or published, on the grounds that they are only estimates and could be misleading. Younger, more aggressive developers are anxious to see them published, partly to convince investors that development corporations are far more profitable than their operating profit figures seem to indicate.

Some developers do note the size of their appraisal surplus profits in their annual reports, and often information of this kind is provided in prospectuses issued for new debentures or when controlling shareholders are attempting to buy back the shares of minority shareholders. Daon is one developer that reports both its operating profit and its appraisal surplus profit every year. In 1973, Daon reported that it had accumulated appraisal surplus profits totalling $17 million. In 1974, the figure was $21 million, up $4 million in the year. By 1976, the amount was $55 to $60 million, an appraisal surplus profit of about $35 million in two years. In 1977, it was $126 million, meaning an appraisal surplus profit of an amazing $66 million that year. Daon's operating profit in 1977, for comparison, was $21.5 million.

Developers and financial institutions. Financial institutions play an absolutely key role in the operations of the land developers by adding investment capital, usually in the form of mortgages, to the developers' own cash. Mortgage money permits developers to undertake projects which cost many times the amount of cash they own in the form of equity or profits.

The development industry is the joint creation of government and Canada's financial institutions. Though government, particu-

---

by borrowing against the appraisal surplus value of 62.9 acres of land which cost the company $1,458,535 and which were appraised at $18,477,600. (S. B. McLaughlin Associates Limited, *Prospectus* dated 27 November 1975, p. 12 and *Prospectus* dated 4 May 1978, p. 13)

larly the federal government, took the initiative in creating and supporting the development industry after the Second World War, government alone was not sufficient to generate this new form of business enterprise. The willingness of banks, trust and loan companies, life insurance companies and other lenders to provide mortgage money to finance the projects of the developers has been essential to the industry's success.

Financial institutions are strictly regulated by the federal and provincial governments. One element of the government policy of promoting the establishment and growth of the land development industry was regulations to permit and encourage these lenders to increase substantially the amount of investment capital going into urban real estate. The most obvious way in which mortgage lenders, mainly life insurance companies, trust and loan companies and the chartered banks, have contributed to the development industry's growth has been through their willingness to make available substantial amounts of new investment capital every year for mortgage lending, and to offer developers large amounts of borrowed cash for every dollar of the developer's own cash invested in a land development project. In ordinary commercial mortgage transactions, first mortgages are provided for 75 percent of the market value of an urban property. Developers can often obtain second mortgages for some portion of the remaining value of the property, though at higher interest rates. A 75 percent first mortgage means that three dollars of mortgage lender's cash is lent against every four dollars of the property's value. It does not mean that the developer must have one dollar of his own cash invested for evey three dollars of borrowed cash, because often the actual total creation cost of a development project to its developer is significantly lower than its market value once it is completed.

First mortgage lenders in the housing field habitually provide mortgages of 90 percent of the market value of an apartment building or a new house. They do so knowing that their loan is safe even if the borrower defaults and even if the property involved is sold for less than its total mortgaged value because the mortgage lender is protected by insurance provided by CMHC under the National Housing Act. These lending practices have permitted the developers to get enormous amounts of leverage from their relatively limited cash resources. Indeed there are many instances, as we will see in Part II, where developers build projects which were financed entirely with mortgage funds and have none of the developer's own cash invested in them after they are completed. This is almost the ultimate in leverage.

A second major effect which mortgage lenders have had on the development industry comes from their policies regarding the types of projects they will finance, and the types they will not finance. Once the profitability of the major types of development projects was established by entrepreneurs willing to take major risks and able to find lenders who would offer them some support, mortgage lenders were willing to provide funds for similar projects as long as these did not deviate substantially from the proven form. William Zeckendorf showed everyone how to produce a profitable downtown development with Place Ville Marie; since then, Canadian mortgage lenders have been willing to put billions of dollars into downtown developments, provided they follow the type that was pioneered by Place Ville Marie. The availability of government insurance against risks on certain standard housing development types reinforced this conservatism of the mortgage lenders.

A third critical effect which mortgage lenders have had on the development industry is a combined result of their willingness to provide relatively large amounts of mortgage funds for every dollar of a developer's own money, and the necessity to ensure that their loans are reasonably safe and secure. Mortgage lenders generally will provide a mortgage for an income property project only when accurately prepared financial projections demonstrate that from the very first year of its operations rent levels in the project will generate sufficient income for the developer to be able to cover all his expenses, make his mortgage payments (including both principal and interest) and have a cash surplus left over to cover contingencies and unexpected difficulties. If a developer cannot predict that kind of financial picture, a mortgage lender will not agree to finance his project. This practice protects the mortgage lenders' interests, but it also has the effect of ensuring that any project which receives mortgage financing will yield a very high percentage profit on the relatively small amount of his own cash which a developer has invested in the project.*

Financial analyst Ira Gluskin sums up the view of Canadian developers (and no doubt of Canadian mortgage lenders as well) of the relationship between developers and their mortgage lenders:

> There is an old adage in real estate circles that 'developers will build as much as lenders will lend.' The U.S. experience is valid testimony to the truth of this statement. We believe that many of the Canadian public [development] companies were prevented from reckless over-expansion and bankruptcy [after 1972] by the fact that Canadian lenders refused to provide the funds.[12]

Though it might seem that small developers would be most dependent on mortgage lenders, in fact even the largest development corporations are subject to substantially the same policies as others in the industry. When the large corporate developers use means other than ordinary mortgages to raise money, from debentures to preferred shares and other devices, they only get this cash if they fulfil strict conditions about their operations and provide convincing security to the lender. Often the relationship between a large

---

* The measure of control of the development industry exercised by the mortgage lenders extends well beyond simple decisions about which projects to fund, and how much mortgage money to make available to the industry every year. Smaller development firms feel the weight of mortgage lenders when they negotiate to obtain funds for new projects, and in the conditions they have to accept in order to obtain those funds. An example of this relationship was provided in an industry seminar for would-be developers by Larry Robbins, president of a small land development company, Paramount Development Corp. Ltd., in the Toronto area. Robbins provided copies of correspondence between Paramount and its unnamed mortgage lender for a small suburban land development project called Clearcreek Heights. Paramount wanted to leave $323,320 of its own money in the project, and to borrow an additional $1.8 million to finance servicing the land. In its original negotiations with the unnamed lender, Paramount and the lender talked about an interest rate of 11¾ percent on the money.

  After formally making the request for the loan, and enclosing a detailed and comprehensive set of financial statements and projections for the project, the lender agreed to Paramount's request — on

developer and a major lender is cemented by the lender's having a representative on the board of the development firm. No doubt this may in some instances give the developer easier access to further financing from the lender, but it also gives the lender a continuing supervisory role over the activities of its developer-client.

In chapter 1 we noted the key role that government played in creating the land development industry. In the light of the internal financial structure of the corporate developers, it is clear that there has been a partnership of government with Canadian financial institutions to generate the development industry as it now exists. At first Ottawa had to exert considerable pressure combined with impressive inducements to persuade mortgage lenders to put the necessary amount of investment capital into urban land development. After some years of experience with this kind of lending and with the profitability of the development project types the industry produced, the financial institutions began to become involved directly in the business with their own development projects (the bank towers in every major Canadian city are usually joint ventures with the large corporate developers) and to direct far more investment capital into urban property than anyone would have dreamed possible twenty or thirty years ago.

---

condition. There were in fact twelve detailed conditions for the loan. One was that Paramount maintain one dollar of its own money for every three dollars of the mortgage lender's in the project. Interest would be, not 11¾ percent, but 13 percent per annum. "We require," specified the mortgage lender, "audited financial statements no less frequently than annually, with the right of access to records concerning the development at any time." The owners of Paramount also had to put themselves on the line personally for their borrowed money. "We will require the guarantee of Paramount Development Corp. Ltd., together with its principal shareholders." The developer had to pay the lender's legal fees for setting up the mortgage: "Our solicitors in this matter will be O'Brien, O'Brien, O'Brien and Rabinowitz. Legal fees and other costs will be your responsibility." And, to cap it all, the lender took a "processing fee" off the top, from the first advance on the loan: "Our processing fee of $2,800 will be deducted from the first advance." There is little doubt about the dependent relationship of the developer on the mortgage lender in this kind of situation. (UDI seminar materials, correspondence between Paramount and the unnamed mortgage lender dated 1 April and 15 May 1975)

Corporate concentration. It was not just a new industry which Ottawa set out to create after the Second World War, but a new industry characterized by large, rationalized, efficient corporations. Ottawa didn't want to have to rely on thousands of "hammer-and-nails" contractors to produce the needed new urban accommodation, and Wartime Housing Ltd. had demonstrated the potential of large corporate building firms.

It took a long time for the process of corporate concentration in the new industry to begin to take hold. Through the 1950s, however, some of the new companies both entrepreneur-owned and investor-owned were growing particularly quickly. Speeding up this growth was continued demand for houses, high-rise apartments and other forms of new urban space, financial arrangements that permitted the developers to keep their income properties rather than having to sell them off to other investors, very good operating profits on their small amounts of cash equity, and a tax structure that permitted them to keep all their operating profits and pay little or no tax.

Like a snowball, once the new development corporations were able to accumulate reasonably large amounts of equity cash through operating profits, their rate of growth increased dramatically. They used their cash to speed up the construction of new properties, and to take over smaller development firms. From the mid-1960s onwards, the pace of growth by takeovers accelerated and giant firms began to emerge out of constellations of small and middle-sized ones. The larger that large corporations became, the larger was their flow of operating profits, and the easier it was to raise cash from debentures, sales of shares to the public, and preferred shares. With that cash plus annual untaxed operating profits, the companies could increase the pace of development and takeovers simultaneously.

Ottawa took a key step in promoting the process of corporate concentration in land development in 1972 when major changes were made in the Income Tax Act. The CCA concession, which until that time had been available to every property investor, was removed for all but the large development corporations. Commented investment analysts Lafferty, Harwood in November 1972 on the implications of this change:

Progressively it seems to us that large individual capital will migrate from this field and that the ownership of land and property will become increasingly institutionalized. This assumedly is the government's social intent.[13]

By the early 1970s it was obvious too that the new development corporations were making most of their money out of high urban land values, not construction. Had Ottawa decided that large corporate builders, not large corporate land developers, were indeed what the country needed, changes could have been made in tax policy to tax away the bulk of these land profits and to discourage high land prices while retaining concessions to permit profits on construction to go tax-free. This was not done. Apparently the federal government was happy with the outcome of its policies, and was eager to see the process of corporate concentration of land developers proceed quickly.

The new corporate city. It is not just the land development industry itself which is a postwar creation of government policy and financial institution lending practices. The five major types of development projects which have been the mainstay of the developers' activity, and which have provided the bulk of the enormous amount of new urban accommodation in Canada's fast-growing postwar cities, are also new. Each of them — the corporate suburbs, high-rise apartments, suburban industrial parks, office towers, and shopping centres — involves a building form introduced to Canadian cities after 1945, and perfected by thirty years of practical experience.

Although each of these development project types fulfils a different need, it is essential to understand how they interrelate to produce maximum profits for their owners. Each depends on the others for its success. Shopping centres, to take one example, depend on the suburbs. There have to be thousands of people living in large subdivisions of suburban houses, all with the use of cars, and all of them many miles away from the traditional retail downtown, for the large regional shopping centres to come into existence. High-rise apartments are dependent for their success on the fact that virtually the only other type of new housing which the development industry was producing in postwar Canadian cities was detached houses in the suburbs. If the developers had been building a whole range of types of new housing in between the two extremes of high-density but reasonably affordable apartments, and very low-density (and highly desirable) but relatively expensive single-family suburban houses, it would not have been possible to market high-rise buildings nearly so successfully. The success of the postwar suburban industrial park as a location for manufacturing and warehousing was crucial in freeing up large amounts of downtown land for redevelopment for office towers.

The new corporate city is made up of the five major types of development projects which the developers have been producing since 1945. New construction of work, living and shopping space has not been limited exclusively to these five types of projects since 1945, and there are still many instances of the traditional urban building types being erected. The bulk of all new urban accommodation, however, has come from the development industry, and it has been via these five development project types.

There is of course more to the corporate city than development projects. Tying it all together is an infrastructure of services provided by municipal, regional and sometimes provincial governments: trunk sewage, water and transportation systems. Arterial roads and expressways have been the single most important innovation in the Canadian urban infrastructure since 1945. They are a key element in the corporate city. Without them, the city could not have taken the form that it has. With them, it is almost inevitable that a city will grow according to the building forms of the corporate developers.

Another somewhat less obviously related element of the public side of the corporate city has been a new form of city government, one which concentrates enormous planning and financial powers into a regional, metropolitan or single-tier city government that is difficult for ordinary city residents to influence or control. Alongside the process of corporate concentration in land development has gone a parallel process of political concentration in urban government. Local government reforms in this direction have been unpopular and widely opposed. In the few cities where urban government has not been restructured along these lines, the corporate developers have had far less success in taking over the process of urban growth.

The term "corporate city" which I am using to refer to the kind of city built by the developers since 1945 is intended to reflect the fact that it is a new and different kind of city, and to stress that it has been constructed by corporations, in ways compatible with their business interests. There is no doubt that the corporate city's fundamental logic is the logic of the development corporations. Whenever there has been a choice to make between providing people with what they want and need on the one hand, and pursuing a strategy that would increase the short-term and long-term profits of the development corporations on the other, the developers have chosen to pursue their own interests. Nor would it be reasonable to expect them to do anything else. The consequence of this arrangement, however, is that the corporate city and its interlocking pieces are designed not to provide a humane and livable city, but rather to maximize the profits to be made from urban land and to capture as much control over the process of urban growth as possible for the development industry. The corporate city as it has been built by the development industry since 1945 is not so much a place for people to live and call their own as it is a machine rationally and effectively designed for making money. How this has been accomplished and what its implications are we will see as we look in turn at each of the major types of development projects that make up the corporate city.

PART II

4

CREATING
THE CORPORATE
SUBURBS

The suburbs are the developers' proudest and most successful creation. These single-family houses on large lots are almost everyone's ideal form of housing. They have only one flaw in most people's eyes: they cost too much. For families with average or below-average incomes, a suburban house is an unattainable dream.

The explanation of the high price of new suburban houses in most cities is to be found in how the corporate suburbs are developed. When the federal government set out to create a large housebuilding industry in postwar Canada and to encourage the emergence of private developers capable of matching the output of Ottawa's own Wartime Housing Ltd., it set in motion a chain of events that led thirty years later to suburban houses whose prices were far higher than they needed to be. In this chapter we look at the suburbs the developers have built: where the idea came from, what's new about them, why people like them, how raw land is turned into serviced lots, and how developers set their prices. This sets the stage for the next chapter, where we investigate the question of why suburban houses cost too much.

Where the corporate suburbs came from. Before 1945, most new housing in Canadian cities was built in streetcar suburbs. The houses were on twenty-five-foot lots, everyone was within walking distance of local transportation, stores were in low-density commercial strips, and industrial, commercial and residential facilities were intermixed.

There was, however, an alternative pattern of land subdivision which was tried by land speculators in the early years of the century. An area called Uplands in the new municipality of Oak Bay on the outskirts of Victoria, for instance, was laid out by the famous Olmsted brothers in 1906.[1] The Olmsteds laid out curving streets, with houses on larger lots, in an attempt to bring the country into the city. Strict land use controls kept out all but wealthy residents and large single-family homes. Most Canadian cities have older suburbs in this style: some, like Vancouver's Shaughnessy and Calgary's Mount Royal, built by that pioneering corporate land developer, the CPR, others like Winnipeg's Tuxedo, Toronto's Rosedale, Ottawa's Rockcliffe, and Montreal's Westmount, the projects of speculators and developers.

One particularly influential plan for a new style of urban development was British planner Ebenezer Howard's scheme for garden suburbs.[2] Howard believed that more desirable urban environments — and far cheaper housing for working people — could be built by assembling large tracts of farm land at farm land prices on the outskirts of major cities, and developing them into self-contained satellite towns. The first garden city built in Britain according to Howard's ideas was Letchworth, and the secretary of the development company from 1903 to 1906 was a young planner, Thomas Adams, who arrived in Canada in 1914 and was influential in spreading Howard's ideas on town planning in this country.

It was, however, not a British planner but rather a British brewing family who pioneered the first large-scale Canadian suburban development project. The Guinness family bought four thousand acres of land on Vancouver's north shore for $75,000 in the 1930s, built the Lion's Gate Bridge to provide access to downtown Vancouver, and began to develop lots in their British Properties project.[3] The corporate suburb really came into its own with the development of E. P. Taylor's Don Mills project, started in 1947 and ready with the first houses in 1953.[4] Don Mills established a prototype for the postwar corporate suburbs that other developers have been imitating across Canada ever since.

Growth of the postwar suburbs. There are three key characteristics of the postwar corporate suburbs which distinguish them from anything that was built in Canada before 1945. First of all they are designed on the assumption that every family owns an automobile. Since everyone no longer has to live within reasonable walking distance of local transit, houses can be built further apart. Lots grew in size so that the standard postwar suburban lot, fifty by one hundred feet, is twice as wide as the standard streetcar suburb lot. The novel street layouts of the postwar suburbs, which abandon the traditional right-angle grid system for a maze-like pattern of curving streets, are designed to discourage through traffic and channel it onto high-capacity arterial roads outside of the development.

Second, new house designs. The standard prewar house had been two storeys, either detached from its neighbours on a narrow lot, or semi-detached or built as part of row housing. The standard postwar house is a single-storey bungalow, broadside to the street and fully detached.

Third, a new development process.[5] Traditionally, Canadian cities had grown by expanding at their edges. Rural land on the outskirts was owned by a host of speculators, would-be home owners and house builders. City engineers extended the existing grid road system into the vacant land, installing roads and services. The municipality financed the cost by borrowing capital funds and repaying the loan with the proceeds of special local improvement taxes levied for a period of years on the owners of the lots which had been serviced. The Don Mills approach was different. One large developer assembled a large tract of land, several hundred or thousand acres. The developer (not city officials) planned the new suburb, and financed the installation of the necessary services with his own money. The developer sold the lots to homeowners who wanted to build their own houses, to small house builders, or kept them and built houses himself. The lot price included the cost of servicing, instead of being paid off as a supplement to property taxes.

The change from old to new patterns of suburban development didn't come overnight. In the early postwar years, many cities had supplies of empty serviced lots that provided an adequate quantity of land, and initially municipalities continued servicing new lots until the strains imposed by growing debt burdens led city after city to relinquish land servicing to the corporate developers. In most cities (Montreal was a notable exception), the transition was complete by 1970 and the corporate suburb was the way that the bulk of the new suburban lots in major urban centres were being produced. Suburban housing now accounts for the majority of all the new land absorbed by cities as they grow.*

Why people like the suburbs. Numerous studies of people's housing preferences have shown that people generally like living in the suburbs. For almost every Canadian family, a home of their own in the suburbs is their first urban housing choice. One Toronto study financed by a high-rise apartment developer showed, not surpris-

---

* Montreal, for instance, grew in size from 53,146 acres in 1952 to 113,284 acres in 1964. Of that 50,138-acre increase, 40,110 acres were used for suburban housing, with the balance split three ways between industry, "quasi-urban" and other uses. Of the 28,000 acres of land absorbed by Metro Toronto from 1958-1971, 15,000 were used for suburban housing. Not only is suburban housing the largest single consumer of new urban land; the suburbs are also where virtually all urban population growth has taken place. The highly visible residential redevelopment projects in central city areas have done little more than replace the housing accommodation demolished to make way for redevelopment and public works projects; net increases in population have been in the suburbs. While the Vancouver region has been growing at a rate of 2.9 percent annually overall, the city of Vancouver itself has been growing at the rate of only .77 percent while outlying suburbs have been increasing population at rates of 8.8 percent, 11.9 percent, and up to 17 percent per year. (*Urbanization: A study of urban expansion in the Montreal region* [Montreal: City of Montreal, 1968] p. 29; Matthew Lawson, *Jobs and the Economy* [Toronto: Metropolitan Toronto Planning Department, 1975] p. 36ff; *The Livable Region 1976/1986* [Vancouver: Greater Vancouver Regional District, 1975] p. 5)

ingly, that the first choice of people currently living in single-family housing in the suburbs was exactly what they had: single-family housing in the suburbs: 91.9 percent of the people in one sample and 93.5 percent in a second favoured this over all other housing alternatives.[6] What was surprising about the Toronto survey was that of the two sample groups of high-rise apartment tenants surveyed, a majority of both, 54 percent of one and 64 percent of the other, also preferred single-family home ownership over any alternative — including the option of high-rise rental living.*

Most people want to own their own home. In a Vancouver housing preference study, the moderate-income families who were the focus of the survey said they were willing to pay an additional $100 per month *for the same housing unit* in order to buy it on a long-term mortgage instead of renting.[7] The other attraction of suburban housing besides ownership is that its design provides many key features that people want, and which are not available in most other forms of housing: soundproofing, visual privacy, convenient parking, a front and back yard, lots of light and ventilation.[8] In most people's eyes, then, there is only one major problem with the houses being built by the development industry in the suburbs — their price. The alternatives — town houses, high-rise condominiums, and rental apartments — are the second choices of people whose incomes do not allow them to purchase a suburban house.[9]

The corporate land banks. This new postwar pattern of suburban development in Canada used up farmland at a very rapid rate. Thousands of acres were absorbed by the rapidly expanding postwar cities, most of it for suburban houses built at a ratio of five

---

* Much the same result was obtained in a sophisticated housing study of a randomly selected sample of people conducted in Vancouver. There, 71 percent of the sample put a single-family house in the suburbs as their first and ideal housing choice. In contrast, only ten of the 774 people surveyed put high-rise apartment living at the top of their housing preferences. (L. I. Bell and Jan Constantinescu, "The Housing Game: A study of consumer preferences in medium-density housing in the Greater Vancouver Region" [Vancouver: United Way of Vancouver, 1975] p. 12)

house lots (plus necessary land for public services) per acre. The appetite of suburban house-builders for raw land and the refusal of most municipalities to continue their practice of installing the necessary local roads and sewers led larger house-builders to get into the land business. They realized that they needed a continuous supply of serviced lots for their construction operation, and the only way of guaranteeing a supply of lots was to buy up raw land in suitable locations on the fringes of the city, obtain the necessary planning approvals to convert the land to house lots, and carry out the financing and the servicing themselves.

Starting in the 1950s, some larger house-builders like Robert Campeau in Ottawa began to assemble land banks for future suburban development. Other developers not involved in housing or participating only marginally in housing saw the long-term potential for profit in suburban land, and also put together other large land banks. Markborough Properties, a consortium of major financial interests, imitated E. P. Taylor's style in the Meadowvale assembly northwest of Toronto. Bruce McLaughlin's land holdings in Mississauga were far greater than needed to supply his modest house-building activities. Smaller house-builders who could not individually finance a land bank sometimes set up co-operative firms to buy up land and do servicing like Carma in Calgary and Ladco in Winnipeg. In the 1950s and 1960s modest prices were paid for these land bank purchases, often $1,500 to $3,000 per acre. At five lots per acre, that is only $300 to $600 per lot. Only a fraction of the purchase price was laid out in cash in most instances, minimizing the actual amount of cash required.*

---

* Looking at the figures for the basic Erin Mills land assembly, seven thousand acres northwest of Toronto purchased in the mid-1950s by E. P. Taylor's development corporation after Don Mills, prices range from $600 an acre for the Rutledge farm, $750 for the Stephens farm, $900 an acre for the McCracken property, $1,200 an acre for the Cook farm and so on. Putting together its 1,100-acre assembly in Thunder Bay, Headway Corp. paid about $2,000 an acre in 1965 for 193 acres that it developed as the County Park subdivision, and about $300 an acre for the 680-acre Anderson farm. In Calgary in 1964, BACM paid about $700 an acre for 640 acres pur-

The major corporate land banks are now extremely large. At the end of 1975, for example, Genstar owned 17,300 acres of development land in western Canada which had cost, in purchase price and carrying charges, an average of $5,500 an acre.[10] Abbey Glen owned 17,792 acres of development land at an average of about $8,000 per acre when Genstar took Abbey Glen over and doubled its land holdings.[11] Daon Development held 12,818 acres outright or under option in 1974, which had cost an average of about $10,000 per acre.[12]

The result of these corporate land assembly activities was that by the early 1970s in most large Canadian cities a few large developers held substantial acreages of land well suited for suburban development. The only important exception is Montreal, where land ownership is still highly fragmented, and some smaller centres, particularly in slow urban growth regions where the corporate developers have not yet taken up substantial positions in the local land market.

Relatively little information is available on these corporate land banks. In 1973, CMHC researcher Peter Spurr put together all the data available from public and other sources and identified corporate land assemblies totalling 103,092 acres around twenty-two cities.[13] In many of the cities surveyed, Spurr found that a small number of corporate assemblers held enough land to supply all the new suburban lots that would be required for the next five, ten or even fifteen years. The incomplete figures contained in Spurr's report (published in 1976 as *Land and Urban Development*) supplemented by other public sources (such as company reports and prospectuses) reveal the identities of many of the corporate developers and the size of some of their land holdings around various cities. More complete information is available on a few cities, including Winnipeg, Edmonton and Calgary. These confirm the

---

chased from Victor Ross Giles and Conrad Keith Giles, both farmers, for land developed ten years later as the Marlborough Park subdivision. (Erin Mills figures from 1976 title search of original land assembly by Jeff House; Headway Corporation Limited prospectus; Calgary title searches February 1976)

dominance of the few large corporate developers in the local market.*

Until full and accurate information is available on land holding patterns around all large Canadian cities, it is difficult to know how typical the Winnipeg and Calgary examples are. Private land banks may be somewhat larger in terms of the overall consumption of urban land in these two cases than in other cities. Incomplete information on some other cities like Toronto, Ottawa, London, Van-

---

* In Winnipeg, the "big four" developers owned 12,878 acres in 1976. The four were: Genstar's subsidiary BACM, with 5,219; Qualico, with 2,950; Metropolitan, with 1,763 and Ladco with 2,946. With Winnipeg using about 750 acres a year for residential growth, this land bank is sufficient to provide all the land needed for seventeen years. Public land assemblies totalled an additional 7,700 acres, but these were farther away from the path of growth than the developers' holdings. The assemblies were mapped in a confidential report by a provincial government researcher.

In Calgary, a 1976 report identified ten corporate developers with major suburban land holdings. Nu-West and Carma (Nu-West is Carma's major shareholder, with just under 50 percent of the company) owned 4,070 acres inside the city limits at the time of the report and 5,400 acres outside, a total of 9,470 acres. Genstar subsidiaries BACM, Kelwood and Abbey Glen together owned 2,780 acres inside the city limits and 6,270 outside, a total of 9,050 acres. Daon owned 1,600 acres inside and 2,840 outside, a total of 4,440. Qualico owned 1,220 inside and 1,760 outside, totalling 2,980. Three smaller firms were also involved: Melton with 2,250 inside the city limits, Jager with 1,010, and Premier with 170. These seven together owned 12,110 acres inside the city limits and 16,360 outside, a total of 28,470 acres.

At Calgary's minimum density figure of twenty-two persons per acre, the corporate land bank inside the city limits would accommodate an additional 266,000 people. The holdings outside the city limits would house 360,000 additional people. Calgary's projected growth over the next twenty years is 365,000 people, and at that rate of increase the 1976 corporate land bank was sufficient to provide all suburban house lots needed in Calgary for the next thirty-five years. Genstar and Nu-West-Carma alone have more than half that total acreage, and enough land between just the two of them to provide for all Calgary's housing needs for about twenty years. (Bill Bloxom, "Housing needs and development potential of existing landbanks," [Winnipeg: Leaf Rapids Corporation, June 1976]; *Calgary Albertan* 27 April 1976 reporting data from a 1976 Calgary city hall report)

couver and Victoria suggests that the land assemblies are not as large in relation to absorption of land and, in the largest cities, there may be six to eight corporations of relatively equal size with a dominant position in the local market, in contrast to Calgary's giant two and Winnipeg's big four.[14] Incomplete local studies in many cities, however, point to the same conclusion that is indicated by the detailed Calgary and Winnipeg information: that a few large development corporations own substantial assemblies of land, well-located for urban expansion and sufficient to supply all the lots that will be required over the next five, ten or fifteen years.[15]

Keeping ahead of red tape. Turning land banks into serviced suburban lots ready for house construction takes time. This long lead time means that every large suburban developer has to plan carefully several years ahead, with one eye on the housing market and the other on the other major firms in the local market.

The process of suburban development has two major stages. The first is the approval process. Every new suburban development requires a considerable number of approvals from city councils and other public bodies, seventy to one hundred in southern Ontario according to the developers' lobby, the Urban Development Institute.[16] The approval process is frustrating to developers because it isn't completely within their control. It can take an indeterminate length of time and a requested approval can be refused. But seeking approvals for a suburban development costs the development firm very little. In the circumstances, developers have every reason to seek approvals for development of their land assemblies as soon as it is reasonable to expect that these will be granted, so that they have a ready supply of land on hand for servicing.

As the report of the Winnipeg suburban land inquiry noted, "Once a major developer acquired land he would seek approval for development at the earliest possible time."[17] This can be many years before actual development is anticipated. In the late 1960s, Genstar subsidiary BACM went to Edmonton city council seeking city approval of development of a 2,500-acre land assembly, Castle Downs, which they projected developing between 1970 and 1985 or later.[18] If developers anticipate a slow-up in the approval process, they move more quickly. Winnipeg's land development industry knew that the Unicity reorganization of municipal government in 1972-73 would create a hiatus in their approval process. "Anticipating difficulty with the new approval process, they... sought and obtained an unusually large number of approvals in 1971," reports the Winnipeg land inquiry.[19] Development corporations learn from experience and operate so as to avoid problems arising from the approval process. Reported an industry trade publication in 1975, "In Cadillac Fairview's specific case, a mass of long-range projects initiated three or four years ago is coming clear of government red tape and the company has stepped up land-banking activities to avoid a similar slowdown in future projects."[20]

Servicing. Deciding on how much land to put through the servicing process is a good deal more complicated than pressing ahead getting land through the approval process. Servicing land involves laying out considerable amounts of cash to pay suppliers of engineering services, sewer and road contractors, and so on. Some of the cash involved will be the developer's own, but most is borrowed. Interest on the funds borrowed to finance servicing is an expense that can be minimized only when land is serviced quickly and the resulting lots are sold to builders for construction as soon as they are ready. Valuable cash cannot be tied up for too long in serviced lots.

Large development corporations have to estimate the market for new suburban houses six to twenty-four months in advance. The servicing process takes six to eighteen months, the construction process another six to eighteen months. Explained the Winnipeg land inquiry report: "Characteristically, [the developer] would service and offer for sale each building season the number of lots that, in his estimate, could be sold at the prevailing market price. He would likely be careful not to service more lots than would be currently required, since he would thereby incur extra and unnecessary interest charges."[21]

In making advance plans for suburban land servicing, the only reasonable assumption for each major developer to make is that the market price for suburban lots in the future will be what it is today. Anticipated demand for lots can then be forecast on the basis of previous years' demand, with some allowance for expected changes in conditions which would somewhat increase or reduce people's willingness to buy new houses. With a forecast of the size of the total demand, each major developer usually assumes that his firm will capture about the same share of the total market as it has held in the past. Using these assumptions, each developer decides every year what quantity of new suburban lots to supply from its land assembly.

When lots are serviced and ready for construction, the corporate developer has three choices about what to do with them. First, they can be retained by the company and used by its house construction division, if it has one, as sites for homes it builds itself. Second, they can be sold to another of the large corporate developers. This is common industry practice, permitting each large firm to spread its house-building activities into several sectors of the city instead of specializing only in the sector where the firm's land bank is located. Third, serviced lots can be sold to small home builders who depend on the big land developers to obtain lots so they can stay in the house construction business.

The land oligopoly. With ownership of large amounts of suburban land for future development held by a few corporate developers, there are in most cities only a handful of firms capable of producing a significant quantity of suburban house lots. In Thunder Bay, it is one; in Winnipeg it is four; in Calgary is four; in Edmonton, seven. The existence of large developer-owned land assemblies around major cities does not on its own prove anything about the suburban land market. The key fact is who is turning raw land into serviced suburban land for house construction — how many developers are active in this field and how they share the market. Large land assemblies held by a handful of corporate developers give them the *potential* to dominate the development business in that locality. Whether in fact they do so depends on the share of the total of serviced lots they actually produce, on the role of smaller developers in the local market, and on the contribution, if any, of public land banks to the housing lot supply.

As it turns out, there is little adequate information on who is actually supplying the new house lots in most Canadian cities. In the only three cities, Calgary, Winnipeg, and Edmonton, where reasonably comprehensive information is available, the large corporate developers are indeed using their private land banks to produce enough lots to be also the dominant suppliers of new house lots on the local markets.*

And, while there is an overall oligopoly in the suburban land development business in many cities, the tendency of the corporate land assemblers each to take a sector or two of the city and to concentrate their holdings in those areas adds to their potential market power. There may be four or five large firms producing 80 percent of the new lots, but in practice this often means that one firm is producing 100 percent of the lots to the south of the city, a second has the west to itself, and so on. Notes a 1976 Calgary planning study: "Some sectors of the city are virtually controlled by one or two developers and, therefore, although there may be

---

* A 1976 Calgary planning study notes that, "According to the City records, since January 1, 1973, there have been twenty-four developers active in Calgary but of these, the top five have 81 percent of the lots in outline plans and 85 percent of the building permits issued." In fact, of the five largest firms, Genstar subsidiaries BACM and Kelwood accounted for 26 percent of all lots for which building permits were issued in the three-year period from 1973 to 1976. Daon received permits for 20 percent, Carma 30 percent, Qualico 9 percent and all the other developers added up to another 15 percent.

In Winnipeg, according to the final report of the provincial land inquiry, "over 80 percent of the residential lots built on each year were produced by the four major developer-builders out of land which they owned."

In Edmonton, analyzing city figures, seven firms supplied 66 percent of all the lots developed by private firms from October 1972 to March 1976. BACM alone accounted for about 30 percent of all serviced lots developed by private firms during that period. (Planning department, "Housing in Calgary, Background paper No. 4" [Calgary: City of Calgary, April 1976] p. 23; Ruben Bellan, *Report and Recommendations of the Winnipeg Land Prices Inquiry Commission* [Winnipeg: Queen's Printer, 1977] p. 19; Edmonton figures calculated from city reports on lot production by planning area from October 1972 to March 1976 using information from city officials on ownership of land in the planning areas)

competition between developers on a city-wide basis, very often there is little competition in a development area."[22]*

How the suburban developers set lot prices. To decide how many new serviced lots they should produce each year, the major developers have to make some assumption about how many lots people will buy. To do this, as we have noted, they have to make an assumption about what the market price will be. The simplest and most sensible assumption is that the price over the immediate future will remain at its current level.

When the new lots are produced and the developer has to set a price for them, he is likely to list them at the price the company estimated in its planning. As long as the lots sell at about the pace the developer forecast, the price will stay where it is. But if other corporate developers decline to buy these lots in the usual quantities, or if small builders pass them by, the company will look for the explanation. If it is that sales of finished suburban houses have slackened, inventories of completed but unsold houses are building up, and builders are being more cautious about starting new construction, the developer will sit tight and hold prices where they are. If unsold lots build up, the company responds by cutting back on planned production, and reducing the amount of land be-

---

* This same point was noted by the authors of Calgary's controversial Genstar report, who mapped land holdings around the city. Said the report about Genstar's holdings in the southwest sector of Calgary: "The combined land holdings of BACM and Quality [Qualico Developments Ltd.] constitute a complete dominance of this sector of the city."

Winnipeg's land inquiry noted the same pattern. "A certain degree of regional specialization [in suburban land assembly] occurred, each firm having acquired holdings chiefly in one or two sectors beyond the built-up area. BACM developed land primarily in the north, in Transcona and the Kildonans; Winnipeg Supply and Fuel largely concentrated on its Westdale development in Charleswood; Ladco's holdings were largely in the south and east, in Fort Garry and St. Vital." ("Report of the preliminary investigation on activities of Genstar Limited" [Calgary: City of Calgary, December 1973] p. iv-31; Bellan, *Land Prices Inquiry Commission Report*, p. 16)

ing serviced. If, however, it turns out that every other development corporation's serviced lots are selling, the explanation for slow sales is that this particular developer overpriced his lots, and an adjustment will be made to get his price in line with the others. No matter how slowly lots are selling, however, the major developers will not make substantial cuts in their list prices. Instead, they hang on, waiting for the market to absorb the lots they've produced. While they wait, they cut back on the production of any new lots.

While lots may sell more slowly than forecast, they may also sell more quickly. When this happens, the developer must determine why. It may be that his prices are a bit too low, slightly out of line with everyone else's, and they will be adjusted upwards. It may also be because new homes are selling faster than expected, overall demand is higher than the industry had forecast, and home builders are looking for more lots than they had expected to need in order to keep up with demand. In this situation, the corporate developer can respond two ways. First, the company can speed up the production of new lots to keep up with demand. But given the time lags involved in the servicing process, speeding up work will take six to twelve months to have any major impact. Meanwhile there are more builders and other developers willing to pay the price that has been set on the developer's serviced lots than there are lots for them to buy. The alternative response? Increase the price. If demand is in fact strong, builders try to find lots at the old price from other developers, but if they discover that there are not enough lots being offered by the large developers, they are prepared to pay the higher price. They figure, correctly, that they can pass on the increase to home buyers.

The other big land developers, seeing that one local firm is getting a higher price for its lots, will have no reason to maintain their lower prices, and every reason to increase them to the new level. Their explanation? Strong consumer demand, not enough lots at the old price to satisfy everyone, and a shortage of serviced lots. Of course once a higher price is set, no corporate developer stands to gain by reducing its price below this level. Every new price increase soon becomes the minimum price for the local market.

The major corporate developers don't have to conspire together (as the gypsum wallboard manufacturers in western Canada did) to find out how much each is charging for new serviced lots or to set prices. As the Winnipeg land inquiry pointed out, they often buy lots from each other, so they know each other's prices. Nor do they need a formal agreement to fix prices. It is obvious that, when demand is strong, they all benefit by raising prices if one firm does so successfully. Once prices are raised, it is in none of the large developers' interests to lower them and spark off a round of price-cutting.

Ready for the price explosion: The transformation in the process of suburban land development which got underway in the 1950s moved ahead quickly in the 1960s. Municipality after municipality abandoned their efforts to keep up with demand for serviced land, and pushed the onus for servicing onto the developers. The greater cash requirements of this kind of development and the advantages that came from dealing with large parcels of vacant land gave a substantial edge to the large developers, and froze many of the small-time speculators and developers out of the market. The supply of vacant land owned by smaller property owners was rapidly used up, while the corporate land banks were poised to absorb projected house-building needs for several years. The large house-builders who got into suburban land assembly and development did so, as they often point out, as a defensive move to ensure a regular supply of serviced lots. Others got into the business because of its profit potential.

Many of the developers may not have realized the implications of a transformation of the suburban land development business from one with hundreds of small owners of developed lots to one where a few large corporate developers dominated the supply of lots. A few, starting with E. P. Taylor himself, certainly did understand the potential of this situation. After all, Taylor had discovered how much greater the profits were in the beer industry when he was able to merge several small breweries into one giant firm with power to influence prices. Taylor led the way to applying the same principle to the suburban land business with Don Mills. Other developers may have been only following in Taylor's footsteps, but they certainly have not been disappointed about where they led. This new pattern of suburban land development is directly responsible for the house price explosion that occurred from 1971 to 1976 in most Canadian cities. The results: unaffordable prices for suburban houses and incredible profits for the suburban land developers.

5

WHY SUBURBAN
HOUSES COST
TOO MUCH

Ralph Scurfield's Nu-West Development Corp. had a TV commercial running in Calgary in the summer of 1976 featuring an ordinary-looking house in a development grandiosely named Chateaux on the Green. After extolling the virtues of the house and the project, the ad got to the point. "Prices start at $63,000," said a gravelly-voiced announcer. He paused, then added: "For a very few lucky families."

The implication was that anyone able to buy a $63,000 single-family house in Calgary's suburbs in 1976 was getting a terrific deal. In fact, that house and lot cost about $20,000 more than they needed to. My research that summer indicated that Calgary's land developers were making a profit of about $20,000 on every house lot they sold, over and above normal profits earned in the construction of the house itself, and in servicing the land.

What has happened to the suburban land business in Calgary, and in most other large Canadian cities, in summary, is this:

☐ As we saw in the last chapter, a few large development corporations, from one to about eight in most cases, have assembled land banks in strategic locations which are large enough to supply all the suburban lots that will be developed over the next five to fifteen years.

☐ These same large development corporations are producing most of the privately developed new suburban house lots in these cities.

☐ The joint decision-making power of these corporate land developers enables them to determine the supply of new suburban lots, and to exercise an effective measure of control over prices.

□ The developers have used their market power in ways which led to enormous price increases for suburban house lots in the last decade, and particularly from 1971 to 1976, so that land was a major factor in the house price explosion which doubled new house prices in most cities between 1971 and 1976.

□ Most of the price increases on suburban house lots resulted not from higher costs of production, but rather from astonishing increases in the profits made by developers on those lots.

□ Profits by the large suburban land developers on their lots added $7,000 to $10,000 to the price of new $50,000 homes in cities like Regina and Winnipeg as of 1978, and $15,000 to $24,000 to the price of $60,000 to $65,000 houses in Victoria, Vancouver, Calgary, Edmonton, London, Hamilton, Toronto and Ottawa and other high-priced cities in 1978.

□ When high prices and a depressed economy substantially reduced demand for housing from about 1975 on, the developers used their market power to prevent suburban lot prices from falling significantly and bringing new house prices down to affordable levels

Many of the people who are in the best position to know, particularly the developers themselves, deny the accuracy of this analysis of what's happened in the suburban land business. "It is not true that developers are taking an excess beyond normal profits," Edmonton Urban Development Institute president Dave McDougall said in September 1974.[1] Said former Calgary chief commissioner Dennis Cole in 1973: "I don't think there is any way developers are making excessive profits on the development of land they buy."[2]

More recently the industry has taken to saying nothing at all about their profits. Comments Ira Gluskin, in his analysis of Cadillac Fairview for the Royal Commission on Corporate Concentration:

There can be no doubt that the absolute level of profits in the development industry has inclined sharply over the past five years. The author has made this statement quite openly and disagrees with the statements of industry spokesmen who fail to acknowledge the high profit levels.[3]

The industry also generally fails to acknowledge the market power it has developed in the suburban land development business, even though the occasional developer like Genstar admits to a corporate strategy of becoming "a major factor" in every business it is involved in. Rhys Smith, director of the Calgary Regional Planning Commission, said in a June 1976 report, "Bluntly, the few large developers control the supply now, the market now, the price now, and the future. In the future, an even greater proportion of land will be under control of the few large developers."[4]

The trend to corporate concentration has been stronger and better documented in Calgary than in most other cities, but Smith's analysis holds true for most of the rest of the country.

Suburban land prices and profits.[5] In February 1976, I was in Calgary looking at suburban houses and analyzing the prices of new house lots. I found a house being built by Engineered Homes, a subsidiary of Genstar, on a lot in the Marlborough Park subdivision on the east side of the city. The house, called the Monterey model, was a plain, three-bedroom bungalow, 1,120 square feet, with a semi-finished basement, no garage, no fireplace, one and a half bathrooms, and a narrower than usual forty-foot lot. The price was $54,000.

I estimated the cost of construction, including normal builder's profit, on the basis of figures from local CMHC officials and people in the industry at $30 per square foot, $33,600 for the house. So the price of the lot was $20,400.

The land on which the house was built was purchased by BACM, a Genstar subsidiary, in 1964 for $745 per acre. The cost of the raw land for one lot (plus a share of the land required to provide for roads, parks and so on) was $138. Carrying costs on that land for twelve years were another $160. Taxes cost $60. The services installed by the developer, including fees for planning and engineering, taxes, levies and other expenses cost $150 a frontage foot in this subdivision, $6,000 for this forty-foot lot. The carrying costs of the servicing between the time it was installed and the time

SUBURBAN LAND DEVELOPMENT COSTS AND PROFITS

	Calgary Marlbo- rough Park Feb. 76	Vancouver Harbour Village summer 1976	Toronto Erin Mills summer 1976
Raw land	$ 138	$ 757	$ 909
Carrying costs	160	250	836
Taxes	60	150	620
Servicing	6,000	13,800	5,134
Servicing carrying costs	400		616
Selling costs	1,000	1,000	1,500
Other	—	—	3,053
Total cost	7,758	15,957	12,668
Selling price	20,400	30,804	33,934
Profit	12,642	14,847	21,266

the house was ready for occupancy were about $400. Selling costs are estimated at $1,000. So the total cost to Genstar of producing this lot was $7,758. With a selling price of $20,400, that means the developer's profit on this lot was $12,642.

In July 1976 I did more research in Calgary. The local market was still booming, and new suburban house prices had risen substantially since February. I called the real estate broker who had shown me the $54,000 house, and asked him if he had a similar unit available for a similar price. The best he could come up with was not a Monterey but a Loyalist, the same house in every respect except for the front windows, a fireplace, and its fifty-foot lot. The price: $69,000. Using the same cost figures, taking account of the higher servicing costs on a wider lot, and including the cost of the fireplace, my estimate of the price of the house was $34,500. The price for this lot was $34,500. The cost of producing that lot was $10,800. The developer's profit: $24,600.

In spring 1976 Genstar's Engineered Homes was selling houses in the Harbour Village subdivision in Vancouver's suburbs. The house I looked at was the same basic three-bedroom unit, but with some fancy extras like sliding glass doors. Its price: $68,000. My estimate of the construction cost of this house was $37,196. The price of the lot: $30,804. The land had been assembled by Genstar in 1972-73 at a cost of an average of $3,030 an acre. So the raw land for this lot cost $757. Carrying costs added another $250; taxes $150. Servicing, fees and related carrying costs I estimated at $13,800 on the basis of costs in a similar municipal land development project in nearby Port Moody plus figures from a developers' association study. Selling costs, an estimated $1,000. The developer's profit on this $30,804 lot: $14,847.

In June 1976 a similar but more modest three-bedroom bungalow with a garage in the basement was being sold by Cadillac Fairview in their Erin Mills development near Toronto for $63,995. The construction cost (including normal builder's profit) for the 1,140-square-foot house alone was $30,061. The lot price was $33,934. Analyzing prices and profits in Erin Mills, I was able to make use of a very detailed study of developers' costs in this area recently completed by planners working for the regional municipality.[6] It is the best such study I have encountered.* Using those figures, total production cost of this lot was $12,668. The developer's profit: $21,266.

Of the costs involved in suburban land development, the original price paid by the corporate developer for land bank land turns out to be a relatively modest factor. Even at prices of $10,000 per acre, raw land costs only $2,000 per lot assuming that an acre yields the usual five standard lots plus necessary public land. Carrying

---

* When the developer purchased the raw land for the Erin Mills lot in 1956, the cost was $909. Carrying costs to 1976, as indicated in the developer's financial statements, were $836. Servicing costs were $5,134, using figures from the regional government study obtained by surveying the actual experience of developers in the area. Carrying costs on servicing added another $616; fees to engineers, surveyors and others, $681; property taxes $620; levies imposed by the local municipality $2,272; land transfer tax $100; and selling costs $1,500 yield a total production cost of $12,668 for this lot. (Canadian Equity & Development Co. Ltd., *Annual Report* 1973; servicing and other cost information from an unreleased study by housing planners of the Regional Municipality of Peel, 1975)

costs on the acquisition price and property taxes are also relatively minor factors. Servicing costs are a substantially greater component of costs. Servicing costs do vary substantially from city to city, depending on the standard of services required by local authorities, and the ease of installation. Standard servicing costs for a fifty-foot suburban lot in 1975-76 were about $4,600 in Winnipeg, $8,300 in Edmonton, $6,000 in Toronto, $5,000 in Halifax, $11,000 in Thunder Bay, $13,000 in Vancouver on difficult terrain.[7] Fees to engineers, planners, surveyors and other professionals are a relatively minor share of these servicing expenses. Selling costs covering the cost of selling the lot and the house are often high as a cost item, though they are much lower for large developer-builders than for individuals who use the services of real estate agents.

The production costs in developing suburban lots, as these few examples illustrate, bear no relationship to the selling price of those lots. The corporate developer's expenses are a minor portion of that selling price. Nor can the increases that occurred in suburban serviced lot prices between 1971 and 1976 be related to any similarly substantial increases in costs.

Public land banks: the difference profit makes. The profits being made by the corporate developers on their suburban land assemblies are so large that is is sometimes difficult to believe that the figures are accurate. Indeed, in my own estimates of profits in specific cases I have tried to ensure that every conceivable element of direct costs has been taken into account, and that all estimates (particularly estimates of construction costs) are conservative so that the final profit figures are, in fact, minimum estimates.

There is, however, external evidence available which confirms the accuracy of these profit figures. It arises out of the operations of public authorities in many cities who are involved in producing serviced house lots out of public land banks. These public land assemblies were usually purchased at market prices by their owners, sometimes by negotiation with landowners, sometimes by expropriation. The purchase prices paid for public land bank lands are in exactly the same range as the prices paid by the corporate developers. The money to finance these purchases is almost always borrowed, sometimes at something less than the market rate for

DEVELOPER PROFITS AND SUBURBAN HOUSE PRICES

City	Project	House and lot price	Lot price	Developer's profit on lot
Toronto	Erin Mills (Malvern public land bank)	63,995 —	33,934 —	21,266 (24,000)
Calgary	Marlborough Park Feb. 1976	54,000	20,400	12,642
	Marlborough Park July 1976	69,900	35,400	24,600
Vancouver	Harbour Way	68,000	30,804	14,847
	Port Moody Barber St. (public development)	—	28,000	11,755
Edmonton	Mill Woods (private portion)	60,000	24,300	13,025
	Castle Downs	61,100	29,600	15,100
Thunder Bay			20,000	8,500
Winnipeg	Waverley Heights area	53,995	19,600	9,800
Halifax	Forest Hills (comparative price cited by Housing Commission)		11,000	5,000

Sources: Data from investigations of sample houses in summer 1976 supplemented by cost information from municipal and provincial planners and public land bank administrations.

---

private firms, and taxes are not always paid. Land purchase prices and carrying costs are, however, a minor factor in the final cost of developing a suburban lot, so any cost advantage of the public land banks is minor. The major cost element is, of course, servicing. Most public land bank administrations contract out servicing work to the same contractors that are used by the corporate developers, and often planning, engineering and surveying work is also done by the same outside consultants. There is no substantial difference between what the corporate developers pay for servicing and what public land banks pay. The usual practice is also to attribute a portion if not all administrative costs involved in the land assembly operation to land costs, and often public land banks set their prices so as to include a comfortable profit margin to cover unforeseen expenses.

Public land banking operations across the country confirm the large difference between the selling price of new suburban lots and the costs of producing these lots. In one instance, lots in suburban Port Moody near Vancouver were selling in 1976 for $28,000 which cost a total of $16,245 for servicing including an allowance for land at $2,000 a lot. The profit per lot: $11,755. Next door was a private subdivision where lots were selling for $30,000.*

Edmonton's large Mill Woods public land development is a more typical project of its type. In 1976, single-family lots in Mill Woods were being sold by the city for $12,500. This included $3,300 to cover the cost of the land and other administrative expenses, and $9,200 for services. Similar standard single-family lots in the corporate developers' projects were priced at $24,000 to $29,000 indicating developer profit margins of $12,000 to $18,000 per lot.[8]

Like Port Moody, Thunder Bay has developed small subdivisions of single-family house lots on municipally owned land. Its reserve prices on these lots cover all costs, and include an allowance for land based on $2,500 per acre. In 1976 city lots were

---

* The Vancouver suburb of Port Moody was unusual in its public land banking operation, the Barber Street subdivision, because the land involved was municipally owned and had cost nothing. In 1976, a sixty-foot lot in the project was selling for an average of $28,000. The development was managed for the municipality by a consulting engineering firm, Underwood McClelland Associates. Services included the usual streets, sewers and water supply, underground wiring, and sidewalks. Total cost of the servicing, consultants, surveyors, legal costs, advertising, and sales commissions worked out to $14,245 a lot. Assume a land cost of $10,000 an acre, higher than the land cost the municipality would have incurred if it had bought the land a few years earlier, and that adds $2,000 to total costs, making it $16,245. The profit per lot sold: $11,755. Port Moody estimated its total profit on the 138-lot subdivision at $1,767,024. (R. H. Blackwood, "Report to the City of Port Moody planning committee from the municipal administrator" 8 January 1976)

being produced at a cost of \$11,500; the suburban developers were selling theirs for \$20,000.[9] Profit margin indicated: \$8,500.

In Halifax-Dartmouth, the Nova Scotia Housing Commission has been relatively aggressive in the land assembly and development business, with two large projects providing serviced lots at selling prices which cover acquisition costs, servicing and administrative overhead. In summer 1976 the Commission was selling fifty-foot lots in the Forest Hills project for \$6,030. The commission's estimate of the price of a similar lot from a Halifax developer was about \$11,000, suggesting a profit margin of \$5,000.[10]

In Toronto, the Malvern public land assembly project assembled in the 1950s, about the time that the corporate developers were starting to put together their large holdings, was being developed in 1975. Malvern assembly costs were typical for the period, and the costs to the Ontario Housing Corporation of installing services were the same as those encountered by private developers in the Toronto area. For a single-family lot in Malvern, the provincial government estimated in 1975 that the difference between its market value and the total cost of developing it was \$24,000.[11]*

An indication of the impact of the developer's profit on people's ability to afford suburban houses came in Edmonton in 1976 when the city announced it would sell 725 serviced lots in the Mill Woods project that summer for \$12,500. Three thousand families sent in applications to purchase one of these lots.

---

* These reasonable (from a cost point of view) but low (from a market price point of view) public land bank prices create their own problems. Some public land banks, like Port Moody's, sell their lots for the going market price and pocket the profit. Others, like Thunder Bay's, set a price mid-way between costs and the private market price so that the developer's profit is split between the purchaser and the land bank. Still others, like Halifax and Edmonton, set a price which is intended only to cover all costs. The purchaser pays a price that covers the full cost of his lot, but finds himself paying far less than purchasers of lots from private developers. Land bank administrators have tried to find ways of giving home buyers the benefit of reasonable land prices while ensuring that the lucky few who are able to get public land assembly lots do not turn around and sell their lots, pocketing the profit that normally goes to the developer. So, for instance, the Ontario Housing Corporation placed an interest-free mortgage on its Malvern lots for the \$24,000 difference between the cost of the lot and its market price.

Costs, prices and profits. Prices of suburban houses in 1976 in most
Canadian cities were at least double the 1971 level. Profits on suburban lots played a far larger role in final house prices in 1976 than
in 1971, but land profit increases accounted for only a portion of
the total price rise. Construction costs went up substantially, and
so did the cost of servicing land. The average cost of constructing
an 1,100-square-foot standard suburban house went from $16,500
in 1971 to $29,700 in 1976, a jump of $13,200.[12] The amount of
this increase varied somewhat from city to city.

The increase in lot prices in many cities was even greater in this
period. Figures reported by CMHC for standard suburban lot
prices in 1971 compared with sample prices I recorded in mid-1976
for ordinary lots show the extent of the increases in lot prices in
four high-priced cities.* When construction cost increases were
adding an average of $13,200 to the final price of a suburban
house, lot price increases were adding $17,400 to $29,200 in the
four cities. Similar increases were recorded in other high-price
cities.

There were cost increases in the suburban land development
business during this period, so the lot price rise is not accounted
for completely by an increase in developers' profits. Wages in the
construction industry went up by an average of 80 percent from
1971 to 1976; materials were up by 65 percent.[13] Basic services for
a standard suburban lot in Winnipeg, for instance, went from
$2,600 in 1971 to $4,600 in 1976.[14] But, as we've already seen,
services make up a relatively small portion of the total price of

---

* My experience in investigating suburban lot prices has been that the
figures reported by CMHC in its annual publication *Canadian Housing Statistics* for average lot prices in different cities are currently
substantially less than the minimum prices being charged by the developers for standard fifty-foot lots in typical suburbs. The 1976
prices reported in my table for Toronto, Calgary, Edmonton and
Vancouver are all considerably higher than those reported by
CMHC. CMHC's underestimates apparently result from a combination of factors: including under-market-priced land bank lots in
cities where these are available, restricting the sample to only those
single-family houses financed under NHA-insured mortgages, and
perhaps a tendency by builders to under-report land prices and over-
report construction prices in some cities.

suburban lots in 1976, and the increases in servicing costs that occurred between 1971 and 1976 account for only a few thousand dollars of the price jump. The other cost components also rose relatively modestly during the period, even though the percentage increase was often large. The bulk of the lot price increase was a result of increased developer profits.

Intensified demand. To explain why suburban land prices exploded between 1971 and 1976, and why the developers were able to add such enormous mark-ups to their costs of land development, we must understand the relationship between intensified demand for housing during those years and the response of the developers to this situation.

Demand for housing strengthened considerably in the period. Some of the factors involved were entirely beyond government control. The baby boom generation of the postwar years was seeking the sort of housing they wanted to raise their own families in. The general economic climate, price inflation everywhere and a sense that house prices were going to rise even higher encouraged people to buy houses earlier than they would have otherwise.

But what is extraordinary about the 1971 to 1976 increase is the contribution made by governments, particularly the federal government, to intensify even further what was already strong consumer demand for housing. Look at the list of government measures and programs implemented in this period:

☐ Changes in NHA rules reduced the cash down payments required for many new houses. As the Winnipeg land inquiry pointed out, in 1972 the buyer of a $45,000 new house had to make a down payment of $20,000. By 1976, a new $45,000 house could be bought for a down payment of just $2,250.[15]

☐ Mortgage lenders, most of them under the direct regulation of Ottawa or provincial authorities, increased the percentage of family income that new house buyers were allowed to spend on mortgage payments, and liberalized practices about counting second incomes as part of total family income. Both these changes added to the demand for new suburban housing.[16]

☐ Federal capital gains tax legislation which became effective

THE SUBURBAN HOUSE PRICE EXPLOSION 1971-1976

—standard three-bedroom suburban bungalow prices—

	1971	*1976*	*Increase 71-76*	*%*
Vancouver				
house[1]	19,178	37,196	18,018	94%
lot	8,179	30,804	22,625	277%
total price	27,357	68,000	40,643	
Calgary				
house	18,055	34,500	16,445	91%
lot	5,848	35,400	29,552	505%
total price	23,893	69,900	45,997	
Edmonton				
house	19,049	31,500	12,451	65%
lot	6,663	29,600	22,937	344%
total price	25,712	61,100	35,388	
Toronto				
house	20,539	30,061	9,522	46%
lot	12,107	33,934	21,827	180%
total price	32,646	63,995	31,349	
Montreal[2]				
house	15,655	28,949	13,294	85%
lot	2,179	3,229	1,050	48%
total price	17,834	32,178	14,344	
Average NHA single-detached construction cost, Canada	17,506	30,665	13,159	75%

Sources: The 1971 figures are as reported by CMHC in *Canadian Housing Statistics 1971.* The 1976 figures are from my own research, except for Montreal which is from *Canadian Housing Statistics 1976.* The Canada-wide construction average price is from the same CMHC sources.

Notes to table

1. The house prices in this table are for a standard suburban three-bed-room bungalow. The houses vary somewhat in size and quality from

in 1972, by exempting profits made on a person's principal residence from capital gains tax, encouraged people to invest in owning a house.[17]

☐ The federal RHOSP program beginning in this period added to housing demand by permitting middle-income families to avoid paying substantial amounts of personal income tax if they put away money for a down payment on a house.[18]

☐ The federal Assisted Home Ownership Plan (AHOP) provided government cash contributions to down payments and monthly payments for purchasers of relatively low-priced new houses starting in 1973.

☐ Provincial governments contributed to intensified housing demand by offering one-time grants to purchasers buying their first home.

Many of these government programs were instituted to enable people to buy housing at a time when house prices were rising. Other measures, like changing the rules about second family in-

---

city to city, and details of the variations for the 1971 figures can be seen in the CMHC table from which this information is taken. Details of the variations between the 1976 houses are given in the text. In general, the Calgary, Edmonton and Toronto houses were very similar, and the Vancouver house used was finished to a slightly higher standard.

The large discrepancies in the increases in construction costs among the cities is accounted for more by variations in the size and quality of the houses than in substantially different rates of increase in construction costs in those cities. The average Canada-wide construction cost increase shown on the table indicates a more accurate measure of the contribution of construction cost increases to the final price of suburban houses during the period.

2. The Montreal lot price does not include services, whereas lot prices for all other cities in this table do include services. Servicing in Montreal is paid for not as part of the house-plus-lot price as in the other cities, but as an additional local improvement charge added to a new home purchaser's property tax bill by the municipality. Servicing adds another $5,000 to $6,000 to the price of a three-bedroom Montreal house in 1976, so the correct comparison between Montreal and the other cities in the table would be between a total price of about $37,000 to $38,000 in Montreal and $61,000 to $69,900 in the other cities.

comes in computing ability to pay mortgages, were appropriate liberalizations of outmoded policies. Coming at the time they did, however, these policies and programs served to add to the demand on the suburban housing market.

The developers' response. In most Canadian cities the intensified demand for housing from 1971-76 ran up against the large suburban developers. The developers' response was not to scramble to increase the number of lots they were supplying at the market price. Instead, they raised prices, and charged more for the lots they had already planned to produce. This failure to substantially increase supply is evident in housing starts. In Vancouver, single-family-housing starts went from 5,283 in 1971 to 8,729 in 1973, declining after that and then rising slightly to 7,777 in 1976. In Toronto, single-family starts went from 6,972 in 1971 to a high of 9,101 in 1972, declining to 6,216 in 1976.

Indeed, in most cities the quantity of lots being supplied by the suburban developers rose from 1971 to 1973 or 1974, but then declined again even though consumer demand was still strong. Often it was *after* supply declined that the most massive price increases came.* The only significant exceptions to this pattern are Edmonton, where a sizeable public land banking operation was producing a significant number of new lots by 1975, and Montreal.

Intensified demand for suburban housing was at least as strong in Montreal as in most other large Canadian cities; so was inflation. Construction costs went up by the same amount in Montreal from

---

* In Calgary, 5,229 single-family lots had houses started on them in 1974. That was the highest figure for the period. The Calgary price explosion came in 1975-76, and it was during those years that the supply of serviced lots was *reduced*. In 1975, 4,887 single-family lots had houses started on them. In 1976 the figure was down again, to 4,111.

  In Toronto, housing starts on single-family lots jumped from 6,972 in 1971 to 9,101 in 1972. Prices exploded from 1972 to 1974. But in 1973, housing starts on single-family lots were down to 8,039, and down again in 1974 to 6,656. In 1975 they rose somewhat to 7,338 and in 1976 they were down again to 6,216. (Central Mortgage and Housing Corp., *Canadian Housing Statistics* 1971 through 76)

URBAN SINGLE-FAMILY-HOUSING STARTS, 1971-1976

	1971	1972	1973	1974	1975	1976
Calgary	3,441	4,367	4,678	5,229	4,877	4,111
Edmonton	3,154	3,955	4,643	3,486	4,974	5,278
Hamilton	2,155	2,820	2,862	2,155	1,890	1,471
Kitchener	1,323	1,772	1,593	1,347	1,764	1,891
London	1,339	1,950	1,770	1,249	1,574	1,235
Ottawa	1,613	1,657	1,491	784	996	1,098
Thunder Bay	275	403	598	623	491	590
Toronto	6,972	9,101	8,039	6,110	7,338	6,216
Vancouver	5,283	7,311	8,729	6,658	6,443	7,777
Victoria	998	1,241	1,427	1,270	1,481	1,178
Winnipeg	2,129	2,925	3,061	2,665	2,381	2,927
Montreal	5,293	9,324	9,412	11,795	12,109	13,110

Source: Canadian Housing Statistics 1971 through 1976

1971 to 1976 as in the rest of the country, so the average suburban bungalow that cost $15,400 to construct in Montreal in 1971 cost $29,100 to build five years later. Even with increased housing demand (Montreal housing starts went from 22,300 in 1971 to 37,500 in 1976) suburban lot prices went up by just $1,000, from $2,260 in 1971 to $3,200 in 1976. As demand for housing intensified in Montreal, spurred on by the same factors that were active elsewhere in the country, suburban lot prices rose only modestly and the city's small developers rushed to provide as many lots as builders (and, in the end, consumers) wanted without a huge increase in price. In 1971, 5,293 single family houses were started in Montreal. The quantity rose every year to 1976 when it reached 13,110. The house and lot that cost $55,000 to $65,000 in other Canadian cities in 1976 cost $32,300 in Montreal plus another $5,000 or so in local improvement charges paid to the municipality for services.

Was it red tape that restricted supply? Why was the supply of suburban lots not vastly expanded by the developers in response to intensified consumer demand? In Montreal, the hundreds of small developers who provide house lots did expand the supply and the result was a total increase of just $1,000 in the price of a lot over five years while the quantity supplied more than doubled. In most other cities, however, we've seen that supply expanded only slightly and often actually declined in this period.

The developers have often argued that they wanted to expand supply, and would have done so if the approval process had not snarled their land up in red tape and prevented them from servicing an increased number of acres from their land banks. Said David Jenkins, an official of Nu-West, pointing the finger at Calgary city hall in 1973, "By placing limitations on the amount of land available, a scarcity... has been artificially created."[19] Said Ross Nunn, vice-president of Daon, in another Calgary debate about alleged lot shortages, "Let the industry supply the demand, and we'll get the prices down."[20] Asked in an interview whether developers were restricting the supply of new lots, CMHC chairman William Teron told *Executive* magazine in 1976; "Definitely not. They spend sleepless nights trying to get land on the marketplace, etc. The interest costs and all the rest of keeping it off the market is quite extreme; that is a totally erroneous notion."[21]

Yet the large corporate developers do not rush every piece of land through the servicing process as soon as it has gone through the approval process. The industry plans far enough ahead to ensure that the approval process does not become a bottleneck, as we have already seen. Though occasionally for a specific large developer the approval process does prevent them from supplying their accustomed quantity of lots in a given year, generally the industry is successful at keeping comfortably ahead in getting the approvals they want. To claims by Winnipeg corporate developers that the short supply of serviced lots was the result of city hall red tape, a courageous and unusual firm of municipal consulting engineers, Templeton Engineering Ltd., replied testily in a brief to the Winnipeg land commission: "If developers really felt that there had not been enough serviced lots over the recent period, they had only to increase the annual production of land for which development agreements and the major trunk systems have existed."[22] And, just to make clear the fact that these engineers knew what they were talking about, they went on to list the cases in point. "Developments such as Westdale, The Maples, Southdale, Valley Gardens, and Fort Richmond are examples where the annual volume of serviced land could likely have been increased if the developer had so desired."

Calgary's home-builders' association complained to city hall in a brief in early 1973 that there was a "critical land shortage."[23] But a city hall count in June 1973 found fifteen thousand house lots already approved or on their way through the approval process in a city where only four thousand to five thousand single family houses are built annually.[24] Complaints in other cities have led to investigations with similar findings. The corporate developers keep well ahead of the approval process in their management of the supply of serviced lots.[25] To keep their large organizations operating, they must do so. They cannot afford to run out of lots.

Nevertheless in periods of intense consumer demand, there are some real shortages of serviced lots. These shortages exist for small house builders, who want to respond to increased demand for finished houses by stepping up production of new units. They often find that they are unable to buy any more lots than usual from the corporate developers, and indeed they may be cut off completely as the developers reserve a larger share of their total serviced lots for their own house-building operations. As the same firm of consulting engineers noted in Winnipeg in 1976, "Although there is no shortage of serviced land, there is a genuine shortage in the number of serviced lots that the major developers have made available to private builders. Of the big five, only BACM has made a significant quantity of serviced lots available to private builders."[26]*

Why developers restrict supply. Evidence from the pattern of house lot production from Canadian cities for the 1971-76 period and evidence from investigations of the approvals provided by municipal governments both lead to the same conclusion: in those cities where a few large developers dominate the supply of suburban house lots, those developers decided to increase modestly, hold

---

* The same situation existed for small builders in Edmonton. Edmonton Housing Association executive director Peter Burns noted in April 1976 that the shortage of lots had forced many of the area's one hundred small builders out of business. In Calgary, city council tried to ensure a supply of lots for small builders by discussing a requirement that would allot a portion of a corporate developer's new serviced lots to small builders. (*Edmonton Journal* 27 April 1976)

the line, or even decrease slightly the quantity of new serviced lots they were producing between 1971 and 1976 in the face of rapidly intensifying consumer demand. Only in one city where there is obviously still a very competitive suburban land business did intensified demand lead to the classic response expected by economists: a substantial increase in supply and only a moderate price increase.

Why did the large developers decide to maintain their production of serviced lots at historical levels through this period? They did so partly because it was clearly in their individual and collective interest. This was the most effective way to maximize profits. The profits earned by this strategy were far greater than those that would have been earned by the alternative response of maintaining prices and increasing supply.

As we have seen, the profit margins on suburban lots by 1976 were enormous for the large developers. They had doubled, tripled, and quadrupled from their 1971 level. In order to generate the same total amount of absolute profit by the alternative strategy of holding profit margins constant and increasing supply, the developers would have had to double, triple or quadruple their output and sales of suburban lots. Even if they had had the financial capacity to do so, the market for suburban housing was not sufficiently strong to absorb double, triple or quadruple production levels. The number of lots purchased by consumers would have increased substantially, as the statistics for Montreal show, but it could not have increased to this extent.

The other reason why the developers declined to increase supply dramatically was because it would have been difficult and complicated for them to do so. The problem was not city hall red tape, but their own internal organization and financial structure. Obtaining the cash necessary to sustain a greatly increased flow of serviced lots would have been a severe strain on the developers' financial resources, and would have restricted their ability to maintain their involvement in other types of profitable development. Increasing supply would also have meant using up the developers' valuable land banks more quickly than they anticipated.

Even if they had wanted to, increasing supply dramatically as in Montreal would have taken some doing for the large developers. But they had no incentive even to try to do so. The alternative strategy of holding the line on supply maximized their profits and generated a substantial flow of cash from suburban land development, conserved their land banks, and promoted corporate concentration in house building.

Strictly speaking, the developers did not *restrict* the supply of new suburban lots. They merely *maintained* supply at the usual level, or increased or decreased it modestly, in the face of heightened consumer demand. They chose the low-quantity high-profit strategy over the high-quantity low-profit alternative, knowing that their choice would lead to maximized profits.

Squeezing the small builder. There was another advantage for the large corporate developers in adopting the strategy of not increasing the supply of new lots in the face of greater consumer demand. It helped hasten corporate concentration in the house-building field and the squeeze-out of small builders. The small builders were last in line to obtain the serviced lots being produced by the large developers when consumer demand for housing was strong. The corporate firms were able to use the existence of a strong market to increase the market share of house building held by their own house-building divisions and those of the other large developer-builders.

Small builders, not much different in scale from the "hammer-and-nails" builders described in the 1940s, were until recently the major suppliers of single-family housing in most cities. The corporate developers have been expanding their house construction operations quickly, and they aim to continue this expansion.*

---

* Statistics on the share of the house-building market held by small builders of direct-loan NHA units show a declining share in most cities. Their share went from 63 percent to 32 percent between 1961 and 1973 in Halifax; from 34 percent to 19 percent in Montreal; from 44 percent to 3 percent in Toronto; from 34 percent to 12 percent in Winnipeg; from 59 percent to 12 percent in Vancouver. In Calgary and Edmonton, their share stayed constant. Meanwhile large builders were growing, often from zero, to capture a large share of the market; 49 percent in Halifax in 1973, 74 percent in Ottawa, 87 percent in Toronto, 59 percent in Winnipeg, 48 percent in Vancouver. These figures do not fully and accurately reflect what was happening in the suburban house construction industry in total because they are limited to NHA-financed housing starts, but they indicate a familiar pattern. (Peter Spurr, *Land and Urban Development: A preliminary study* [Toronto: James Lorimer, 1976] p. 191)

Ironically, in cities with sizeable public land banking operations it is the public land bank that provides many small builders with serviced land. Land banking authorities rarely discriminate in favour of corporate builders. One implication of public takeovers of the existing private land banks would be a dramatic slow-down in the trend towards greater concentration in the suburban house-building business. Small builders would no longer be at a disadvantage to their large competitors in obtaining supplies of serviced land to build on.

The market collapse. If a clinching argument were needed to confirm the analysis that the suburban land market in most Canadian cities is now dominated by a few large developers with oligopoly powers, it was provided by the response of the developers to the collapse in the suburban market which came after the price explosion in 1974 in most cities, and by 1976 everywhere. House builders suddenly found themselves with unsold inventories of completed housing, and developers found they had serviced lots on hand that no one wanted to build on. The Calgary and Edmonton markets were the last to continue booming, and the last to collapse, but even they had cooled down by the end of 1976.*

---

* Daon Development reported in its 1974 annual report: "The demand for building lots in Vancouver is decidedly weak, the vacant and unsold inventory of detached single family houses for sale is at record high levels, and new home construction has virtually ceased. Daon has no serviced lots for sale in Vancouver and until the mortgage climate improves we will stay out of this market." There were 1,653 vacant new houses in Vancouver at the end of October 1974, compared with 455 a year earlier.

Reported the national research director of the Canadian housebuilders' association, HUDAC, in October 1976: "The Vancouver market is very, very soft. There is an over-supply of condominium apartments. Winnipeg is a little better in the sense that there is no large inventory buildup, but demand there is also very soft. In Ontario inventory of unsold units is double what it normally is at this time — largely because starts are up by about 35 percent compared to last year... Starts in the Atlantic region are running about 42 percent ahead of last year and demand is good for AHOP units. However, builders there are starting to worry about growing inventories of higher priced homes." (*Vancouver Province* 14 January 1975; *Globe and Mail* 22 October 1976)

With serviced lots that wouldn't sell, finished houses sitting vacant, and little consumer demand for new housing compared with a couple of years earlier, what would be expected in a highly competitive market whose prices had temporarily raced ahead of costs would be rounds of price-cutting until the unsold units were disposed of, demand picked up and the industry could resume servicing land and building houses. For the large corporate developers, undercutting the prices charged by their fellow oligopolists would always be an attractive strategy if it could gain them a larger share of the total local market. The problem is of course that it invites retaliation, a round of price-cutting by every large firm, with the end result that everyone ends up with lower prices but profits per lot have been reduced. In a depressed market, the attractions of price cutting are even greater for the large firms and sometimes they succumb, hoping to be able to get away with it without their competitors noticing.

There were some instances of price cutting by the corporate developers in particularly soft markets after the collapse of the boom, though usually these were disguised as "bonuses" and "special offers" to new home buyers. In Winnipeg, for instance, some major firms were reducing prices on new homes in fall 1976 by $2,000 to $3,000. Brian Hastings, marketing vice-president of Qualico, one of Winnipeg's Big Four, explained they'd done it "to perk up sales."[27] "We have more unsold homes than anyone else, most on land we developed." With new projects getting close to completion, Qualico was worried by its inventory. But Hastings was careful to note that Qualico hadn't started the price cutting. "Engineered did $2,000 reductions on selected units, though they didn't advertise their cuts," he said. Engineered Homes is a Genstar housebuilding subsidiary.

Suburban lot prices sagged somewhat in 1976-77, but in general the large house builders held the line on prices on their inventories of unsold units, preferring to absorb higher costs on carrying charges than to reduce overall market prices. Their principal strategy for coping with diminished demand was not to cut prices but rather to reduce the number of new lots being supplied to the market. Single-family housing starts were down dramatically in Montreal, and substantially in Edmonton, Toronto, Vancouver and Victoria in 1977 compared with 1976. The price increases had come to a halt, for a while, but the corporate developers had managed to avoid substantial price reductions which would make significant cuts in their profit on suburban land development.

It was obvious to the development industry and to government after the slump in demand in 1974 in many cities that the problem was that house prices were too high for most families. The federal government quickly stepped in with new housing programs which started from the premise that the developers' per-acre profit on serviced suburban land should be protected. Still, there were ways of reducing the per-house land cost and hence the final price tag on new housing units. The most obvious was to build semi-detached and row housing units on smaller lots. While single-family-housing starts in major urban centres hovered around 60,000 units from 1973 to 1976 and hit 52,000 in 1977, semi-detached housing starts increased from 9,300 in 1973 and 7,000 in 1974 to 11,000 in 1975 and 1976 and 13,600 in 1977.[28] Row housing starts in major cities also jumped, though there was a slight decline from 1976 to 1977. Many of these were financed under CMHC's AHOP program, which limited the land price component in overall prices, leading developers to slice their land thinner but maintain at least the same profit per acre as they had made on single-family lots.

The unaffordable dream. Single-family houses in the suburbs have always been relatively expensive in terms of people's incomes. Yet it is not the high cost of *housing* which makes suburban living unaffordable for most Canadians. It is the high price of suburban *land*.

The best illustration of this fact is to look at who is buying houses in the few Canadian cities where suburban lots are still reasonably priced. In these cities, suburban single-family houses are still affordable for moderate-income families. This is the case, for instance, in Montreal and Quebec, because there is as yet no oligopoly in the suburban land development market. It is true also in Saskatoon and Halifax, probably because of the impact of public land banking which keeps land prices reasonably low. In Halifax in 1976, 66 percent of all new house buyers under NHA had incomes of less than $15,000.[29] In Saskatoon, 56 percent of new home buyers had incomes below $15,000. In Quebec, 68 percent were below that figure. In Montreal, 53 percent. Average family income for Canada in 1976 was $17,400.

The contrast between these cities and high land-price cities is startling. In Toronto in 1976, only 7 percent of new house buyers had incomes of less than $15,000; in Vancouver, 31 percent; in Winnipeg, 8 percent; in Ottawa, 13 percent; in Edmonton, 4 percent; in Calgary, 3.8 percent.

Eliminating the high developer's profit being made on suburban lots would have a dramatic impact on the prices of new housing. Houses selling for $60,000 to $65,000 in larger cities like Victoria, Vancouver, Edmonton, Calgary, Hamilton, Toronto and Ottawa could be priced at $15,000 to $24,000 less. Houses selling for $50,000 in cities like Regina and Winnipeg could be priced at $7,000 to $10,000 less.

In spite of the increases in family income since 1961, the ability of people in most Canadian cities to afford a house in the suburbs has actually declined. A Winnipeg researcher, Steve Jacobs, who compared 1961 with 1975 prices in that city found that family incomes had increased by 100 percent in that time.[30] But the price of a new house in the suburbs had increased by 152 percent. The increase in monthly payments, reflecting the impact of both higher house prices and much higher mortgage interest rates, was 219 percent.

The role of government. Governments at all levels have played a key role in promoting and fostering the corporate suburbs and the emergence of large developers with their sizeable land banks which push house prices far higher than they need be. Ottawa set the stage for this pattern of development by its policies of the immediate postwar period to promote demand through low-interest, low-down payment, government-insured mortgages and parallel measures to encourage the supply of suburban houses.[31] When municipalities balked at the enormous capital costs of providing the expensive trunk sewer and water services required to open up suburban acreages, Ottawa came up with loans and subsidies to assist. As the corporate developers began to build up their inventories of suburban land, Ottawa offered encouragement with tax policies on the developers' carrying cost expenses that made large assemblies more attractive.

The 1970s produced a new problem in the suburbs: demand for housing was increasing due to underlying factors in the country's population structure, and the developers were exercising their new market power to push land profits and house prices up. This problem had been foreseen by the federal government's 1969 housing task force headed by housing minister Paul Hellyer, and Hellyer had proposed a realistic set of measures that would have headed off this rapidly emerging monopolization of the supply of suburban lots with an aggressive program of federal-municipal land banking funded by Ottawa. A combination of senior federal civil servants headed by Robert Bryce, then deputy minister of finance, Tom Shoyama, now deputy minister of finance, and Herb Hignett, then president of CMHC, combined with Pierre Trudeau and his inner circle of political advisers to kill the idea and force Hellyer out of the cabinet.[32]

When the predicted rapid price increases came, Ottawa instead produced a whole new set of government subsidies that permitted house buyers to pay for the developers' high profits. When an opportunity inadvertently came Ottawa's way in 1975 to regulate the developers' profit margins on suburban land development and force prices down through the Anti-Inflation Board, the response was for the AIB to find a way to protect the developers' high profit margins from being interfered with by AIB regulation in any significant way.[33]

Another potential difficulty for the suburban developers came to a head in the 1973 Calgary study suggesting that the power of Genstar and its subsidiaries in the Calgary suburban land market might be in violation of the federal Anti-Combines Act. When Calgary city politicians finally forwarded their study to federal officials for investigation, Ottawa's response was to decide that there was nothing about the Calgary situation (and, by implication, the emerging oligopoly in other cities) that violated federal legislation. "We looked at all possibilities relating to abuse of monopoly power, and came to the conclusion that no violations of the Act had occurred or were about to occur," George Orr of the Consumer and Corporate Affairs services branch told Calgary reporters in 1976.[34] Monopoly power and profits are themselves no violation of federal legislation; it is only when monopoly power is used in ways that are considered to harm the public interest that an offence occurs.

Provincial governments have been, with a few notable exceptions, equally supportive of the corporate suburbs and the large suburban developers. They have often been instrumental in providing the necessary public infrastructure — trunk sewers, trunk watermains, sewage treatment plants, expressways, bridges, highways, and commuter transportation systems — required by the corporate suburbs. Equally important, they have used their powers over municipal government structures to establish the regional and metropolitan governments and the regional planning authorities which have removed many key planning powers from the hands of smaller, local municipalities. The unified control of these new governments over an urban market and the concentration of political power which they represent have enabled the large developers to use their land assemblies to dominate the supply of new house lots.

As we have seen, a key factor in the takeover of suburban land development by large developers was the withdrawal by municipalities from the business of installing services to raw land and recovering the expense through local improvement taxes. Had provincial governments wanted to prevent the emergence of corporate power in the land development business, they could have ensured that municipalities had access to the necessary capital to continue their servicing activities.

Municipal governments are the public bodies most directly involved in suburban development, and here too support for the large developers has been strong. Municipalities provide much of the immediate infrastructure needed to support the conversion of farmland into suburban lots. They make most of the decisions about where growth occurs. They regulate densities, street layouts, servicing requirements, and many other details of the suburban development business. In a few instances, municipalities have taken the only effective step of any level of government and have levied taxes of $1,000 or $1,500 on the profits of the suburban developers (often called imposts) on every new lot approved. The taxes are very modest in relation to the enormous per-lot profits earned by the developers, but the industry has vigorously opposed them arguing that they push land prices up higher rather than admitting that they take away a modest portion of the developer's total per-lot profit. In spite of these occasional efforts, and the sense that individual developers are often in conflict with municipalities because they want even more than the officials and politicians are prepared to give them, municipal governments have provided support in terms of services and regulation which have permitted the corporate suburbs to succeed.

Why Montreal is an exception. Montreal (with Quebec City) is the only large Canadian city where corporate concentration has played no significant role in the suburban land development business so far. Why this is so underlines the key contribution of government in permitting and supporting this pattern elsewhere. Unlike most other cities, municipal government in Montreal is still highly fragmented. There are thirty different municipal governments with relatively independent powers over planning and development in the 191 square miles covered by a relatively weak regional government authority, the Montreal Urban Community, and the full Montreal regional area of 1,032 square miles includes more than one hundred municipalities.[35] Also, suburban land development in Montreal is undertaken in the way that has been abandoned in most other Canadian cities. It is the municipalities, not the developers, that install services to new suburban lots. The cost is recovered through local improvement charges levied on property taxes.

These arrangements mean that Montreal developers can operate with more limited financial resources. Equally, with many small municipalities making independent decisions, small developers have greater success in ensuring that the servicing of lots proceeds in advance of supply and that there is always an ample supply of lots ready at current market prices. A developer with a very large land bank in the Montreal area could provide a significant share of the total supply of lots, but as long as small developers have local councils who will service their land when they see a market there is no way a large developer can earn above-normal profits.

Embarrassing profits. Most developers were genuinely astonished by the size of the profits they were able to make in suburban land development beginning in the early 1970s. They had little notion that the market power they had been slowly developing would permit them to generate so soon such fantastic lot price increases by holding supply to traditional levels. Occasionally developers would deny they were making unreasonably high profits. Once in a while, they would attempt to justify their profits by referring to the long approval process, the allegedly high cost of land being added today to their land banks, and the "risks" of the business. At a public meeting in Calgary called to discuss whether a land assembly owned by Daon should be annexed to the city and thus start on its way through the long approval process, farmers complained that they had received low prices for their farms and that Daon would make immense profits on the land. A Daon representative jumped to his feet: "If that annexation doesn't go through, we're going to be the biggest grain farmers around here . . . We're taking a risk."[36] A corporate developer's risk on its land bank is very modest, the difference between the purchase price plus carrying costs compared with its value in some non-urban use. With the financial resources to hang on until urban growth eventually reaches his land, a large developer doesn't have much to lose if he can wait for his ship to come in.

The occasional developer has admitted to high profits in suburban land development. "We don't need the high price level to be highly profitable," Toronto developer Bruce McLaughlin said in July 1974.[37] The occasional politican has also pointed to those high profits as a major cause of the unaffordable price of suburban housing. One of the few is Bill Yurko, Alberta's housing minister, who has described how he gave a speech in 1976 to Alberta's housing developers dealing with the profit question. "Their profits were immoral," Yurko said. "I told them. They knew it."[38]

CMHC chairman William Teron has agreed that fantastic profits are being made in suburban development. Teron told *Executive* magazine in mid-1976, "The developer is not beyond taking as much as there is going, and then you start seeing lots at $20,000 and $25,000 and this is unconscionable. This is terrible and I know that we here are devoting our entire attention [to it] . . ."[39]

Barney Danson, when he was Ottawa's urban affairs minister, was also concerned about suburban land profits, though his position was more qualified than Teron's. "Mr. Danson refused to attribute high housing and land costs solely to big developers, saying that a number had made a 'great contribution' to housing in the country," reported the *Globe and Mail* in August 1976. "If developers such as William Teron, now president of Central Mortgage and Housing Corp., made some money along the way, 'good luck to them,' Mr. Danson said. He was more concerned that they didn't make too much money.''*

The suburban reality. The suburbs are the creation of postwar technology, politics, planning and economics. They are most people's housing ideal not because they are the best housing form in the best neighbourhoods, but rather because they are the best urban option that the developers have produced. In many ways, they provide people with the housing features that are most important to them, and they are obviously far more successful at doing so than the developers' major alternative, high-rise apartments.

Just when suburban house prices were rocketing out of the reach of most families, other factors were changing fundamentally the assumptions on which the suburbs have been built, such as cheap energy and the continuing supremacy of car transportation. Suburban densities require universal car ownership and use, but the oil price revolution of 1973-74 signalled the beginning of the end of the era of cheap and easy access to car travel. The assumption that Canada's resources are abundant, and that the economy is prosperous enough to permit the consumption of large amounts of agricultural land for housing and to generate the incomes needed to purchase suburban houses, is now in question. The new economic difficulties which Canada faced in the 1970s, combining inflation with unemployment, a slow rate of real growth, and a difficult balance of payments situation, indicated that affluence was not an assumption that could be easily made for the future. Another and more subtle change was occurring at the level of family and social life. The underlying social concept of the suburbs dictates a more rigid adherence to nuclear family roles than other

---

* The news media, which were full of reports about rising house prices in most Canadian cities during the 1971-76 period, played an extremely dismal role in reporting on this phenomenon. In almost every case, the media went no further in explaining house price increases than quoting the comments of industry spokesmen and their references to red tape, the rising costs of servicing and inflation. Only when the industry came under criticism from politicians or outsiders did the media reflect any other point of view.

kinds of neighbourhoods. More and more people, women and men both, are becoming less willing to accept and follow those roles.

In most people's eyes, however, the most serious problem with the corporate suburbs is a simple one: the houses are too expensive. In most cities, as we have seen, the reason that suburban houses cost too much is because the developers have staged a successful takeover of suburban land development. A few large developers have captured an effective monopoly on the supply of new house lots in many cities. These firms took advantage of their collective market power to hold the supply of new house lots after 1971 to roughly historical levels, and in the face of this limited supply intensified demand pushed prices up enormously. Developer's profit is so substantial a portion of the prices of new suburban houses that these could be reduced by $7,000 to $24,000 in most large Canadian cities if suburban land developers were restricted to a margin of 10 percent on their development costs, or if lots were being developed by non-profit agencies.

Commented Calgary Regional Planning Commission director Rhys Smith in 1976:

> The present situation [in Calgary] is a far cry from that of ten to fifteen years ago when there were a large number of developers placing relatively small developments on the market ... Lot prices in a situation of a few suppliers is largely a function of control of the market place. There is not a free market ... The problem is how to return sanity and equitability into a very disturbing picture. Measures have been suggested such as capital gains, windfall profit taxes, municipal land banks, and even the requirement that a land developer become and operate under public utility regulation ... The real issue is how to get back on the market reasonably priced land for general housing requirements.[40]

The corporate developers have used the very desirability and success of the suburbs to force people to pay far more than is necessary for the privilege of living there, and to close off the possibility of suburban living to a majority of families. The developers themselves know they have gone too far in squeezing profits out of suburban land. Said Robert Keenan of Headway as he worried out loud about developer profits: ''They're going to kill the goose that laid the golden egg.''

6

HIGH-RISE APARTMENTS

[Le Corbusier] dealt like a giant with the landscape of sky and sun and rolling hills. The family is not to be enclosed by small hedges and picket fences; it is to be lifted up and shown the horizon from the upper floors of the great city Habitation. The whole building is itself lifted from the ground on stilts so that the landscape goes rolling on right through and underneath.[1]

High-rise apartments are the corporate developers' second major housing innovation. As for the suburbs, the inspiration was a planner's dream, convincingly conveyed in this quote by CMHC's influential housing planner Humphrey Carver. High-rise was to be a new, more humane way to live that met people's housing needs better than the familiar forms of congested cities and crowded streets.

The developers have built at least 450,000 high-rise apartment units in Canadian cities since 1945.[2] In Hamilton, Ottawa, Regina, and Toronto these account for more than half of all apartments. In 1977, there were 10,700 new apartment units in non-high-rise apartment buildings built in Canadian cities, 7,000 of them in Montreal alone. In contrast, there were 22,000 high-rise apartments built that year.

In many ways, high-rise apartments are the opposite extreme to the suburbs. Instead of being built at very low densities, they are extremely high-density. Instead of land costing $25,000 to $35,000 per housing unit as for single-family suburban houses in some cities, land for a high-rise apartment unit costs $2,000 to $6,000 per unit. Instead of providing most of the features which people want in housing, high-rise apartments provide almost none of the key housing features people look for. While suburban houses are everyone's first housing choice, high-rise apartments come last on most people's list of preferences.

High-rise apartments have only one undisputed advantage over the other types of housing provided by the corporate developers: relatively speaking, they are affordable. Rents in high-rise buildings certainly are not cheap, but the monthly cost of an apartment unit is considerably less than the combined monthly carrying costs of a similar-sized house.

The fact that it costs less to live in a high-rise rental apartment does not, however, mean that the development industry is making smaller profits from these projects. The financial structure of apartments as income properties provides a substantial annual return to the developer. It also helps provide the paper losses (in the form of the capital cost allowance) which permit the developer to avoid paying tax on other profits made in suburban land development. And, over the long term, apartments offer the additional potential for enormous appraisal surplus profits for their developer-owners.

The dream. Canadian advocates of high-rise apartments cite French architect-planner Le Corbusier as their intellectual mentor. Writes Humphrey Carver:

> The threat of dispersal of the great city into the ever-expanding spider's web of satellite towns made Le Corbusier the first proponent of a massive programme of urban renewal. The packed, narrow-corridor streets of the central city must be removed to open up wide green spaces as the setting for towering residential blocks exposed to the sun and the wind and embracing wide views of the sky. He shows that three million people could live in a green and radiant city of inner Paris with space left over, and so fulfil the destiny of the city as a great centre of thought and administration and commerce, housing its incomparable force of talented people ... The garden city movement was frankly an escape from the big city as something monstrous and beyond comprehension ... Then,

suddenly, there burst upon the world an altogether new revelation of the big city as a bold and exhilarating place, a fitting
challenge for the technical skills and healthy bodies of a new
urban generation... Le Corbusier seized the problem of
Town and Country and raised it out of the romantic and
dainty scale of the suburban garden city.[3]

Le Corbusier's own designs for high-rise buildings attempted to
incorporate many of the attractive features of ground-related living. When his prototypes were translated into the harsh commercial reality of constructed buildings in Canadian cities, however,
there was little evidence of Le Corbusier's humanism. What was
bold and exhilarating about high-rise apartments was not the accommodation they provided, but rather the dramatic new scale of
operation they permitted apartment developers.*

High-rise land. For the developer the appeal of high-rise apartments is simple: money. High-rise provides the industry with a way
of squeezing new profits out of every acre of urban residential land
they're built on, without conflicting with the profits the industry
makes building single-family houses in the suburbs.

As in the suburbs, the real money in high-rise apartments is not

---

* Poetic descriptive language and dramatic architectural drawings have
  always been key to developer presentations of high-rise projects.
  The small-time developers who latched onto this idea did their best
  to imitate the language of advocates like Humphrey Carver, but
  their efforts were less convincing. Julie Hanson, an officer of the
  Meridian group that built the ten-thousand-unit St. James Town
  project in central Toronto, produced this description of his project:
  "A park-like atmosphere of winding trails, plush foliage, and...
  special features placed throughout the project: a free form concrete
  fountain... and a ten-foot statue." Winding trails and plush foliage
  are not how anyone would describe St. James Town or any other
  central-city high-rise project anywhere in Canada. "In other
  words," Hanson went on, "modern luxury accommodation." Most
  tenants of high-rise apartments do not consider them to be "luxury" accommodation, though there's no doubt that's how they were
  promoted and sold when the idea was introduced to Canada in the
  late 1950s and 1960s. (Robert Collier, *Contemporary Cathedrals*
  [Montreal: Harvest House, 1975] p. 45)

in the construction of the building, but in the land. The way the industry works, every apartment unit in a new high-rise building is considered to have a value that's made up of two components: the building component, which is valued at the cost of construction (including normal profits), and the land component. Relative to the cost of construction, the cost of land in the value of a new high-rise apartment is relatively modest. In 1976-77 when Toronto's housing authority was purchasing completed high-rise buildings from developers to use as senior citizen housing, it was paying prices of $16,283 to $18,600 for the apartment units, and $3,000 to $5,529 per unit for the land.[4] The construction cost per square foot for high-rise apartments is about the same as a standard suburban house. But there is a big difference in the final price when land for a suburban house costs $30,000 and land for a high-rise apartment unit costs only $5,000.*

The value of land for a high-rise apartment unit varies from city to city, and from location to location. Generally, there is a rule-of-thumb figure that is used by developers and the property industry

---

* Land for high-rise apartments does not come in single lots with $5,000 price tags the way suburban house lots are divided and sold one at a time for $30,000. Instead, high-rise buildings are put up on large parcels of land that are subject to zoning and density maximums. For example, a 3.3-acre site in the Toronto suburbs was zoned by the local municipality in 1977 for a maximum of 301 high-rise senior citizen apartments units, just under 100 units an acre.

Considered as a site for a high-rise apartment, the value of a piece of land can be quite easily determined. If the standard value at a particular time and place for land for high-rise apartments is $4,000, the value of an acre of land zoned to permit fifty apartment units is fifty times $4,000, or $200,000. Increase the zoning to permit the construction of one hundred units instead of fifty, and the per-acre value jumps to $400,000.

Density maximums are established by city planners in two different ways. Sometimes the total area of building is regulated, and related to the total size of the site. Under this system, if the density maximum is three times coverage, a developer can construct three square feet of building for every square foot of land on the site. The other method often used is based on the number of dwelling units permitted per acre of land.

No one knows how many hundreds of millions of dollars have been made by the development industry by converting land into

for a standard location in a city at any one time. Everyone in the industry knows that high-rise land is worth $2,000 or $3,000 or $5,000 a unit in various cities at the moment.

That market value of high-rise land is a residual figure, the result of the interrelationships between apartment construction costs, interest rates, and local rent levels.[5] A change in any one of these affects high-rise land values. If rents go up, high-rise land goes up. If construction costs go up and rents stay the same, high-rise land goes down — or it would if mortgage lenders and developers weren't so anxious to keep it up.

High-rise triumphant. In terms of the number of housing units constructed, high-rise apartments surpassed single-family houses in many Canadian cities in terms of construction starts in the late 1960s and 1970s. Single-family starts for Canada were 78 percent

---

high-rise apartment use. On that 3.3-acre site in Toronto rezoned to permit 301 high-rise apartments for senior citizens, the land involved had been purchased by the previous owner for $513,500 in 1975. Two years later, zoned for high-rise use, the Metro Toronto Housing Company paid $1,238,100 for it. The increase in value was $724,600 in just two years.

The fact that the developers and the property industry generally value high-rise apartment land on a per-unit basis makes it very easy to see what is really at stake when developers go to city councils seeking rezonings on land they have purchased or hold under option. Their control of the land means that the cost of the land to the developer is fixed. Decisions by municipal governments on how many apartments to allow on a developer's site are really just decisions about how much that land is to be worth, and therefore what the developer's profit on the land assembly is to be. If high-rise apartment land in that location is worth $3,000 an apartment, a battle between the developer, neighbourhood residents, city planners and city politicians over whether a site should be zoned for two hundred apartments or four hundred determines whether the land should be worth $600,000 or $1,200,000. It's astonishing that the developers manage to persuade most city officials and their friends at city hall that it's not proper to discuss publicly this aspect of rezoning decisions. It is always money that is really at stake, and usually the amounts involved are enormous. (Letter from R. R. Tomlinson, Social Services Commissioner, Municipality of Metropolitan Toronto to Alderman John Sewell, 28 February 1977)

of all housing starts in 1951.[6] By 1961 the figure was down to 61 percent, and by 1971 to 42 percent. In contrast, apartments (both small and high-rise) were 14 percent of housing starts in 1951, 28 percent in 1961, and 45 percent in 1971. After 1971, in response to federal housing policies, apartment construction declined somewhat in favour of both single-family houses and other types of smaller scale housing.

High-rise apartments have been successful mainly in medium and large cities. In the cities in the Windsor to Quebec City corridor, for instance, dwelling units increased by 923,376 units from 1961 to 1971.[7] Apartment units accounted for more than half of this increase, a total of 481,441 units. An estimated 80 percent of the new apartment units were in high-rise buildings.

By 1977 there were 323,000 apartment units in Canada's metropolitan areas in buildings of 50 to 199 units, most of them high rise.[8] Another 132,000 units were in buildings of 200 units or more. But these large high-rise buildings were by no means evenly distributed across the country. Toronto alone had 190,000 of the units mainly in large high-rise buildings. Only sixty thousand of Toronto's apartment units were in buildings of fewer than fifty units. In Montreal, by dramatic contrast, there were 353,000 units in smaller buildings, and only 65,000 in large. Vancouver had 34,000 apartment units in large buildings, 54,000 in small. Other cities with a large number of apartments in large mostly high-rise buildings are Calgary, with 10,000, Hamilton with 26,000, London with 12,000, Ottawa with 29,700, and Winnipeg with 22,300.[9]

The high-rise apartment building boom began in the largest cities in the late 1950s. Often it was government that led the way, with large-scale public land assemblies for residential urban renewal followed by the construction of high-rise public housing. In Toronto, for example, it was only after Regent Park South and Moss Park high-rise public housing projects had been completed that the massive St. James Town private redevelopment project got underway. By 1971, a total of eighty-eight high-rise public housing apartments had been erected across Canada.[10] Of these, sixty-five were in Toronto, sixteen in Ottawa and eight in Hamilton. Row housing and walk-up apartments were the forms used for public housing in other cities.

Vancouver's dramatic concentration of high-rise apartments in the West End also commenced in the late 1950s. With municipal zoning that permitted buildings with floor space 3.0 to 3.35 times the area of the lots, and no height restrictions, buildings shot up.[11] The boom reached its pitch in 1968-69 when, as Donald Gutstein reports in his book *Vancouver Ltd.*, thirty-seven buildings were started in this one-mile square area adjacent to Vancouver's downtown.

The high density maximums permitted by city governments were the key to the success of high-rise buildings and to the profits made by the developers. Those high densities produced enormous differences between the value of urban land in low and medium densities traditional to Canadian cities and its potential value in high-rise use. Aware of the profit potential, developers put together land assemblies using a wide range of techniques. The most innocuous involved posing as ordinary home owners and offering somewhat higher prices than usual. The most vicious involved block-busting tactics that residents' groups across Canada tried, often unsuccessfully, to combat: random demolitions of houses, showing that the area had no future except for high rise; installing motorcycle gangs as tenants in developer-owned houses; ceasing all maintenance and repair work; harassing visits and sales tactics by agents of the developer; and even arson to convince the recalcitrant homeowner to sell.[12]

The pressures generated by the redevelopment of existing residential neighbourhoods distracted attention from the fact that high-rise apartments are by no means a central-city phenomenon. Whether in the downtown or in the suburbs, the secret to their success lay in the fact that this housing form results in lower land costs per unit than other housing forms built at lower densities. Given that high-rise apartments have been the only form of high-density housing which most city plans permit, they have been at least as successful in the suburbs as in central areas of most cities. "Between 1959 and 1974, for instance," notes George Nader in *Cities of Canada*, "531 of the net addition of 740 buildings with ten or more storeys in Metro Toronto were built outside the City of Toronto [in the suburban boroughs]."[13]

Fitting people in. What makes the success of high-rise apartments surprising is that they have been widely and vigorously opposed by residents in areas where they are to be built, and more important they are the *least* desired form of housing.

Neighbourhood opposition arose from the impact of the buildings themselves (more traffic, parking problems, shadows) and, more important, the instability which is generated as high-rise developers put together land assemblies for these buildings. In Vancouver, people often fought high-rise buildings because they would obstruct views of the sea and the mountains.* In Toronto mayoralty candidate David Crombie's promise that he would work to protect neighbourhoods against the threat of redevelopment was a key commitment in 1972 when resistance to high-rise buildings was at its peak.

Neighbourhood residents are, however, by no means the only people unhappy about high-rise projects. Housing studies have produced a substantial amount of evidence that most people do not want to live in high-rise buildings and prefer other forms of housing. This is true not just for people who live in other housing types; it is also true for people now living in high-rise. In a carefully conducted Vancouver study which analyzed the housing preferences of a sample of 775 low and moderate income families, for instance, only ten of the 775 people put high-rise apartments first on their list of housing preferences.[14] Of the group in the sample who were currently living in high-rise buildings, "less than 10 percent ... thought it was a good place to raise children."[15]

People have definite reasons for their aversion to high-rise living. The Vancouver study identified the housing features people consider to be particularly desirable, and are willing to pay for. Among these key considerations are privacy, adequate space, a private yard, private parking, and quiet.[16] None of these features is usually available to the high-rise tenant.

---

* This led Vancouver architect Arthur Erickson to produce a plan for what he called a "see-through high-rise", a building twenty to forty storeys high with holes and gaps in it so people living behind it could catch glimpses of the mountains they could already see without obstruction. Erickson won an architectural prize for the design, but public opposition helped kill it. (Donald Gutstein in *The City Book*, ed. James Lorimer and Evelyn Ross [Toronto: James Lorimer, 1976] p. 63)

Other evidence confirming the fact that high-rise apartments are generally an undesirable housing form comes from a study by a York University researcher, Peter Homenuck, commissioned and paid for by high-rise developer Deltan Realty in 1973.[17] Homenuck looked for people who preferred high-rise rental living to the alternatives, and particularly to single-family housing. Perhaps not surprisingly, people not now living in high rise showed little taste for it: only 0.5 percent of Homenuck's sample of people living in townhouses, single detached houses or high-rise condominiums said they would prefer to live in high-rise rental units. Even high-rise tenants showed a marked inclination towards other housing types.[18] There were just 20 percent of the high-rise tenant group who said their first housing choice was high-rise rental living. Another 5 percent opted for high-rise when it was owned through a condominium arrangement rather than rented. But 21 percent said they preferred townhouses and duplexes, rented or owned. And a majority of the high-rise tenants group, an astonishing 60 percent of the total, put single-family detached suburban houses as their preferred housing type. The only category of people grouped by their life cycle who showed substantial interest in high-rise renting were one-parent families with children at home (18 percent put high-rise first, but 54 percent put a detached house first) and one-parent families with no children at home (24 percent for high-rise, 54 percent for detached housing).[19]

Usually in housing studies, no matter what people's housing preferences are, they report that they are generally satisfied with their current housing. This indicates that they think they have made the best housing choice open to them, not that they would not prefer some other housing option. Homenuck did not ask high-rise residents about general satisfaction, but he did ask whether they were satisfied with the size of their current housing, and 87 percent of his high-rise sample said they were.[20] Answers to other questions in the survey revealed specific problems with high-rise living. The physical design of the building discourages social relations, with the result that high-rise residents are much less likely to have friends in their neighbourhood than detached house residents. And, as political workers who have canvassed high-rise buildings know well, there is less interest and concern about neighbourhood questions among high-rise tenants than elsewhere.[21]

Who lives in high-rise buildings? Given their general unpopularity, it might seem surprising that high-rise buildings so easily fill up with tenants. Most high-rise residents are in fact there on a temporary basis, waiting until they can find or afford more satisfactory housing. High-rise buildings are often holding zones for young single people and young families, saving money to buy more desirable housing, and for older people who can no longer afford or cope with another, preferred housing type.[22] High-rise tenants generally have relatively lower incomes, aren't as likely to own cars, and are often new arrivals to the city. In a 1970 study of Vancouver's West End residents, Marathon Realty found that most of the people living there were from Canada east of the Rockies or from abroad.[23] Only 10 percent had incomes over $10,000.

It is the high price of housing alternatives, and particularly new suburban houses, that effectively forces people to live in high-rise apartments. As one analyst studying the cities in the Windsor to Quebec City corridor noted, the cities with the highest proportion of high-rise apartment construction are exactly those cities where new house prices are highest:

> The greatest concentration of apartment construction has been in those urban areas where the price of single detached homes is the highest, which tends to reinforce the argument that it is not just demand related to the general stage in the life cycle of the population that has encouraged this apartment boom, but also the prohibitive cost of alternative forms of housing in some cities.[24]

In effect, the developers set up a squeeze play. Only two choices were offered in new housing: a single-family house in the suburbs, which almost everyone wanted but only a few could afford; and a high-rise apartment, which almost no one wanted but most could afford.

Either way, however, the urban resident lost. Buying a new suburban house, the purchaser paid far more than was required by the cost of constructing the house and producing the lot giving the land developer a profit of $8,000 to $24,000. Renting a high-rise apartment, the tenant paid a rent that covered a substantial profit made in the land assembly for the building and that effectively purchased the property outright for the developer over the next twenty to thirty years. On top of that, the tenant got a kind of housing accommodation that didn't suit his needs or tastes. Either way, the developers won.

High-rise profits. Like other types of income properties, high-rise apartments produce annual operating profits for their developer-owners as well as long-term appraisal surplus profits.

The developer obtains mortgage financing from a financial institution for a high-rise building in either "conventional" (which means uninsured by government) or National Housing Act insured mortgages. These provide cash equal to 75 to 90 percent of the *market* value of the finished project. Since the cash cost to the developer of assembling the land and erecting the building is usually less than its finished market value, the cash obtained from the mortgage lender is generally almost enough to cover all the cash it cost the developer. When all the cash needed to create the project is obtained from mortgages, the project is said to be "mortgaged out" and the developer ends up with none of his own cash invested in it. Sometimes mortgage funds are actually greater than costs, meaning that the developer finishes the project with a cash surplus. The industry calls that cash surplus "negative equity."

To obtain mortgage financing, the developer prepares sample financial statements for the proposed project (called pro formas), which set out expected revenues and expenses. Revenues are rents, assuming normal local rent levels, and include an allowance for vacancies. Expenses are operating expenses of the building plus mortgage interest. Strictly speaking, mortgage principal is not an expense, but often developers include a depreciation expense which is equal to the amount of the mortgage principal they have to pay off every year. High-rise buildings are expected to return an operating profit to the developer after his operating, interest and depreciation expenses. That profit is return to the developer on his cash equity invested in the building. Even if the building has been "mortgaged out" and the developer has no cash tied up in it, he is likely to be earning some operating profit every year. From the point of view of mortgage lenders, that profit is a safety margin for the developer to run into some problems and still have enough rental income to be able to cover his mortgage payments. Yet an operating profit of any size, given the fact that the amount of cash the developer has left in the project is likely to be small or even non-existent, results in a very high rate of return on his investment for the developer.

Over the years, the only expense which increases for a high-rise developer is operating expenses — property tax, maintenance, repairs. Mortgage payments are fixed for the period of the mortgage. Rents, of course, can be increased as market levels increase, and generally this is more than enough to cover hikes in operating costs. The prospect is, then, for the developer's rate of operating profit which starts out quite high to increase during the building's lifetime. This is true even when rent controls limit rent increases to 5 to 10 percent per year.*

The condominium wrinkle. Faced with escalating construction costs rising faster than rents and wanting to prevent the value of high-rise apartment land from falling, the developers began to switch from rental to condominium projects in the early 1970s. High-rise condominiums were usually no different from high-rise rental buildings, but instead of renting occupants purchased their units.

The early years of the condominium business were relatively free of the government "red tape" and regulation that the development industry complains about constantly. The result of this absence of regulation was that purchasers were constantly running

---

 * The developers do not usually provide sufficiently detailed information in their financial statements to yield a clear picture of the profitability of their high-rise rental business. Though it has to be read and used keeping industry thinking and terminology in mind, the data provided by the study on Cadillac Fairview by Ira Gluskin commissioned by the Royal Commission on Corporate Concentration provides for the first time some reliable information on the financial side of the high-rise business to a large developer. Cadillac went into the merger with Fairview Corporation owning 7,472 rental apartment units which cost it an average of $12,325 per unit to develop. Gluskin breaks down Cadillac Fairview's 1976 rental income to show that total residential rents were $44.7 million, and operating expenses were $21.7 million. The interest expense for money borrowed to finance these apartments he sets at $12.4 million. Gluskin also divides the corporation's general and administrative expenses into its various activities, and estimates that these total $1.9 million for rental apartments. Operating profits after all these expenses are

PROFITS IN HIGH-RISE APARTMENTS — CADILLAC FAIRVIEW'S 1976 RESULTS

Rental income		44,700,000
Less: Operating expenses	21,700,000	
Interest	12,387,000	
General and administrative	1,922,000	
Total expenses		36,009,000
Operating profit		7,691,000
As a percentage of rents		17%

Source: Ira Gluskin, *The Cadillac Fairview Corporation Limited, A Corporate Background Report.* Study No. 3, Royal Commission on Corporate Concentration pp. 45-8.

into incredible examples of profiteering and sleazy business practices by developers.[25]

Buying a high-rise apartment unit appealed to a few people, but on the whole the high-rise condominium experiment was a disaster. Ownership alone did not compensate for all the other deficiencies of the high-rise building form. Condominium high-rise apartments stood vacant literally for years while mortgage lenders waited anxiously for them to fill up. One typical project at 350 Parkway Terrace in suburban Toronto, built by developer Bruce

---

$7.7 million, 17 percent of the rents paid by tenants.

Gluskin offers a "hypothetical" example of profits made by developers on high-rise apartments built in 1967, 1972 and 1976 at prevailing construction and land costs. His 1967 apartment cost $12,000 to construct, close to Cadillac's actual average figure for its apartment buildings. Gluskin estimates the developer's cash equity in the building at $2,400, much higher than in practice. Even so, the apartment produces an operating profit of $978 a year, a 40.8 percent return on this assumed $2,400 cash equity. Had Gluskin assumed a more realistic cash equity of $1,200, the annual rate of return would be about 80 percent. Similar conservative assumptions for a 1972 apartment produces a rate of return of 16.7 percent. On a 1976 unit costing $25,000 to construct, the rate of return would be negative. (Ira Gluskin, *The Cadillac Fairview Corporation Limited* A corporate background report: study no. 3 [Ottawa: Royal Commission on Corporate Concentration, Supply and Services, 1977] p. 8, pp. 45-8, p. 120)

McLaughlin, was only 45 percent sold after being on the market for two years. Stockbrokers Burns, Fry in an investment letter in summer 1976 noted that there were unsold condominiums everywhere:

> The situation has reached serious proportions in some smaller centres. For example, condominium sales in London, Ontario, are almost negligible at present, according to one builder. Yet there is an inventory of more than 1,000 unsold units...[26]

In September 1976 there were 17,000 unsold condominium units in Toronto, the majority high-rise. There were 2,500 unsold in Ottawa, and 3,000 in Vancouver.[27] Marcel Lalande, a Campeau Corporation executive, was quoted as agreeing that the difficulties arose because most people did not want to live in a high-rise condominium. He went on to say that he thought the old squeeze play would be what would force people to buy them in the end: "High housing costs may well force buyers to accept condominiums, 'possibly as a last resort'."[28]

High-rise millionaires. Though the developers cut back on high-rise rental construction in the early 1970s because they were unable to make their accustomed rate of return on these projects, most of the developers have substantial numbers of high-rise buildings in their portfolios. These generate respectable operating profits every year, as we've already seen. That is not, however, their only attraction.

Consider the prospects for a developer who owns just one high-rise building, a small fifty-unit building which cost $19,000 a unit for land and construction in 1972 and which was valued at $20,000 a unit as a completed project, or $1 million. Assume the developer put in $1,000 of his own cash per unit, $50,000 in total, and obtained a mortgage for $18,000 per unit to be repaid over twenty years to 1992. If the developer manages to clear $300 per apartment in the first year in profit, just $25 a month, his rate of return on his cash investment is a healthy 30 percent. Over the years, as rents go up faster than expenses, that profit will increase, so that every year the building is earning him a solid rate of return on his money.

By 1992, however, something wonderful has happened. While making his annual profit, and without any investment beyond the initial $50,000, the developer has also used his rental income to pay off completely the mortgage on the building. He now owns the building outright. Its value? It was worth $1 million when it was built in 1972, and it's very likely that continued inflation and rising urban land values will make it worth much more than that in 1992. But make the conservative assumption that it is still worth only $1 million. From an initial investment of $50,000, one fifty-unit high-rise building has made one developer into a millionaire in just twenty years!

It's worth noting that the requirements of mortgage lenders who insist on a minimum level of return on high-rise projects that covers all operating expenses and mortgage payments, leaving a modest cash surplus, are key to the profitability of high-rise apartments. As long as lenders demand this relationship between rents and expenses, and as long as they are allowed by government to mortgage buildings for high proportions of their actual cost, the developers are certain to make high profits.

The role of government. Governments at all levels have played an essential role in supporting the takeover of the business of providing rental housing by the developers using high-rise apartments. Ottawa led the way in providing directly and indirectly an ample supply of mortgage money to developers who wanted to build rental housing, with no requirements that building forms adequately provide for people's needs (a step that would have ruled out high-rise or drastically limited its appeal compared with other housing forms). Indeed Ottawa helped teach builders how to put up high-rise buildings by including them in early publicly financed urban renewal schemes. Even after practical experience made many people doubt the suitability of high-rise as a housing form, particularly for young families, the federal government did not take the steps open to it that would have cut off much high-rise construction in favour of other housing types by not providing subsidies and NHA mortgage insurance for these projects.

Provincial governments generally also provided support for this development form. Provincial housing agencies erected high-rise buildings themselves for public and senior citizen housing, and purchased completed buildings from developers. With their review powers over municipal land-use plans, provincial governments permitted density maximums and rezonings that paved the way for high-rise buildings. Often controversial projects were reviewed and approved by provincial cabinets. When in the 1970s the developers decided to try to use the appeal of home ownership to make high-rise living more attractive, provincial governments across the country obliged with the necessary condominium legislation.

Municipal governments have been equally important in supporting high-rise apartments as a building form. Planning and rezoning policies have been set up to permit construction of these buildings, and to regulate the supply of high-density residential land so as to maintain a substantial profit margin. Even though their rezoning decisions create millions of dollars in property values, municipalities have made no attempt to capture a portion of these increases through taxation. They have often provided indirect subsidies to large high-rise development projects by selling public land to developers at less than its market value. And though municipalities have extensive powers to regulate building and design standards, they have not attempted to use these to enforce regulations that would pose real problems for high-rise buildings and push developers towards other housing forms.

Intermission or the end? Federal housing politicians have been nervous about high-rise apartments for some time. Paul Hellyer, during his brief tenure as urban affairs minister in Ottawa, used the evidence of citizen hostility gathered by his task force on housing as the basis for objecting to new high-rise public housing projects in Ontario, where these were concentrated.*

---

* Complained Ontario housing minister Stanley Randall, a better friend of the development industry than Hellyer, in a testy letter to Hellyer's successor: "Hellyer completely stopped housing in this province because he said we were not building the right kind of public housing for the needs of the people and they must have a front door and a back door, and no more high rise ghettos." (Michael Dennis and Susan Fish, *Programs in Search of a Policy* [Toronto: Hakkert, 1972] p. 150)

Beginning in the early 1970s, Ottawa and some provincial governments began to encourage the construction of housing types which were mid-way between high-rise apartments and detached houses in density and hence in land price. Semi-detached and row houses began to show up substantially in new house construction statistics. City governments in Vancouver, Toronto and some other cities by the mid-1970s were less ready to support large-scale high-rise redevelopment projects, and willing to go along with high-density projects that did not follow the standard high-rise pattern.

The reason the developers paused in constructing high-rise buildings was not, however, that people didn't like them. It was because rent levels had not risen quickly enough to restore the traditional relationship between rents, expenses, and developer profits. Even if developers were willing to accept lower profits, however, the buildings could not be built because mortgage lenders would not provide the necessary funds without the guarantee of high profits.

Rather than change the way the rental housing business works, Ottawa scurried around developing schemes to subsidize developers and other property investors so that they could make the same high profits in rental buildings and go on building them. This resulted in the federal Assisted Rental Program (ARP), which combines repayable loans to apartment developers with enormous indirect subsidies through income tax concessions to persuade developers and investors to get back into rental construction. Investors were offered returns of 50 or 60 percent on their cash through the ARP program to attract them to rental housing construction.[29]

As long as there are ways to make the usual profits, high-rise construction will carry on. The condominium gambit was a disaster, but the ARP federal scheme is assisting high-rise construction. The fact that many city residents oppose high-rise construction, and that most people don't want to live in high-rise buildings, is not enough to stop them. Developers continue to assemble land and erect buildings where they can, mortgage lenders provide financing if the financial projections meet their usual requirements, and city politicians usually come through with the needed rezoning.

Toronto mayor David Crombie may have termed the city's St.

James Town project's westwards extension "obscene and insane," but he and the city's planners negotiated a southwards extension of the same project which will look like more high-rise buildings to the ordinary eye. In the summer of 1977, when a proposal was made for a temporary downzoning of Edmonton's Garneau area during a planning period, twenty developers showed up at city hall to argue that the downzoning would reduce the value of their high-rise land assemblies by $5 to $6 million.[30] While the provincially appointed commisioner reviewing municipal government in Ottawa recommended against stuffing old people into high-rise senior citizens' projects in 1977, the Toronto municipal government was busy bailing out local developers from Cadillac Fairview on down by buying high-rise apartments from them outright — for old people's housing.[31]

And in Calgary, in 1977 the liveliest real estate market in Canada, Campeau Corp. was pushing for city approval of two thirty-one-storey buildings in a suburban area of their city. Their architect, Martin Cohos, was doing his own imitation of Le Corbusier as if the previous twenty years of experience with high-rise buildings in Canada didn't exist. Said Cohos: "Everyone sees these things as some sort of monsters, but I truly believe they will be a beautiful thing in the landscape. I'm convinced that what we're doing is correct and is far superior to what's happening elsewhere in the city."[32] High-rise apartments may be temporarily down in many parts of Canada, but they are far from finished. And there are already at least 450,000 Canadian families living in them, most of them wishing they could afford to live somewhere else.

7

INDUSTRIAL PARKS:
WORK GOES
TO THE SUBURBS

Industrial parks, large tracts of land owned by a single developer and planned to accommodate one-storey factories and warehouses sprawling over acres of land, are a third major postwar innovation of the developers in Canada. As in medieval fiefdoms, businesses located in industrial parks are usually not owners of the land their premises are built on. Perhaps it's not surprising to discover that one of Canada's first large industrial parks was developed near Vancouver by the Duke of Westminster, owner of one of the largest and oldest estates in Britain. Explains British journalist Oliver Marriott:

> The Duke of Westminster, who had fought in the South African war at the turn of the century and was full of zeal for the Empire, was allowed to export five million pounds, part to Canada, in 1950 because of the good character of the [family-owned] Grosvenor Estates... In 1950 he bought Annacis Island in the Fraser River, just off Vancouver in British Columbia. This was a continuation of the policy of the rich families, started in Victorian times, of buying estates in the Empire.[1]

Industries which located in the Annacis Island project had to become tenants of the duke, because Grosvenor Estates refused to sell any of their land-holdings there.

Industrial parks are the technique by which the developers have fostered a major change in the geography of postwar Canadian cities. Across the country industry has moved out of its former central-city locations and gone to the suburbs. The shift has been dramatic. In just ten years in Montreal's central area, for instance, industrial use declined from 11 million to 8.5 million square feet.[2] In the downtown core itself, the change was even more drastic:

from 4.6 million square feet in 1962 to 2.4 million in 1972. In Toronto, by 1970 10,000 of the 13,500 acres of developed industrial land in the Metro area were located in the three outer suburban boroughs.[3] Note Calgary's planners, "Development of industrial space in the downtown stopped in the 1960s and has declined steadily ever since."[4]

More than just the location of industries has changed since 1945. From multi-storey buildings, on ordinary city streets, in central areas, serviced by rail and with most workers relying on public transit to get to work, industry has gone to single-storey buildings in designated industrial areas served by expressways and roads as well as rail, with many workers travelling to work by car and parking in lots adjoining their factories. Until 1945 the typical industry owned its buildings and land or aimed at doing so eventually; now it is quite common for industry to be the tenant of an industrial park developer who may own both the land and the buildings on it.

Where the idea came from. The industrial park idea has a long history. "The concept of the industrial estate," writes a U.S. analyst of the phenomenon, "dates from the end of the nineteenth century, with the development of Trafford Park in Manchester (1896) and the Clearing Industrial District in Chicago (1899). Their use as industrial planning devices has increased substantially in recent years, and there are now over one thousand operating in the United States and almost half this number in the United Kingdom."[5]

Early Canadian company towns were similar in concept to developer-owned industrial parks. Industrial parks themselves became an important phenomenon in this country only in the 1950s when demand for new industrial space was strong, changes in factory production methods had occurred that made single-storey buildings more attractive, road transport was developing to the point that it was an alternative to rail for goods and to public transit for workers, and growing suburban municipalities were anxious to welcome industries to supplement their residential assessments.

E. P. Taylor's prototype suburb, Don Mills, included industrial acreage. The development company had a number of stringent restrictions about the kind of industries it would sell to, and the design of their factories.[6] Another early industrial park was Calgary's

Manchester Industrial Park, developed by the city itself beginning in 1954.[7]

Why industry likes industrial parks. A number of factors explain the shift of industry to the suburbs, and the ready acceptance of industrial parks as the way in which much of this shift takes place. Virtually all of these elements are included in this ad for the Grosvenor Estate's (in partnership with Laing, a British construction firm) Annacis Island:

> Annacis is remarkable in its capacity to meet all transportation demands of industry. A regional freeway network, direct connection without switching charge to all five major railroads servicing the region, year-round deep sea and barge depth docking capacity and close proximity to Vancouver International Airport provide industry with excellent access to the rich markets of the West Coast and beyond. Annacis is situated fifteen miles north of the United States border.[8]

Industrial parks start with large tracts of serviced land which is, compared with central-city prices, relatively cheap on a per-acre basis. This enables the construction of single-storey industrial buildings which are themselves cheaper to build per square foot of construction than multi-storey buildings. One-storey buildings also provide a higher percentage of useable floor space, permit more flexible layouts and more efficient flows of production goods, resulting in lower production costs.

Transportation facilities are a second attraction. Many industrial parks have railroad connections, though few can boast the five railways offered by Annacis. Even more important, however, is a connection to an expressway road system for inter-city truck transportation. Notes an American study:

> Nearly every industrial park developed since 1955 has been adjacent to, or in close proximity to, a major arterial highway. Highway access is virtually indispensable. In addition, over 90 percent of the industrial districts in operation are still served by rail. Air, water and pipeline transportation are important for specific types of users.[9]

Industrial parks have some additional social and political attractions for industry in the U.S., and though some of these have little relevance to Canada they are influential in the decisions that are made by U.S. subsidiaries about the location of their operations in Canada. American analysts have noted that industry often wants to get out of central-city areas because of "urban blight" and racial tensions. Two U.S. geographers have noted "a social dynamic" that involves "the avoidance of the central city by the majority white residents."[10] The suburbs offer opportunities to capitalize on what another writer termed "the advertising and PR value of a handsome plant on a landscaped setting."[11] There are more mundane considerations as well. Referring to the largest industrial park in the U.S., Chicago's Elk Grove Village, a real estate agent selling the project said: "I say that the principal reason we have five hundred new companies in Elk Grove Village is that it is close to where the boss lives."[12] He noted that blue-collar workers are less enthusiastic about suburban factories. "Many of the workers, particularly the blue-collar ones, still live in Chicago, while many of the northwest suburbanites still work in the city."

A significant portion of the industrial expansion that has occurred in Canada since 1945 has been by foreign-owned, particularly American, companies. Research by geographer Michael Ray has established that U.S. subsidiaries are particularly cautious and conservative in their decisions about where to locate in Canada.[13] They strongly prefer locations just across the border, as close as possible to the head office of the U.S. parent. This pattern is one reason for the attractiveness of southern Ontario for American branch plants.

Once in Canada, these branch plants seek locations that are similar to the locations of their parent firms. Industrial parks offer exactly the kind of accommodation they're used to.* With southern Ontario as the industrial heartland of the country, and with foreign firms playing such a large role in Ontario's manufacturing employment (they accounted for 61.6 percent of the value of Ontario's manufactured goods in 1970, compared with 41.6 percent for the rest of Canada)[14] the subsidiaries' contribution to the dramatic success of suburban industrial parks has been substantial. No

---

* Toronto suburb Mississauga noted in its advertisement in the *Guide to Industrial Parks and Area Developments* published in the U.S. that residents of its five industrial parks "include American Can, Union Carbide, Kohler, Hyster, Capitol Records, Douglas Aircraft, Haywood Gordon, Sperry Rand, Mallory Battery, to name but a

wonder, then, that Grosvenor Estates pointed out that Annacis Island "is situated fifteen miles north of the United States border.",

How industrial parks are developed. Developing a suburban industrial park is similar to developing suburban house lots. The first step is to find a large enough tract of land that is well located for industrial needs. Transportation facilities are paramount, but there are other more subtle considerations as well. Wrote an experienced American developer in an article for his developer associates entitled "Twelve Common Mistakes in Industrial Land Development":

> A careless developer may find, too late, that his property is just outside the free local delivery zone, or the rail switching limits, or the telephone local call area, or the twice-a-day mail area. Any of these factors can sharply reduce a property's market potential.[15]

The developer produces the basic service infrastructure for the land he owns, installing services, roads and so on. These specifications have to be carefully geared to industrial requirements. Once planning and zoning permissions are obtained, the developer commences marketing the project often before or at the same time as installing the services.

A feature of every industrial park is the minimum requirements set out by the developer or the municipality or both for potential tenants or purchasers. These function like municipal zoning requirements, but they are often enforced by covenants or other legal devices by the developer. A key restriction governs the maximum coverage permitted of the lot. In general, coverage and densities are very low. Noted one U.S. developer:

> Each developer has his own firm notions on the subject. The normal range is from 1 [square foot of land] to 1 [square foot of building] to 5 to 1; in our district we hit upon the 3 to 1 figure and we have been very well satisfied with it.[16]

---

few." With neighbours like that, it's not hard to understand why U.S. subsidiaries would feel right at home in southern Ontario's suburban industrial parks. (*Guide to Industrial Parks and Area Developments 1970-71*, Princeton, N.J.)

The developer may control the design of buildings on sites in the project, establish landscaping minimums to ensure attractive surroundings, regulate the storage of materials outside the building, set out parking lot requirements and so on. Though industrial developers sometimes cite social and aesthetic motives for these restrictions, in fact they are governed by hard-headed economic considerations and the developers' desire to maximize their profits. The restrictions prevent an industrial park occupant from taking cost-cutting or efficiency measures that might reflect badly on neighbouring businesses and reduce the value of their properties (or the developer's, if he has leased the land rather than sold it).

Even if an industrial developer doesn't enforce restrictions on land use in his development, they are likely to be required by mortgage lenders who finance the project. "If the park is well-restricted and will be properly developed, the lender is more likely to give a long-term loan," a Detroit mortgage banker explained to U.S. and Canadian industrial developers.[17]

Though some industrial park developers offer only leases on land or land and buildings, often industries have the choice of renting or buying in an industrial park. Industrial developers usually construct space for a tenant on the strength of a lease. Financing the development requires funds for land servicing and for some construction. As usual, industrial land developers try to maximize their leverage by putting as little of their own cash into these projects and borrowing as much as possible. Note two U.S. authors, "The basic objective of the developer's financing plan is to conserve his own cash, and to maximize the use of others' funds. This makes his own equity funds go further and last longer for larger development activities."[18]

Prices and profits. In some Canadian cities, well-located suburban industrial land sells for prices that generate substantial per-acre profits to developers who assembled the land at relatively low prices years before it was ready for development. A good indication of the profit potential of industrial land development is given by the range in per-acre land prices within a fifty-mile radius of Toronto.[19] The cheapest serviced land in the region in 1976 was selling for $15,000 an acre in Bowmanville, east of Toronto. In eight other industrial parks in the region at some distance from Toronto, land was available for $30,000 an acre or less. Depending on servicing standards, the developer's servicing costs run from about $14,000 to $25,000 an acre. Land located closer to the city near the airport, however, was selling for $65,000 an acre, and just inside the Metropolitan Toronto boundary it was $85,000. The highest price reported for serviced vacant land in 1976 was $150,000 an acre, up from $125,000 an acre just two years earlier. Servicing and other development costs did not vary substantially from one location in the region to another. The main variable accounting for the difference between the low prices of $15,000 to $30,000 and the higher prices was land profit. Profits on land assembled some years ago at $5,000 to $10,000 per acre were running at $35,000 to $100,000 an acre in many developments. This is much the same profit on a per-acre basis that developers are accustomed to making in suburban housing land development.*

---

* Confirmation of these profit levels in industrial land comes from Cadillac Fairview, which owns 1.2 million square feet of rentable industrial space in Canada, 2.8 million square feet in the U.S., and has 212 acres of serviced industrial land in its portfolio in Ontario and 680 acres in the U.S. as of 1977. Cadillac Fairview vice-president Martin Seaton provided detailed pro forma financial statements for one of its U.S. industrial parks, Orange County Industrial Center in southern California, to Canadian developers at a seminar in 1977 sponsored by the Urban Development Institute. Cadillac projected that development of the 132-acre project would involve a cash investment of $2.0 million beginning in January 1976, rising to $3.5 million in July 1977 when cash in the project would reach a maximum. By July 1978 most of Cadillac's cash, about $2 million, would be back in its hands as revenue from land sales and by 1980 it would have received back in full its cash investment — plus a total profit on the project of $9,680,000. Cadillac Fairview calculated its overall return on its investment in the project at 37.2 percent per annum. A more careful calculation, taking into account that different amounts of cash were invested in the project at different times during its life, indicates a rate of profit on investment averaging 75 percent per annum over the five-year period. Cadillac Fairview's projected profit on the development was $74,000 per acre on land expected to sell for an average of about $110,000 an acre. (Presentation by Martin Seaton, senior vice-president, Cadillac Fairview, "Orange County Industrial Center. Calculation of rate of return on investment.")

The industrial land developers. Most of the corporate developers in Canada involved in suburban land development are active in both residential and industrial land. Several of the large British development firms with modest suburban land banks who are active in house construction are also involved in industrial development. The eagerness of suburban municipalities to receive commercial and industrial development property taxes encourages suburban industrial development. The suburban Toronto municipality of Mississauga, for example, obtained agreements from the large developers operating within its boundaries providing for a minimum ratio of industrial to residential development projects. Don Mills was a forerunner of this practice.

Most municipalities possess substantial inventories of vacant land properly planned and zoned for industrial use, awaiting only servicing and construction. In Vancouver, for instance, the 1976 regional plan noted, "There is plenty of industrial land available in the region, about 12,000 acres of vacant land zoned for industry outside of the Agricultural Reserve. At the rate we expect to use industrial land, about 250 acres per year, we would not begin to approach limitations on industrial land supply by 1986."[20]

The willingness of municipal governments to approve land for industrial use has not, however, led to low industrial land prices. There are indications that the control of a few large developers over suburban land extends from residential to industrial land in some cities, and that they are using the same practices to keep prices (and profits) high. This point was asserted, indirectly, by a 1976 Metro Toronto planning study:

> In recent years much of the designated industrial land in and around Toronto has come to be owned by individuals and companies who are in the business of industrial development. In many cases they want to develop these lands as part of their business rather than sell to industries that might buy sites and build for themselves. In addition some of these industrial development companies have come to regulate the amount of land they will put on the market to give themselves the best long-term financial position. In both these ways they have come to exercise a constraint on the market supply.[21]

Unlike the suburban housing market, high industrial land profits are not paid for by ordinary consumers. Instead they are paid for by the industrial and manufacturing sector of the business community to the land development-financial sector, though no doubt they are often passed on eventually to consumers. This conflict of interest between manufacturing and industry and developers (with their financial backers) has had fascinating consequences in some cities. It has produced many municipal non-profit land development schemes for industry, similar to the residential land banks operated in some cities like Saskatoon, Edmonton and Halifax. The difference between the two kinds of public land development operations is that the same local politicians who oppose non-profit public land development for housing are usually enthusiastic supporters of non-profit public land development for industry.

Cheap serviced land for industry is available in many cities. In Calgary, for instance, the city has no housing land bank but operates an industrial land bank that owns about fourteen thousand acres. The city develops three hundred to four hundred acres of industrial land a year, making it "the leading industrial land developer in Calgary."[22] In Winnipeg, an apparent shortage of serviced industrial land in the early 1970s led the city to acquire a large badly located site on the east side of the city. In London, Ontario, a 1976 summary of available industrial land showed 132 acres of city-owned land and 109 acres of developer-owned land for sale.[23] In these and other cities, industries are able to buy serviced suburban land at reasonable prices even if ordinary house buyers cannot.

No one knows what share of total industrial growth since 1945 has taken place on land assembled by industrial land developers, or what share of total new industrial space is leased by developers to industry. Much suburban industrial development around Canadian cities has been a lower-key version of the full-fledged planned and rigidly controlled industrial park. The enthusiasm of municipalities for suburban industrial growth and the over-supply of approved land waiting for development has made it easier for a wider range of speculators and developers to operate in the industrial land business than in residential land development where controls are tighter. As the supply of land owned by smaller operators is used up, however, and as the large corporate developers control a larger share of available industrial land, it is inevitable that they will use their improved bargaining position to obtain higher profits and to maximize long-term profits by leasing rather than selling land. Corporate developer-owned industrial parks are bound to play an increasing role in the growth of industry in cities without public land development for industry.

A hint of the implications of this trend is given in a planning study done in Metro Toronto:

> The overall effect is that while there is a large amount of land designated for industry in and around Toronto only a limited amount is available for development at any one time and this is likely to be tied to developer-built industrial estates. The majority of companies are well-satisfied with this arrangement but some that want to buy their own site and build and own their plant, especially large companies, may have great difficulty finding a suitable property close to Toronto.[24]

The impact of suburbanized work. Suburban locations for new industrial space have meant that more and more blue-collar jobs are located in the suburbs. Central-city locations are increasingly reserved for white-collar workers, and in fact urban planners have encouraged large corporations to split their operations by locating offices downtown and plants and warehouses in the suburbs. Ironically, this is the reverse of the residential pattern, so that inner city low-income earners are commuting, often by inadequate public transit, to suburban job locations, while more affluent white-collar suburbanites are adding to urban traffic congestion by driving to downtown office jobs.

Before the emergence of industrial parks, industries were typically owner-occupiers of the buildings and land they used. Businesses that were not owner-occupiers aimed at achieving the stability and security that came with ownership. The industrial park has permanently changed this situation. Businesses that previously had fixed occupancy costs as owner-occupiers are now in the same situation as apartment tenants: as market rents rise, their occupancy costs rise. The profits that incidentally came to industrial owner-occupiers from increases in their property values have been captured by the industrial developers.

The scope of the change is substantial. In Halifax, for instance, there was a total stock of 525,000 square feet of rented industrial space in 1970. Between 1970 and 1975, that stock was increased by 1,373,000 square feet, almost three times as much. As of early 1976, Halifax had just over 2,000,000 square feet of rented industrial space, nearly four times the 1970 figure.[25]

The role of government. The trend towards suburban locations for industry has been supported and assisted by a number of senior government policies. Probably the most important of these has been, surprisingly enough, transportation policy and the strong priority given in the postwar period to road transportation. Industry is attracted to the suburbs in part because of the easier access to these locations by truck transportation, particularly inter-city trucking, while rail transportation does not have the same built-in suburban bias. Urban road systems are equally important because they serve to transport industrial workers from both the central city and the suburbs. Without the enormous investment by governments in both inter-urban highways and urban expressway and road systems, suburban low-density industrial parks would have been considerably less attractive.

Government tax policies have supported the shift from owned to rented suburban industrial premises. By permitting the development industry to enjoy the same tax concession afforded to business owner-occupiers of industrial space through the capital cost allowance provisions of the Income Tax Act, the federal government made renting industrial premises a more attractive proposition than it would have been if developers were not able to use paper losses generated through the CCA concession to avoid tax on profits made elsewhere in their business. Had the tax concession been limited to business owner-occupiers only, the rental terms offered by developers would have been much less attractive compared with the advantage of a business owning its own building and using the CCA concession to reduce taxes paid on its own profits.

Suburban municipalities have been enthusiastic supporters of suburban location for industry and of developers' industrial parks. Through this land development technique, the suburbs were able to add industrial property to their assessment rolls. Municipal officials consider that the cost to a municipality of providing services to industrial land is far less than the tax revenues generated.

Municipalities have usually been eager to zone land for industrial development, provide necessary trunk services, and approve development projects. As we have seen, in cities where it seemed that cheap industrial land could attract more industrial development, municipalities have had no hesitation about going into the land development business and offering industry land at cost. The development industry has not opposed public industrial land development with the same vigour that it has opposed public residential land development, but this may be because public industrial land development has not played much of a role in cities like Vancouver and the southern Ontario Golden Horseshoe area where postwar industrial growth concentration has been aided by federal government economic policies.

Nothing stands in the way of developer-owned industrial parks expanding their role in every Canadian city. Noted a 1976 Toronto planning study, "If present trends continue... entrepreneurial developers will accommodate an increasing share of all industry in industrial estates."[26] The innovator of Annacis Island, the Duke of Westminster, would no doubt find this trend familiar and comforting. So must the industrial park developers, who have discovered one more way of making returns on their investment which are far beyond the profit levels usually earned by the industries occupying space in their industrial parks.

8

THE DOWNTOWN
OFFICE EXPLOSION

Have you ever seen an atomic bomb explode? I've been sitting here for two years now, watching the whole centre of town climb. In bits and pieces, towers have been shooting up to the sky until now I almost feel like I'm on the ground again. I'm thirty floors in the air, but all around I see walls, offices and people on the same level. In the past two years, Montreal has become a vertical city.[1]

This description of the downtown office explosion came from a developer in Montreal in mid-1975. But he could have been in any other large Canadian city. Until over-building and depressed economic conditions produced a temporary slowdown in most cities in 1975-76, large office towers were going up across Canada at an unprecedented speed. In 1967, spending on office construction in Canada was $479 million. By 1974 it was $1,115 million, and $1,541 million in 1976.[2]

This spending, much of it by the corporate developers on a relatively small number of major projects, has transformed the downtowns of every Canadian city. At first these projects were welcomed with gushes of local boosterism, combined with sighs of relief that finally the home town was going to look like New York. Reported the *Winnipeg Tribune* about the construction of a series of insurance company towers in the Broadway area of the city, "The City of Winnipeg, of course, was delighted to see the crumbling old verandahs and lacey porches along Broadway replaced by spanking new buildings."[3] Crowed Vancouver mayor Tom Campbell after a local vote permitting the downtown Pacific Centre pro-

ject to proceed, "You're going to see Vancouver take off like
Montreal and Toronto now."[4]*

These looming new office towers are a perfect visual symbol of
who's really in charge of the Canadian economy and who makes
the decisions about how cities are to develop. In an era where
buildings are measured not by what they add to their neighbourhoods or by their architectural merit but by how tall they are, the
tallest buildings of all are the creation of the biggest corporate developers, often in open partnership with the financial institutions
—life insurance companies, trust companies, and especially the
chartered banks—who stand behind the development industry.

There has been an explosion in the number of white-collar office jobs in the Canadian economy since 1945. Through large
downtown office redevelopment projects like Vancouver's Pacific
Centre, Edmonton's McCauley Plaza, Winnipeg's Lombard Place,
Kitchener's market square project, Hamilton's aborted Civic
Square, Toronto's Toronto-Dominion Centre and later bank
towers, Ottawa's Place de Ville, Montreal's Place Ville Marie, Halifax's Scotia Square, and St. John's Atlantic Place, the corporate
developers and their financial backers have captured a large share
of the market for new office space generated by this economic
growth.

As industrial workers have had increasingly to go to work in the
suburbs, more and more office workers are converging every day
on the downtown areas where offices are concentrated.** The
downtown office towers have replaced a much more diverse pattern of land use and activity downtown. Figures for Calgary, for

---

* Campbell was outdone a year later by Vancouver's deputy mayor
Hugh Bird, who unveiled the model of Pacific Centre for the press.
As the lights dimmed, Bird stepped up to a draped platform on the
stage of a hotel ballroom where the project model was ready. "Finally," proclaimed Bird with a wonderful combination of hyperbole
and mixed metaphor, "Vancouver has a heart and downtown has an
anchor." (*Vancouver Sun* 28 January 1969)

** There were 53,000 workers in downtown Ottawa in 1971; by 1974
the figure had gone up to 76,000, with most of the increase being
office workers. In 1970, Toronto's central area accounted for only
19 percent of all jobs in industry, storage and warehousing, but it
had 63 percent of the city's office jobs. Montreal's downtown had in

example, show that of the buildings demolished in downtown Calgary between 1964 and 1972, mainly for new office, retail and hotel space, 65 percent were single-family houses, 21 percent were commercial buildings, and 14 percent were institutional, industrial, transportation or other types of buildings.[5]

Though most people went along with the local boosterism that accompanied the first of the large postwar downtown redevelopment projects, resistance to them has grown as city after city experiences the effects of this kind of growth. Public subsidies turn out to be the rule rather than the exception for the large downtown projects and every level of government has provided grants and subsidies to assist the developers. Many fine old buildings have been demolished by the developers so that most cities have relatively few old buildings left in the downtown. City governments have used their expropriation powers to assemble land later turned over to the developers, often destroying small downtown businesses in the process. Expensive new transportation facilities (subways in Toronto and Montreal, expressways and bridges in most other cities) have been built to provide the necessary access for suburban white-collar residents to get back and forth to their downtown jobs.

Downtown retail businesses have moved from owner-occupied buildings on shopping streets to tenant premises provided by developers in the basements of the new buildings. Views that urban residents cherished have been obstructed. Instead of seeing the harbour as they go along Spring Garden Road, residents of Halifax now have the pleasure of looking directly into an enormous office

---

1972 buildings totalling 49.6 million square feet. Offices accounted for 25.6 million square feet; retail space was 6.7 million, hotels 3.8 million, parking 3.3 million, and residential just 2 million.

A good indication of the extreme concentration of office use on a small amount of downtown land is given by calculations made by Montreal planners. In that city's central area in 1972, there were 102 million square feet of building space in total, of which 28 million square feet were offices. While offices made up 28 percent of the downtown's building space, they occupied only 9 percent of downtown land. (*Ottawa Citizen* 31 August 1974; George Nader, *Cities of Canada* Vol. II [Toronto: Macmillan, 1976] p. 211; Service de l'Habitation et de l'Urbanisme, "Centre-ville, Bulletin technique No. 8" [Montréal: Ville de Montréal, Octobre 1974] p. 12, p. 15)

project erected by Trizec with Maritime Telephone and Telegraph. Downtown Vancouver now offers fine views of high office buildings, with little more than glimpses of mountains and sea in between.*

By the early 1970s the shine was off what ten years earlier had been "spanking new buildings." As the downtown office explosion reached its height, it was clear to many urban residents that a city pays a steep price for aspiring to look like New York.

Skyscraper cities. Downtown real estate has always been a lucrative field for speculators and developers. In times of economic boom, many fortunes have been made buying and selling downtown land. The most dramatic examples were in western Canada during the railway and wheat boom before 1913. In his fascinating account of the history of downtown development in Vancouver, Donald Gutstein cites many instances of dizzying increases in land values which made fortunes for local operators and foreign investors.[6] High downtown land values encourage tall buildings, because (as with high-rise apartments) only high-density buildings permit high prices to be paid for land while keeping the land cost per square foot of rentable space down to a reasonable level.

There was a boom in downtown construction in most cities during the 1920s, producing tall buildings in the classic skyscraper designs pioneered in New York and Chicago. For decades after its construction was completed, Montreal's Sun Life head office building (built in three stages between 1917 and 1931) was that city's largest office building.[7] In Winnipeg, the Richardson family had plans ready in 1929 for a fourteen-storey office building to dominate the city. The site was assembled and construction was ready to go when the stock market crash came along. The land stood vacant until 1967 when James Richardson announced a thirty-four-storey tower as part of a Lombard Place project. Noted

---

* The developer of Vancouver's black Pacific Centre, a smaller version of the Toronto-Dominion Centre in Toronto, replied to critics of the building's design who labelled it the "dark tower" and complained about its appearance by denying that it was black. Its publicity called it "solar bronze." Said project manager Lorne Cook: "It really is not a black building in my eyes. At times it has an absolutely delightful quality. It's just a jewel when seen from the North Shore or city hall." (*Vancouver Sun* 5 May 1971)

Richardson with no apparent embarrassment, "My father started this project forty years ago."[8]

The Canadian development industry traces the roots of massive downtown office-commercial redevelopment projects to Place Ville Marie and its U.S. developer William Zeckendorf. Place Ville Marie (4.2 million square feet), started in 1959, was indeed the project that firmly established the potential of downtown office towers on a scale previously unthought-of, particularly when combined with retail-commercial space (as in PVM's basement) and hotel space (in the Queen Elizabeth Hotel, connected to PVM and owned by the CNR which owns the land PVM is built on). From 1946 until the start of construction on Place Ville Marie the largest private office tower project in Montreal had been Bell Telephone's 299,000-square-foot eight-storey building on Belmont built in 1947, a seventeen-storey 36,000-square-foot tower on Guy started in 1957, and a fourteen-storey 298,000-square-foot tower built in 1958 by Prudential Assurance.[9] But bigger buildings had been erected by government bodies: a seven-storey federal building in 1950 of 265,000 square feet, and an eleven-storey office tower of 478,000 square feet for the Department of National Revenue in 1957. The same year William Zeckendorf started Place Ville Marie, the CNR itself built a seventeen-storey building of 2.1 million square feet.*

---

* In other cities too it was governments and not private developers who led the way with early large downtown office buildings. In Vancouver, the federal government began the office boom of the 1950s with new buildings for the unemployment insurance commission and the department of national revenue. In both cases, opposition politicians showed that Ottawa paid local Liberals more for the land than it was worth. Vancouver's boom peaked in 1955 with the construction of a large new head office tower by B.C. Electric. In Toronto too, large office projects were pioneered by governments. In 1960 the federal government put up a 570,000-square-foot office project, the Mackenzie Building; in 1964 the new Toronto city hall with 815,000 square feet was started; the next year, a 450,000 square-foot court house was erected. The largest private projects in the early 1960s were 360,000-square-foot buildings put up by Prudential Assurance, National Trust, and the Royal Bank. (Donald Gutstein, *Vancouver Ltd.* [Toronto: James Lorimer, 1975] p. 68; Development Department, "The downtown area — major development projects completed 1960-1969" [Toronto: City of Toronto, 20 May 1970])

Toronto's first large project was the Toronto-Dominion Centre, with its first tower of 1,300,000 square feet started in 1967 and a second tower of 900,000 square feet in 1969. Total Toronto office space went from 13.9 million square feet in 1958 to 27.5 million in 1968, doubling in a decade. It was after 1968 that the market really exploded, with the total increasing to 45.2 million in 1974 and 50.3 million in 1975.[10] In the downtown area, growth was dramatic. From 1946 to 1953, new office construction totalled 1.6 million square feet, less than the size of the T-D Centre. From 1954 to 1963 construction was 5.1 million square feet. In the next decade, it was 11.3 million square feet. In 1974-75 alone, almost three million square feet were added to the downtown office supply.

Perhaps the best illustration of the mid-sixties to mid-seventies office boom in Canada is Halifax. Its total supply of office space at the end of 1974 was 4,450,000 square feet. In 1975 alone, 1,104,000 square feet were added to the total. In 1976-77, another 1,061,000 square feet were added, mostly in a few corporate projects like the Maritime Telephone and Telegraph Centre developed by Trizec (301,000 square feet), the Bank of Commerce (260,000 square feet), and the Toronto-Dominion Bank (104,500 square feet). In just three years, Halifax increased its total supply of office space by 50 percent and greatly increased the potential number of downtown office workers.[11]

Every Canadian city added substantially to its supply of office space in the boom that ended about 1975. Nor was office growth limited to the downtown. Most cities have areas outside downtown where there has been significant office development in the postwar period. A certain amount of new office space has also been built in the suburbs. In Vancouver in 1975, for instance, downtown office space was roughly twelve million square feet. The Broadway office node was an additional four million. Offices in the suburbs totalled about three million.[12]

The office developers' idea. Though it was not the first large office building to be built in postwar Canada, Place Ville Marie is certainly the prototype of the corporate developers' office project. Since the day in early 1958 when developer William Zeckendorf phoned up his financial backer, James Muir, the president of the Royal Bank of Canada, because he couldn't find a major tenant for

Place Ville Marie, Canada's downtown developers have never looked back.[13]* Place Ville Marie includes the four key elements of downtown commercial redevelopment projects.

First, *large-scale buildings*, buildings big enough to dominate the supply of new office space. Place Ville Marie was particularly dramatic in its scale. The biggest private office project in postwar Montreal had been 383,000 square feet up to 1959; Place Ville Marie measured 4,195,000 square feet — more than ten times the size. In 1975 central Montreal had a total of 26.3 million square feet of rentable office space. Place Ville Marie alone accounted for about one-eighth of that amount.[14]

Second, *developers are owners, businesses are tenants.* In Place Ville Marie, the Royal Bank became a tenant of William Zeckendorf, though Zeckendorf reports that the lease was for fifty years at $2.6 million a year, terms far more favourable than the normal lease offered by developers.[15] In other projects, as the success of these developments has been demonstrated and their financial potential assured, major tenants, particularly large financial institutions with no shortage of money to invest, have purchased an equity interest in projects where they are the prime tenants. Of Vancouver's Pacific Centre, for instance, 33.3 percent is owned by Cadillac Fairview, 33.3 percent by Eaton's, and 33.3 percent by the Toronto-Dominion Bank. Toronto's T-D Centre's 3.3 million

---

* As Zeckendorf tells the story in his fascinating autobiography, he called Muir on the weekend at home:

> "Jim, you know we are not getting anywhere with this damn renting."
> He roared back, "Why the hell should you get anywhere. That goddamn Chinaman is stopping you." [The goddamn Chinaman, in Muir's delicate phrase, was I. M. Pei, Zeckendorf's architect who had designed the project.]
> "No, you're stopping us."

Given that the banks are the most powerful Canadian businesses, that the Royal at the time was the largest Canadian bank, and that Zeckendorf was a wheeler-dealer customer of the bank, this was a rather daring conversational ploy on Zeckendorf's part. His account continues:

> "I'm stopping you?"
> "Jim, your enemies, the ones who hate you, won't take space

square feet are 50 percent owned by Cadillac Fairview, 50 percent by the bank. Trizec's controversial development at Portage and Main in Winnipeg is owned 50 percent by Trizec, and 50 percent by the Bank of Nova Scotia. The major financial institutions have the power to insist on partnership in owning these projects; other businesses have no choice except to become tenants of the corporate developers.

Third, *combine offices with other profitable uses:* shopping malls, department stores, hotels. The standard combination is office space over ground level or basement retail space. The retail space is often a bonus for the developer, making it possible to generate more rent out of his site for space that could not be leased at such high rates for other uses.

Fourth, *build on land that is right in the heart of the city.* Canada's five major banks rushed to build new office towers on the four corners of Toronto's King and Bay streets and the Royal Bank lost the game of musical corners. Every Canadian city has its equivalent major downtown corner, with similar if smaller office towers dominating the downtown core.

Why businesses like office towers. Though it sometimes takes the kind of arm-twisting that Bill Zeckendorf applied to James Muir to

---

here. The ones who love you don't believe in us. There is a gang-up on the part of the other banks, the Bank of Montreal, the Imperial Bank, the Canadian Bank of Commerce, the Bank of Nova Scotia, Toronto Dominion..."

He said, "You're crazy."

"I'm not crazy."

Then he said, "Well, what do you want me to do about it?"

"Move."

"I should move? You're mad."

"Move, Jim. We'll call the new tower the Royal Bank of Canada Building in Place Ville Marie. You will be king of the hill, towering over the whole of Montreal. The business will have to come to you."

One problem remained. The Royal Bank already had a head office building:

"You're out of your mind. We have the biggest bank in Canada in the biggest bank building in Canada."

get large corporations into a specific development project, on the whole downtown office towers have been successful because they suit the government departments, large corporations, and professionals like corporate lawyers, accountants, management consultants and so on who rent space in them. The basis of the office explosion in large and medium-sized Canadian cities is the very rapid postwar increase in the number of workers in white-collar office occupations in large cities. Notes Maurice Yeates in his study of the "axis" cities, those from Windsor to Quebec City, "The tertiary sector of economic activity [sales and office jobs, mainly] occupies the majority of the total...labour force and provided seven-tenths of all the new jobs in the axis between 1961 and 1971."[16]

This expansion of the labour force (plus improved standards of accommodation for office workers that have led to more office space per person) has been the ultimate source of the demand for the space the corporate developers have provided. Big government and big business have together filled up these office towers.

The logic of the preference of business and government bureaucracies for downtown office buildings has been spelled out by a study conducted by Vancouver planners in 1974 who interviewed decision-making executives in ten major industrial, financial and

---

I said, "I'll buy it from you."

"You've got no money to buy it, you——Jew."

"Now look here, Jim, think this over. I'm coming up tomorrow morning to a directors' meeting."

It was Zeckendorf who deleted the expletive. The deal they made was that Zeckendorf purchased the Royal's old building, and the bank leased space in Place Ville Marie.

That clinched it. With the Royal Bank in as a major tenant, Zeckendorf went to see his old pal Fred Ecker of Metropolitan Life in New York asking for a $75 million mortgage. He came out with $50 million, on condition. When finding tenants to fill up the project later posed difficulties, the Royal was as committed as Zeckendorf to the success of Place Ville Marie, and they had the necessary muscle to ensure that it was a success. A troop of corporations, law firms and other businesses who were clients of the Royal obediently lined up for leases under James Muir's inspiration. (William Zeckendorf, *The Autobiography of William Zeckendorf* [New York: Holt, Rinehart and Winston, 1970] p. 175ff.)

transportation corporations. Summarized the researchers: "Almost without exception we found that they liked downtown Vancouver as a business location for a variety of good reasons."[17]

□ Proximity to support services; to other activities like shopping, entertainment; to hotels; to clubs; and to residential areas like the high-rise West End.

□ Reduced time needed to get from place to place, and proximity of business associates.

□ Prestige of being located downtown in a big building everybody knows instead of in some obscure suburb.

□ Ready availability of office staff, who for their own reasons find working downtown appealing.

Those interviewed reported that the main problems with downtown locations were traffic congestion and the relatively high cost of space with little flexibility of expansion.

When they are making a choice among downtown office buildings, businesses prefer large well-located prestige buildings even though their rents are considerably higher. Reported the trade magazine *Canadian Building* about the Toronto office market in 1975:

Tenants will continue to show a preference for larger buildings and especially major complexes. During the last few years major complexes like the Toronto-Dominion Centre, Commerce Court and some of the smaller complexes at the major subway intersections have experienced more successful leasing results and considerably higher rental rates than smaller free-standing buildings.[18]

Large office buildings also reflect the increasing dominance of large corporations in the Canadian economy.* In fact, the decisions large corporations make about downtown office locations are

---

* Calgary, where the booming Alberta economy managed to sustain the 1970s office building explosion longer than in any other Canadian city, is a good example of this. The companies that have been growing in Calgary are mostly resource corporations, and their problem is finding office buildings large enough to accommodate their needs. *Calgary Herald* reporter Vern Simaluk noted in a 1976 article that Hudson Bay Oil and Gas was about to move to Scotia Centre

revealing expressions of the realities of corporate power in the Canadian economy. There is more than just symbolism to the dominance of the downtown skylines by the chartered banks, followed by the trust companies, insurance companies, and resource corporations. As many business observers have pointed out, the chartered banks are the key to the Canadian business establishment. William Zeckendorf's raucous out-of-class stories about James Muir offer a glimpse of the realities of the role of the banks in deciding not just to support financially this pattern of urban development, but to take a slice of the action themselves along with the corporate developers, and fill up the space they don't use themselves with their customers.

An explanation of this phenomenon, considerably more understated than Zeckendorf's but underlining many of the same points, comes from an article in a small trade paper:

> There are other factors that decide where firms will locate, George Kee, marketing director of Y&R Properties [one of the large downtown development firms] points out. A company may locate in a certain office building because it's part of a conglomerate, and other parts of the conglomerate are in the building. Or a bank may decide that a certain mining company it's lending money to would be advised to locate in the same building as the bank so it can 'keep an eye on it.' "[19]

How the developers do it. There are three key steps in putting a downtown development scheme together. The first is getting con-

---

being built by Trizec and the Bank of Nova Scotia; that left Hudson Bay's head office building vacant, and it was being eyed by Loram Industries which had its employees spread out around several adjacent buildings. Alberta Gas Trunk, with six hundred employees in six buildings, was getting ready to move into eight floors in a building in the Bow Valley project plus partial space on five more. Shell Canada was getting ready to consolidate its one thousand employees out of five buildings into sixteen storeys in the thirty-four-storey Shell Centre being built by Olympia and York. Dome Petroleum was going to anchor a tower in the Oxford Square project; Home Oil was to anchor the other tower. As Simaluk put it: "A game of corporation checkers is being played in Calgary boardrooms as companies are hopscotching from building to building in search of new office space." (*Calgary Herald* 9 April 1976)

trol of the site. Sometimes, as for Place Ville Marie, this means finding a large parcel of land under single ownership and leasing or buying it. More often, it involves a land assembly operation. These are generally much more sophisticated and smoothly executed than the blockbusting favoured by high-rise apartment developers. Commercial assemblies involve businessmen negotiating with businessmen. Usually elaborate care is taken to disguise the fact that an assembly is being carried out. Dummy companies, front men lawyers and trust companies, even renovations on existing buildings to mislead neighbours about what is really happening are all part of the strategy. Developers can always afford to pay much more for a parcel of downtown land than its current value because of the higher overall densities they achieve with their redevelopment projects. Owners of older buildings usually like selling for demolition because this permits them to treat the sale price as a sale of land only, and to avoid the taxes they would pay if they sold a depreciated building for more than its book value. The only real difficulty in these land assemblies is the bargaining which decides how much of the increase in the value of the land that comes with the redevelopment goes to the former owners, and how much to the developer.

The second key step in a downtown development project is lining up the major tenants for the project. Usually mortgage lenders demand a commitment by a corporate tenant to rent a sizeable percentage of the proposed building. If the project includes major commercial space such as a department store, the developer has to have a tenant committed to this space to get the mortgage money to build it. Aware of these circumstances, "anchor" tenants can demand exceptionally good terms from the developer (like the Royal Bank's fifty-year low-rent lease at Place Ville Marie) or a percentage of ownership in the project. Without major tenants, developments cannot go ahead, because mortgage lenders demand the guarantee of sizeable rental incomes before putting up their money.

The third key step is getting the necessary municipal planning approvals and support for the project. The general rule seems to be the larger the development project, the larger its developer, the more powerful the anchor tenants of the space, the more anxious are local city planners and politicians to give developers everything they ask for and more. More than with any of the other corporate development techniques, downtown development projects often involve direct subsidies from city hall.

Developers prepare pro forma financial statements for downtown development projects that show projected income from rents, deduct an allowance for vacancies, and subtract operating expenses to show the net income that is generated annually by the project. It is this projected annual income after operating expenses that is used by developers and financial institutions to establish the value of the completed project.* The total creation cost to the developer of a project of this kind must of course be less than its market value after completion; how much less determines the amount of the developer's own cash that the project requires. Minimizing the cost of assembling the land, maximizing the rental income of the project by building as much as the developer calculates can be leased on the site and as city hall will permit, adding city-owned land to the project at low cost, persuading city hall to pay for construction of the parking garage needed to service the project and many other strategies are used by downtown developers to keep their cash investment to a minimum while maximizing the final value of the project.

If a scheme is particularly well developed, the developer may keep his total creation costs of the project below 75 percent of its final value. In that case, once the project is constructed and fully rented and the developer has collected the cash for the first mortgage, the developer finishes the project with no cash of his own tied up in it and with extra cash in hand because he has "mortgaged out" the project.[20] In addition, rental income will more than cover operating costs and all mortgage and principal payments, leaving the developer with a cash income from the project every

---

* The calculation is this: the market value (or lending value) of the project is a multiple of the annual net income it generates. The multiple used is a function of interest rates, so that the value of a downtown project generating an annual income of $4 million is the amount of money which invested would yield interest of $4 million. If interest rates are 12 percent, the value of the project would be roughly $34 million (12 percent of $34 million is about $4 million). Large financial institutions generally lend developers 75 percent of the market value of a commercial development on a first mortgage.

year. And, as with high-rise apartments, at the end of the mortgage period of twenty to thirty years, the developer will own outright the building and the land it sits on.

In most cases, downtown developers find that they must invest some cash of their own in their projects in addition to the funds they are able to borrow from mortgage lenders. Because mortgage lenders are anxious to ensure that the net income from the project is comfortably larger than the cash needed to cover mortgage interest payments so that the developer can cover principal repayments and have a cash cushion on top, the rate of return on that cash investment by the developer is usually quite high. Over time, with office rents rising much faster than operating expenses and with mortgage payments fixed, the operating profit on downtown development projects increases.

It is only since 1960 that downtown office redevelopment projects have been a major activity for the development industry in Canada. By the end of the decade, however, developers were far more interested in building office and office-commercial projects than high-rise apartments. Office rental buildings had all of the attractions of high-rise apartments, with one bonus extra: tenants were businessmen and governments, who knew the rules of the game and were not likely to agitate for rent controls or tenant take-overs of their buildings. Developer profits were at least as attractive as in the apartment business, and office projects generated the same paper losses for income tax purposes as apartments. The developers scrambled to get their share of this business while the boom lasted, and by 1976 every major developer in Canada who had begun in the residential field had at least one finger in the office development pie.

9

PUBLIC PARTNERS
FOR OFFICE PROJECTS

The first nation-wide survey of downtown development projects in Canadian cities was published by planner Robert Collier in 1975.[1] Collier recounted the histories of eleven projects from Vancouver's ill-fated Project 200 to Halifax's Scotia Square. Not a single one of the schemes was built without public subsidies and support in addition to the normal rezonings and planning permissions provided for most developments by municipalities. Says Collier about municipal support given one of the projects, Place Bonaventure in Montreal: "The city only stopped short of manning the bulldozers."[2]

The development industry benefits from a wide range of supporting policies from provincial and federal governments, and takes advantage of these in all its activities. What is special about downtown development projects is that almost inevitably they involve additional subsidies from government. The bigger the project, the greater the chance of public subsidy, and the larger that subsidy is likely to be.

Cheap land. The most common public subsidy comes from providing some or all of the land for the project at less than its market value. Public streets and lanes are often closed to make way for large projects. These can amount to a very sizeable proportion of the total site area, and they are usually sold at bargain basement prices to the developer. Or public land may be leased to the developer at far less than market value.

Expropriation. Municipalities and other governments have often helped assemble sites for downtown development projects, and

173

have used their power of expropriation to do it. This speeds up the assembly process. and means that individual property owners cannot extract a share of the speculative land profit from the developer by holding out. Small businessmen who have been owner-occupiers of their downtown properties have often been ousted by expropriating city halls. Their response is understandably bitter. Eddie Dozer, a shoe store owner in downtown Vancouver who was expropriated by the city to make way for Pacific Centre, then being developed by the Bronfman family's Fairview Corporation, told newspaper reporters in 1966 that he still believed in democracy to the extent of giving up his business to make room for a school, a bridge, a highway, but "not to fatten up Sam Bronfman."[3] Bronfman had earlier explained that Fairview's profits were not for himself, but for his children and grandchildren who owned Fairview through Cemp Investments. "If he can do so much for his grandchildren," said Al Miller, a jeweller also expropriated by the city, "what makes the city think I haven't the right to do something for mine?"[4]

Support facilities. Downtown office projects often require expensive alterations or improvements in public services to accommodate them. Sewers and underground services have to be relocated. Intersections and roads have to be improved. Large downtown projects generate the need for expressways to the downtown: Vancouver's waterfront freeway proposal was closely related to the CPR's postponed scheme to build an enormous office complex, Project 200, on waterfront land owned by the railway. Halifax's Scotia Square has a complex and expensive interchange, the Cogswell Street interchange, next door to it. Only stiff citizen resistance stopped the construction of a waterfront expressway to serve the project. Usually municipalities make improvements in off-site public works required for these projects without question, and without charge to the developer. Often they go even further in covering costs associated with the project, like paying for the parking garage. If any justification is offered for this kind of subsidy, it is that the new assessment and tax revenues generated more than cover the costs to the city. This assertion is rarely backed up with a thorough cost-benefit analysis.

Renting space. Governments and public agencies very often provide another form of subsidy for downtown development projects
by signing up as major tenants. If this is done early enough, the
commitment helps the developer to line up his financing.* Given
the financing structure of office development projects, government office rentals are usually more expensive to the public sector
than if public bodies owned their own space, and will certainly be
more expensive in the future. Public bodies sometimes opt to rent
space because it means they can avoid borrowing to finance construction of buildings, and sometimes because they calculate that
the cash cost of leased space is less than the cash cost of owned
space. That ignores, however, the hidden cost to the public sector
of the corporate income tax that goes unpaid because of the paper
losses developers are permitted. to charge on their rented
buildings.

An array of development projects. The histories of major downtown
development projects in Canadian cities offer an amazing array of
inventive and path-breaking techniques for providing public subsidies and assistance to private business. Nowhere do the country's

---

* The federal government's department of public works, for instance,
   prides itself on being the largest "landowner and leaseholder" in
   Canada. In Ottawa alone, the federal government in 1976 owned
   11.3 million square feet of offices of its own, and was leasing
   another 9.7 million square feet from developers. In contrast, the
   private sector in Ottawa was using a total of three million square
   feet. In Halifax, the three levels of government occupied a total of
   45 percent of the city's office space, much of it leased. In one Ottawa
   deal, the federal government was leasing 1.4 million feet of office
   space in a single project developed by Olympia and York for $7.46 a
   year. In a Toronto deal, Ontario Hydro was the prime tenant of the
   Hydro Place development built by Canada Square, owned by developer Gerhard Moog, a good friend of Ontario premier William
   Davis. For its 1.3 million square feet of leased space, Ontario Hydro
   was paying $3.10 a square foot on a long-term lease. (*Ottawa Citizen*
   20 November 1976; Department of Development, *Halifax Metropolitan Area Survey and Inventory of Commercial Space* [Halifax: Government of Nova Scotia, March 1976] p. 4; *Globe and Mail* 2 January 1976)

developers display their entrepreneurial talents more effectively than in the schemes they devise and persuade governments to adopt to subsidize their big downtown projects. Justifying the amazing deal struck between the City of Vancouver and Fairview for the Pacific Centre project, Fairview director Leo Kolber said innocently, "This developer didn't come to the city. We were invited — selected. We made the best deal we could. Everybody was over twenty-one.... "[5] In fact, as the record shows, the bargaining that goes on between developer and city hall is no contest. The developers win every time. The only variable is the size of their winnings.

Vancouver's Pacific Centre. Pacific Centre is as good a prototype of these projects as can be found anywhere in the country. Now completed, it has an Eaton's department store, two huge black office towers, one with the Toronto-Dominion Bank as the major tenant, the second with IBM, an underground shopping mall that connects into other underground downtown shopping, and a parking garage. The developer was Fairview, Sam Bronfman's family development firm. Eaton's was being courted by the city in 1963. Said deputy director of planning Harry Pickstone at the time, "They haven't actually said 'yes' or 'no' to the proposition, but they are following it with interest. Quite surely they will realize that what's good for Vancouver will also be good for Eaton's."[6] By 1966 Charles Bronfman had struck a deal with the mayor, Bill Rathie, which included an Eaton's store. "Our first meeting with Mayor Rathie," said Bronfman, "convinced all of us that we were dealing with a man who talked our language and walked on the same side of the street. That was all I needed.... "[7] The project hit an unexpected snag, however, when Rathie was defeated by mayoralty candidate Tom Campbell who had run on an anti-project platform. Campbell put on a show of tough negotiating with Fairview for a year, then with some minor concessions swung behind it.[8]

The deal that was struck involved an enormous municipal subsidy to the developer. The site was expropriated and assembled by the city. The cost of the assembly was $10.5 million, though its market value as a redevelopment site was certainly higher than the cost of putting it together. Fairview (now Cadillac Fairview) rents the land from the city for just $36,000 a year, about 3.5 percent of the city's acquisition cost. But the city rents the parking garage in the project from Cadillac Fairview for a fixed rent of $31,547 a month, $378,000 a year, and operates the garage absorbing any loss. The city actually lost $500,000 in the first sixteen months after the garage was opened in 1971 before the project itself was built. To cap the deal, Cadillac Fairview has an option to buy the land from the city in 1982 for just $7 million, $3.5 million less than it cost to assemble it in the 1960s when downtown land values were lower. In case Cadillac Fairview doesn't want to buy the land in 1982, it retains its option to purchase for many years at a price that escalates slowly from $7 million.[9]

The deal in summary: the city provided the land for next to nothing. The city took over the parking garage, and guaranteed the developer its rent regardless of whether it made money. And, having financed the purchase of the land at the time when the assembly was speculative, the city agreed in advance to sell the developer the land in the future for a price that was likely to be far below its market value, an option which the developer would pick up only if there was a profit to be made from the land.

Of course Pacific Centre had more than just a financial impact on Vancouver. Its design provoked reactions of outrage. Said *Vancouver Sun* columnist Allan Fotheringham: "It is a bathtub of white tile, upside down at the major intersection of the city."[10] Lack of windows, doors, and an uninviting relationship to the sidewalk were strategies used by the developers to get people off the streets into their shopping mall. After the criticism, the developer made minor design modifications. But when people also objected to the black office towers of the project, there was no compromise. Architect Bill Dahl, brought in from Los Angeles by the developer, told a city hall committee, "We feel very strongly this building is avant garde ... After all, who liked Picasso 50 years ago?"

The small businessmen who had been expropriated by the city for the project were told they could rent space in the mall if they wished. Before Pacific Centre, the merchants said, rents in the block had been $2.50 a square foot. In the mall, they were to be $8.00 a square foot.[11]

Saskatoon's Midtown Plaza. The developer of what proved to be a very large retail-commercial downtown project tied in to a new suburban industrial park in Saskatoon was Canadian National, in partnership with local developer Morris Wiss. Though it is a Crown corporation, CN acted just like any large corporate landowner in its negotiations with the city.

CN emerged with an amazing deal. It persuaded the city to rezone its downtown railway yard land to commercial use to permit an office-retail project. The city agreed to freeze assessment on the downtown land for five years. The city provided free of charge the necessary city services to CN to develop a 180-acre industrial park in the suburbs. Saskatoon guaranteed to provide adequate bus service to the new suburban railway yards constructed by CN. And it provided three hundred acres of land to CN for the yards for $100,000. Finally, the city agreed to pay $2.6 million for about six acres of CN land downtown required for a freeway and a railway bridge the city later had to demolish.[12] In 1963, in an apparently separate deal, the city agreed to pay CN another $250,000 for two acres of land for a site for a new auditorium.

CN did not develop its downtown land itself, but rather leased most of it to local developer Morris Wiss. Wiss developed a very ambitious plan for offices and retail space which would increase Saskatoon's retail space by 25 percent and its office space by about 200 percent. Wiss lined up Eaton's and Simpsons-Sears as tenants, but had tremendous difficulties finding financing, so the site stood vacant for several years. The project finally proceeded in 1966 with Simpsons-Sears financing its own building, and the doors opened in 1968. Only at that point did the rest of the project get properly underway, and construction was completed in 1970.

Shepherding the project along in spite of its difficulties was Saskatoon mayor Sid Buckwold. In 1968, Buckwold justified the city's subsidies to the project by saying that Saskatoon would have been "a ghost town if new development had moved to the suburbs." In 1970, when it was completed, Buckwold described it as "just another indication of the spirit of Saskatoon."[13] Capping Buckwold's achievement, in 1971 Midtown Plaza was one of the thirteen winners of the Massey medal for excellence in urban design. The award was presented in Ottawa to Sid Buckwold, who received

it on behalf of Midtown Plaza and the City of Saskatoon. As it
happened, the prairie representative on the selection committee
was Saskatoon's mayor, Sid Buckwold.[14]

Winnipeg's Trizec project. At the corner of Portage and Main in
Winnipeg, Canada's second-largest public real estate corporation,
Trizec, has a city-subsidized project that took six years to get
underway.[15] At the time the project was first talked about in February 1971, it was a regional headquarters office building for the
Bank of Nova Scotia right at the corner of Portage and Main. By
the time negotiations with the city were completed, the project had
expanded to include a whole city block and was a 1.5 million-
square-foot commercial-hotel-office project on Place Ville Marie
scale.

In April 1972 Trizec president James Soden set out a proposal
for the redevelopment of the entire block. The city accepted
Trizec's proposal and conditions virtually without change. The details of the deal are astonishing. First, the city agreed to expropriate
the site. This was eventually estimated to cost the city $16 million.
Second, the city agreed to lease the site to Trizec for ninety-nine
years for a rent fixed at just 3.5 percent of the city's expropriation
costs for the first forty years, to rise somewhat after that. Third,
the city agreed to construct and pay for a one-thousand car parking
garage under the development, absorbing the full cost, another
$7.7 million. The only commitment Trizec made in exchange for
all this was to erect 300,000 square feet of offices on the city's land.

Though the deal was approved in principle in 1972, Trizec did
not find major tenants lining up to lease space in the project. Four
years later in 1976, Trizec still had no firm tenants apart from its
Bank of Nova Scotia partner but nevertheless it was pressing the
city to begin construction of its parking garage. The city agreed in
December 1976. And, just to sweeten the pot and make it easier
for Trizec to attract tenants, the city also agreed to spend *another*
$6.5 million building an underground concourse beneath the Por-
tage and Main intersection which would connect the shopping mall
in the Trizec project with the Richardsons' Lombard Place project
and a proposed Toronto-Dominion Bank-CPR project on another
corner of the intersection. The city also agreed not to use any

powers it had or might receive to stand in the way of the demolition of three historic buildings on the TD-CPR site. It agreed to pay for the maintenance of the pedestrian concourse and to put up barriers to prevent pedestrians from crossing the street at Portage and Main, "thus eliminating the possibility of short-circuiting the concourse."[16]

London's Talbot Square. In 1964 the federal government got into the business of subsidizing commercial redevelopment projects in Canadian cities through its urban renewal program. Cities eagerly lined up with more and more expensive schemes until the program was cut off in 1969. One of the late arrivals at the downtown urban renewal trough was London, Ontario, which originally proposed a renewal plan for twenty-five downtown city blocks. In 1968, London applied for federal support for an urban renewal scheme on a single city block which was later named Talbot Square.[17]

It took from 1968 to 1974 for London to make a deal with a private developer to put up a project on the site. The urban renewal partnership expropriated the block for $8.25 million, and then the land stood vacant while the politicians tried vainly to make a deal with a developer. Said Mayor Fred Gosnell to his fellow city politicians in 1971, three years into the project with no building in sight, "You can't jump out of the boat now. It's no time to back-pedal, panic, or push the button."

The provincial government decided to build a $9 million courthouse on one corner of the block, and the federal government bought 40,000 square feet of land for just $154,000 to put up a $10 million federal office building. When the third in a series of developers made an offer in 1973, the politicians were desperate. "We were ready to grab at anything that looked viable," Controller Orlando Zamprogna said later. The developer, Talbot Square, proposed a 240-unit hotel, a ten-storey office tower, a 240-unit apartment tower, and 48,000 square feet of retail space. The developer would rent the land for just $51,000 a year for ninety-nine years.

To help things along, the city agreed to pay for the 395-space parking garage that would service the development. The garage was to be operated by the city's parking authority, a curious public-private company named Covent Garden Building Inc., and the city would pick up any deficit in the garage's annual operation. The developer was to construct the parking garage, and Covent Garden was to pay $2.123 million for it. But the city's deal with the developer included an open-ended provision to pick up any excess in costs of the garage over $2.123 million.

Construction started in 1974 after the agreement was approved by the city, but a series of disputes between the developer, his contractors, and labour led to several work stoppages. In December 1975 the city was told by the developer that it would have to pay an extra $1.3 million for the parking garage which would now cost $3.4 million to build. The major cause of the increasing costs was delays in construction which the city had no control over. Nor was there any ceiling on the increased costs the city was committed to cover. In the end, the city paid the developer $834,000 in addition to the $2.123 million for the parking garage. Developer John Ryan received the money graciously. He said it was a compromise figure arrived at "in order that we can continue together in a spirit of cooperation without any delay or hard feelings..."[18]

This did not spell the end of the city's troubles, however. By mid-1978 the developer still had not got construction of his part of the project underway.

Why these deals get made. In an appendix to this book, there is an account of the negotiations that took place between the City of Saskatoon and negotiators for the CNR for the city's Midtown Plaza project. It is based on minutes of the meetings, often verbatim records, kept by city officials. Though these minutes were highly confidential at the time, copies were obtained by researcher Donald Gutstein in summer 1977. They offer a rare glimpse into the secret bargaining that still goes on between cities and developers, with results much the same now as they were in Saskatoon when the Midtown Plaza negotiations took place in 1962.

The bargaining is always done in secret. By the time the details of an agreement are announced, a majority of city politicians have been privately lined up to support it. Opposition politicians at city hall may criticize the deal, and citizen groups may oppose it, but all this happens after the fact and can rarely upset the deal.

The Saskatoon negotiations illustrate what participants in these discussions often do not explicitly realize, that what determines the outcome is the format in which the bargaining takes place and the acceptance by city administrators and politicians of the roles in which they are cast by the developers. The basic rules of the game, laid down by the developers and accepted by city halls, are simple. First, only private developers can undertake downtown development projects; so if the industry won't undertake it, there is no alternative public development. Second, the only design form for downtown development projects is large high-rise office towers combined with shopping malls on large land assemblies. No other design form is considered. Third, there is no financial disclosure by developers, and what they assert about their financial situation is generally taken at face value. Fourth, there is no independent assessment undertaken by the city of a development proposal to reveal to city negotiators the financial circumstances and profit projections of the developer.

On the basis of these rules, all city officials can do is say yes or no to a specific development proposal. If they want to say yes, their only further contribution is to haggle over the size of the public subsidy the project will receive.

Weakening the bargaining position of city officials is their concern about the constituency that supports downtown redevelopment. The large financial and commercial organizations that are involved are of course project supporters, and these are a powerful collection in the eyes of most city politicians: the banks, the mortgage lenders, department stores and retail chains who rent space in these projects, and the prospective office tenants. Downtown property owners are usually also supporters, not only the largest who see redevelopment possibilities on their own land but small business property owners who look more to the impact of downtown redevelopment on land values than to the implications for small business. Not only do city officials feel as if they have little option but to say yes to the project; their ability to haggle over the terms is severely limited by the risk that the developer will pick up his project and leave, and by their lack of the necessary information to evaluate properly the developer's proposal.

In the circumstances, developers have every reason to bluff about their need for subsidies and concessions, and city officials have virtually no way of calling that bluff. Obviously Saskatoon's Midtown Plaza negotiators had no idea whatsoever whether CNR officials would have carried on their relocation-redevelopment project with a city subsidy of only $1 million instead of the requested $3.9 million, or with no subsidy at all. A quick-witted city commissioner and an ordinary city mayor both realized what was happening to them in their negotiating. The commissioner could think only of asking the CNR for information the CNR had absolutely no interest or reason to provide in an accurate form. The mayor could think only of how he could possibly finance the requested subsidy. Many city politicians are of course delighted to provide subsidies to the developers because they are themselves involved in land development, but no matter what their intentions or politics city officials can do little but continue to subsidize these projects unless they unilaterally change the rules of the negotiating game. My own guess about the impact of public subsidies on downtown development projects is that the subsidies are usually large enough that developers invest little if any cash of their own in these projects. The difference between the mortgage money the developer receives from his lender and the total creation cost of the project is largely made up by city subsidies. To confirm this would take access to the financial projections of downtown developers, information I have found impossible to obtain. In deals where mortgage loans plus city subsidies equal the creation cost of the project to the developer, of course, the developer himself has no cash at all invested. The result is that the developer has nothing to lose, and millions to make.

The corporate takeover of the downtown. Using the technology of the large downtown office complex, the corporate developers have since 1960 been successful in gaining control of the supply of new office space, particularly in downtown areas. The consequence of this development is felt not so much by small businesses, who require only modest amounts of office space, or new businesses whose requirements are also often equally modest, but by existing businesses who have outgrown their current accommodation and need new space. Ironically, the effects of domination of the new downtown office supply by a few corporate developers have been felt mainly by medium- and large-sized corporations.*

Adding to the trend towards concentration in the ownership of downtown office space is the process of eliminating the smaller, less well-financed office developers. This occurred as the boom of the seventies terminated leaving the small, under-financed firms first to feel the pressure. Reported the *Globe and Mail* in December 1975:

> A rise in 'distress sales' of large commercial buildings, brought on by overbuilding and the continuing slow pace of business expansion, is becoming evident throughout the country.... Industry officials say the problem is isolated to smaller investors without strong financial backing. The vacancy rate in most urban centres is high at present, forcing greater competition among developers of commercial properties.[19]

To undertake these massive projects has without exception taken sizeable direct public subsidies in addition to overall government policies which give the development industry benefits and subsidies not generally available to business. It has also, without anyone really considering the implications of the change, led to a transformation of the nature of the downtown. As architect Ray Affleck, designer of Montreal's enormous Place Bonaventure downtown office-commercial-hotel complex put it, these projects have turned the city "inside out."[20] What used to happen outside

---

* As a Calgary business journalist explained the situation in that city in 1972, in terms which would apply elsewhere as well: "Anyone requiring more than five thousand square feet and looking for new office space this year really has only two choices: either Palliser No. 1 or Phase One of Bow Valley Square." Both were large office tower developments. Even in the largest city market, the same situation can exist. Just two projects, First Canadian Place involving the Bank of Montreal and developer Olympia and York (1,650,000 square feet) and Hydro Place by Ontario Hydro and developer Gerhard Moog (914,184 square feet) accounted for almost one-half of all new office construction in Metro Toronto in 1975. (*Calgary Herald* 21 April 1972; *Canadian Building* August 1976 p. 14)

on public streets now happens inside on developer-owned malls.

It was the postwar pattern of Canadian economic development which generated the demand for the huge increase in urban office space which has been met by high-rise office towers, most of them downtown. Clearly this work force could have been accommodated in many different ways: in high-rise buildings located exclusively in the suburbs, in buildings more evenly scattered through cities at transportation nodes, in smaller buildings built to less grandiose scale, and in renovated and rehabilitated buildings which instead were demolished to make way for the new projects. Downtowns could have been rebuilt more gradually, maintaining the existing street pattern and preserving the traditional functions of the street. Planning policies, transportation and land use decisions, and public subsidies have permitted and supported the concentration of offices in huge downtown projects. Different policies could have produced different patterns of development, and could have done so without public subsidy.

At the official opening of Vancouver's Pacific Centre, a single demonstrator, John Petrie, picketed carrying a sign which asked "Is this building really necessary?" The leaflet he distributed to guests answered the question: "Skyscrapers are only necessary and beautiful if you happen to own one."[21] That sums up the situation not just for Vancouver, but for every Canadian city.

10

SHOPPING CENTRES: THE MONEY MACHINES

Until 1950, there was no such thing as a shopping centre in Canada. In September 1950, the Guinness family opened the Park Royal centre in West Vancouver on land leased from the Squamish Indian band. Park Royal included a branch of Woodward's, a big downtown Vancouver department store, and twenty-one other shops to serve residents of Vancouver's North Shore and the Guinness's British Properties development.[1] A Woodward's official who was at the opening of Park Royal remembers hearing the comment of one of the senior executives of Eaton's who were invited to the 1950 opening: "It'll never work," said the Eaton's expert.

By 1956 there were sixty-four shopping centres in Canada. In 1973 there were 664 of them, according to Statistics Canada, and many more under construction. Retail sales in shopping centres totalled $233 million, just 1.8 percent of retail sales in 1956. By 1973 the figure had rocketed to $6,736 million, a twenty-nine-fold increase in seventeen years. In 1973 one retail sales dollar in every six was spent in shopping centres, and their share of the market was continuing to increase.[2]

The developers have made brilliant use of shopping centres to dominate the new retail space market in Canadian cities since 1950. The success of shopping centres has produced a host of important changes in the structure of cities, in the retailing business, in the position of independent small businessmen versus the national retail chains, and in the choices people encounter as shoppers.

Shopping centres share many similarities with amusement park midways. As in midways, shopping centre merchants rent concessions on both sides of a pedestrian passageway. As in midways, the concessionaires pay not just a basic rent but a percentage of every dollar they take in. As in midways, the key attractions get placed at either end, so that people are exposed to every enticement to spend as much money as possible. Architect Harry Petroff sums up the essence of shopping centres very simply: "They're machines for making money."[3]

The shopping centre idea. Shopping centres are an American invention, and owe their success to the suburban car-dependent lifestyle. The idea of a large group of stores in the suburbs which people would get to not on foot or by streetcar but by car was a major change from the traditional downtown or local shopping strip. James Doyle, an official of Steinberg's, explained the aim of suburban shopping centres:

> You are, in effect, drawing business that would otherwise go into downtown stores. To say who is getting hurt would be a bit speculative but the traditional, downtown merchants have lost a certain proportion of their trade.[4]

Another radical change was to move stores off the street so that, instead of having frontage on a public sidewalk and roadway, shopping centre stores opened onto a privately-owned mall. Mid-block shopping arcades in downtown areas were a precedent for this, but arcades depended for their success on being short-cut routes for people walking in the downtown. No one ever takes a short cut from anywhere to anywhere through a suburban shopping centre mall.

A third important new element in the shopping centre concept is the changed status of retail businesses from property owners, owning the store they occupy, or tenants who pay a fixed monthly rental, to concessionaires who share their take with the landlord. A fourth is the dependence of shopping centres on large retail chains, particularly supermarkets (for smaller centres) and department stores (for larger ones). These large stores attract the most business to a shopping centre. They are deliberately placed at a maximum distance from each other and the space in between is occupied by stores which capitalize on the traffic generated by the large stores.

A final element in the shopping centre concept, new to the retail trade, is the explicit concern to minimize or eliminate competition coupled with the desire to control the market the centre serves. In principle at least, traditional downtowns and local shopping districts conferred no monopolies on any businessman. If a third department store wanted to build in downtown Winnipeg and undercut Eaton's and The Bay, no one could stand in its way. A successful drug store on a shopping strip could expect at any time that a competitor might open up across the street. Not so with shopping centres. Their developer owners stand to make the highest profits if people *spend as much as possible in the shopping centre*. The developers' concern is to offer the broadest possible range of goods to increase *total* spending in their centre rather than to permit competition between stores for the same dollars. Often shopping centre tenants ask for and get guarantees from developers of no competition in their type of business. Developers also try to ensure that their shopping centre does not face competition from a new centre built to siphon off business from their market area, thus reducing sales.

Though the development industry has been successful with each of the major new building forms it has introduced since the war, it reserves its own superlatives for shopping centres. Says A.E. Diamond, chairman of the board of Cadillac Fairview: "Shopping centres rank as one of the best forms of investment."[5]

From a standing start. Canada's population increased by 83 percent from 1945 to 1973. The number of cars on the road went from 1,161,337 in 1945 to 7,866,084 in 1973, an incredible 577 percent jump.[6] Population expansion was mainly in the cities, since that was where most of the jobs were, and along with the construction of work places and housing went the need for more retail space.

Shopping centre development began in the largest and fastest-growing cities. Of the sixty-four shopping centres in Canada in 1956, forty-one were in Ontario and another ten in Quebec. By 1973, Ontario and Quebec had 420 of the 664 centres in Canada, with the balance spread among the other provinces but heavily weighted towards Alberta (with 72) and B.C. (with 91). Prince Edward Island's first shopping centre was built in 1970.[7]

Shopping centres did much more than provide the kind of local shopping facilities traditional for shopping districts. They also attracted the kind of retail business that had previously gone downtown, and substantially weakened the dominance of downtown businesses over their local markets. In Ottawa in 1977, 75 percent of all retail purchases were reported to be in suburban shopping centres — compared with 35 percent in 1961. Downtown Ottawa's share of every shopping dollar had been 65 cents in 1961, and was already down to 35 cents in 1971.[8] In Winnipeg, the same trend was apparent. Downtown Winnipeg had 87 percent of general merchandising sales in 1961. By 1966 it was already down to 70 percent, and by 1974 had slipped to less than 50 percent.[9]

Most of the growth in retail floor space in Canadian cities since the war has been in suburban shopping centres, or in the downtown shopping mall variants. About 90 percent of the net increase in retail floor space in Toronto between 1952 and 1969, for instance, was in suburban shopping centres.[10]

Developers and their mortgage lenders recognize three types of centres, varying in size and type of stores. Neighbourhood shopping centres have five to fifteen outlets according to Statistics Canada, and are usually focussed around a supermarket. There were 417 of these in Canada in 1973, and the median annual sales volume was $3.7 million. In the typical neighbourhood centre, about half this volume would be sold by the supermarket, and the balance by the smaller stores.[11] Community shopping centres have sixteen to thirty outlets, often with a supermarket and a small department store. There were 146 of these in Canada in 1973, with median sales of $10.4 million.[12]

The largest shopping centres are classified as regional centres. Though the country's first centre, Park Royal, was a regional centre, there were only fifteen built from 1950 to 1959. It was in the 1960s that construction of regional centres took off, and the total went from 15 in 1959 to 101 in 1973. Those fifteen regional centres had sales of $190 million in 1959; in 1973 sales had reached $3,171 million, and had captured almost half of all shopping centre sales.[13] Highest sales in the country were $168 million, chalked up in 1973 by Toronto's Yorkdale, owned by Trizec.[14]

The largest regional centres are enormous. Calgary's Chinook Centre, for instance, built in 1959, has been enlarged twice and now measures 1,020,000 square feet, twenty-four acres of floor space. Its 230 stores include a Woodward's (297,725 square feet), a Simpsons-Sears (177,337 square feet) and a Loblaw's (19,600 square feet). Chinook claims that it serves a prime market area of 250,000 people, with an additional 250,000 in its secondary market area.[15]

Edmonton's downtown Edmonton Centre owned by Oxford Development is the same size, 1,050,000 square feet. Its two anchor tenants are Woodward's (400,000 square feet) and Eaton's (300,000) with ninety-nine other stores. There are 4.8 million shoppers passing through its doors every year.

Suburban Toronto's Square One centre, built by developer Bruce McLaughlin in Mississauga, measures 1,541,000 square feet and has four anchor tenants, Woolco, Simpsons-Sears, The Bay, and Dominion. There are 156 other stores.

By 1975, shopping centre developers were beginning to slow the pace of construction of new projects, largely because department stores were not willing to take on further expansion. As investment dealers Burns, Fry explained:

> Total retail construction expenditures...doubled from 1972 to 1974 and the level of new construction during those three years equalled all expenditures of the previous six years. This wave of building was primarily the result of a strategic move by the major retailing chains to develop prime suburban locations, often with two or more anchor stores and a multitude of smaller-sized outlets. Growth of this nature has clearly peaked.[16]

The right site. Development of a shopping centre starts with finding a good site. Location is the key consideration; and developers must first estimate the number of people who live within a reasonable *driving* distance, for whom the new shopping centre would be the closest one of its size. Beyond this primary trading area is a secondary trading area, which is still within a reasonable distance of the site, but which is also within equally easy reach of other shopping centres.

The people who live within easy reach of one shopping centre, but at a considerable distance from the next, are virtually captive customers of the nearby centre, especially for routine weekly shopping. The more such captive customers there are, and the higher their incomes, the greater the sales and the rents of the shopping centre. Wrote an Ottawa *Citizen* reporter about the attitude of the manager of the Lincoln Fields Shopping Centre in Ottawa towards new housing being built next door to his centre:

> Mr. Saykali's smile stretches from ear to ear when he contem-

plates the tremendous boom in apartment buildings in the area around Lincoln Fields. He can notice the crowds swelling almost daily as a result of the high rises.[17]

To analyze a potential shopping centre site, a developer goes through a statistical exercise. A line is drawn around the centre's primary trading area, census data are used to discover the total disposable income of the people in that trading area, and expenditure data collected about how the spending of those people is divided among food, clothing, furniture and other items. Based on experience and data from other areas, the developer can estimate what percentage of the total spending by people in this primary trading area a new centre in the proposed site can be expected to capture.

What determines the size and wealth of a shopping centre's primary trading area is not distance as such but *time*, the time it takes shoppers to drive from their homes to the centre. Since travel time by car is the crucial factor, the best possible sites for larger, regional shopping centres are next door to expressways.* Notes plan-

---

* Even better than one expressway, of course, are two. For shopping centre developers, expressways are conduits pouring cars of shoppers into their parking lots. Headlined the local newspaper the day of the opening of Sherway Gardens, at the intersection of two expressways in suburban Toronto: "32 Traffic Lanes to Lead Customers to Sherway Gardens." The construction of Toronto's controversial Spadina Expressway was directly related to the fact that its route was to intersect with an existing expressway right next door to the Yorkdale shopping centre:

> When Frederick G. Gardiner, first chairman of Metro Toronto, sought the ultimate argument in favour of the construction of the Spadina expressway [in the late fifties] he pointed to Yorkdale shopping centre. The massive enclosed mall, the first in the Toronto area, was announced in 1958, two years after Metro Council had voted against the idea of the expressway. However, the expressway plan was rapidly revived, and Gardiner regularly instructed councillors that construction should begin in conjunction with Eaton's and Simpsons starting work on the complex "to handle the volume of traffic these two developments will create."

(*Mississauga Times* 16 December 1970; *Toronto Star* 23 February 1960, quoted by Graham Fraser, *City Magazine* vol. 2 no. 5 p. 46)

ner Matthew Lawson; "The location of regional shopping centres is largely determined by the expressway system as the means of access to the market area served."[18]

In the shopping centre hierarchy, smaller centres offer some of the same goods and services of the larger centres, but the regional centres have a wider range of goods than community and neighbourhood centres. Once most cities had been dotted with smaller centres, developers seeking maximum shopping centre profits had to construct larger regional centres to draw business away from the smaller centres and from downtowns. "Today there's more realization in the industry that you need to build a facility that will dominate a market," said Richard Baxter, president of the International Council of Shopping Centres in 1974. "In smaller markets this is necessarily going to mean larger developments."[19] In effect, a small neighbourhood centre has a limited territorial monopoly in the area where it is the closest store for groceries and other necessities. The primary trading area of a regional shopping centre is also a limited territorial monopoly. Inside that territory, a regional shopping centre faces some competition from smaller centres, but it is the sole location that offers a wide range of goods to shoppers. Customers may choose which store to buy from, but no matter where in the centre they buy they pay prices that include rent to the developer who holds that territorial monopoly. The monopoly is not absolute — individuals living in a shopping centre's primary trading area can and of course do often choose to spend their money elsewhere — but the structure of the retail business in Canada is such that the main basis on which retailers and shopping centres compete is not price, not choice of goods, not even types of stores but rather distance. Noting the similarity of stores in shopping centres, marketing professor Donald Tigert told journalist Graham Fraser, "As a consequence [of this similarity in stores and goods sold] the consumer's choice has been greatly simplified. He or she shops at the centre nearest home."[20]

Battling for a site. The worst thing that can happen to a shopping centre developer is to have a rival centre locate half a mile away. The new centre is immediately "nearer home" for a large proportion of the people who were in the old centre's primary trading area. The immediate effect is to cut severely the size of the old centre's primary trading area, and to reduce its total sales. If the new centre is larger than the old one and has a wider range of stores, the effect will be even worse than if the two were roughly the same size.*

Developers are much happier competing with each other for the exclusive right to a shopping centre site in a large trading area than owning rival centres competing for the same trading area. Two giants of the industry, Cadillac Fairview and Campeau Corporation, spent two years fighting over the right to build a new regional centre to serve the southern suburbs of Ottawa.[21] Campeau's South Keys site was in the City of Ottawa; Cadillac Fairview's Blossom Park land was an old gravel pit in the township of Gloucester. Both developers argued the advantages of their own sites and criticized the other vigorously. Politicans from the two municipalities each supported the scheme for their locality. The regional government decided only one of the two should be built, and a majority of the politicians opted for South Keys and Campeau over Blossom Park and Cadillac Fairview. Neither developer and none of their political champions suggested that both centres should be built in order to create a competitive situation. But one regional politician, West Carleton Reeve Don Munro, refused to vote on the issue. He objected to deciding to give a monopoly to one of the two rival developers:

> It would allow the developer to go to the largest corporations in the country and say, "We have control of the only shopping centre in this market. How much will you give us to get in?" They could ask Dominion for two cents a pound for all the meat sold in the centre. . . .

---

* Journalist Graham Fraser described the impact of a major regional centre a mile away on a smaller community centre in suburban Toronto built 15 years earlier. At the older community centre stores were vacant, and maintenance was neglected. Chain tenants — Agnew Surpass, Zellers, Fairweather, Monarch Men's Wear and Woolworths — departed. The chain Tamblyn's drug store severely reduced its stock. Said a long-time employee, "It's a shame the way the plaza's gone down. I started when it opened, and I've worked here off and on for 18 years. Then, it was a gold mine for everybody. The man at Tamblyn's where I worked then, got an award for doing better than any other Tamblyn's." (*Globe and Mail* 27 December 1975)

It would be like Laurier saying fifty years ago that there would be only one major store in downtown Ottawa... with no competition. That's the kind of decision we're making here.[22]

That's exactly the kind of decision shopping centre developers like.

In situations where there is no regional government to choose between two rivals competing for the same primary market area, shopping centre developers play a game of corporate chicken. The first developer to get zoning and planning permissions, tenants, mortgage financing, and to start construction may find that developers with competing projects give up — or are forced to do so by mortgage lenders, who refuse to fund a second project because its sales potential is judged not strong enough.*

---

* Sometimes, though, rival projects do get built close to each other. Until 1972, for instance, Woodward's had the only department store of any consequence in the Vancouver suburb of Surrey. In May that year, Eaton's, The Bay, and Simpsons-Sears all opened stores there. "I think everyone is seeing a potential and feeling they must be in there," a Woodward's official said at the time. "It all takes pieces out of the pie," he added, sounding rather regretful. When they get built, rival centres rarely have sales so low that one or both goes bankrupt. The concerns of mortgage lenders ensure that there is enough spending in the area to support both centres. The main impact is on profits, particularly of the shopping centre developer. His centre is far less profitable than it would be with the extra sales volume and resulting rents that are siphoned off by the rival centre.

Halifax offers an interesting example of rival shopping centres serving the same basic primary trading area. In 1960 William Zeckendorf launched the Halifax Shopping Centre with Eaton's as its department store anchor tenant across the street from a Simpsons suburban store that had relocated from the downtown years earlier. The two centres were not connected; in fact, they are far enough apart that people usually drive from one to the other. Some years later, Simpsons added a shopping mall with a supermarket to their centre. The supermarket tenant in the Halifax Shopping Centre is Sobey's, a George Weston subsidiary. Faced with the prospect of a competitor across the street in a rival supermarket, Sobey's did the obvious thing: it rented the supermarket in the Simpsons mall as well. The result is that Sobey's has two supermarkets in virtually the same location, serving virtually the same territory. (*Globe and Mail* 21 July 1972; *Halifax Mail-Star* 24 August 1960)

A key strategy for shopping centre developers who want to protect their territorial monopoly is to continuously expand their centre as the size and wealth of their primary trading area grows, in ways that increase spending and reduce the possibility of a rival developer competing effectively in the territory. One way to do this is to add a second department store to a centre with only one, and later perhaps a third. As a U.S. textbook on how to develop a shopping centre puts it, "Three department stores... also provide greater security against the possible invasion of new shopping centre competition."[23]*

The tenant "mix". After a shopping centre developer has identified a potential site, the next step is to line up tenants. This is a complex process, and the developer's concern is to make the most out of his location, by getting the combination of tenants who will together maximize the amount of money people spend in that shopping centre. It means getting the highest possible rents, not out of each tenant individually, but out of the centre as a whole. The developer also has to come up with a set of prospective tenants

---

* This is exactly the strategy used by Vancouver's Park Royal centre. Opened in 1950 with 130,000 square feet including a Woodward's department store, the first major expansion came in 1962 when the centre jumped across the street and added 240,000 square feet including an Eaton's and a smaller Super-Valu discount store. In the mid-60s, Woodward's expanded by 40 percent and the north side shopping mall was covered in and expanded. Fifteen years later, a third department store, The Bay, was added in an expansion totalling 260,000 square feet. From 22 stores, the shopping centre had gone to 150. West Vancouver mayor Peter Jones explained in 1975 that the expansion was not intended to attract shoppers to the North Shore from Vancouver across the Lion's Gate bridge, but rather to keep the 160,000 North Shore residents from shopping in Vancouver. Park Royal now shares that rich market with only one other, smaller centre. (*Journal of Commerce Weekly* 3 December 1960, 22 September 1962; *Vancouver Sun* 1 May 1966, 9 June 1967, 16 January 1968; *West Vancouver Citizen* 10 April 1968; *Vancouver Province* 16 July 1968; *Vancouver Sun* 14 March 1969, 30 January 1975; *Vancouver Province* 19 July 1975; *Vancouver Sun* 19 August 1975, 26 November 1976, 12 January 1977)

who look solid enough for a mortgage lender to agree to provide the financing to build the project.

A shopping centre project is made or broken by the success of the developer in signing up "anchor" tenants. For regional centres, anchor tenants are department stores. In community and neighbourhood centres, they are usually supermarkets. The importance of the anchor tenants is that they and not the smaller stores pull in the customers. Explains Charles Tabachnick of Cambridge Leaseholds, one of the major shopping centre developers in Canada, until taken over by Oxford Development, "We in the industry are reduced to following the department stores' lead. We can't build anything without them. They're the draw and they know it."[24]

Department stores use their power as anchor tenants to demand and get special terms from shopping centre developers. Sometimes they are in a strong enough position to demand successfully that they not be tenants of the developer, but that they own their store and the land on which it is built. If they go in as tenants, they pay a much lower rent than mall tenants. The median national department store tenant in Canadian regional shopping centres in 1975 paid $2.84 per square foot in rent for 125,000 square feet of space.[25] In contrast, the median figures for fast food stores was $29.91 per square foot; for ice cream parlours $13.73, for women's specialty stores $9.19, for men's shoes $13.70.*

---

* The U.S. shopping centres textbook offers a checklist of concessions developers make to department stores:

> The department stores are usually subsidized through low rents, high allowances towards construction, purchase of their land at a higher price than they originally paid, sale of land to them at a relatively low price, absence of a percentage rent clause, or some combination of those factors. The subsidy to a department store and the structure of rents to tenants are determined by the place held in the retail pecking order by each of the prospective occupants of shopping centre space.

(William Applebaum and S. O. Kaylin, *Case Studies in Shopping Centre Development and Operation* [New York: International Council of Shopping Centres, 1974] p. 42)

Canadian shopping centre consultant Warren Scott describes the conditions extracted by department stores in a "fictitious" account of the experiences of a developer he names Harry:

> After protracted negotiations, Harry became the owner of an Offer to Lease from the department store. Of course, the Offer was conditional upon Harry changing the site plan to suit their store, and upon zoning and proof of financing, and obtaining a lease from a major supermarket, and obtaining leases for at least 50,000 square feet of mall stores. . . . He was a little upset at these conditions until someone explained that this was rather typical of today's department store lease requirements.[26]

With anchor tenants lined up, the developer looks for smaller store tenants. Decisions about how many of these there should be, and what the right combination of stores is, start with analyzing incomes and expenditure patterns in the centre's primary market area. After estimating how much people will spend in the centre on groceries, shoes, women's clothing, men's clothing and other products, the developer calculates what percentage of these expenditures will be captured by the department store. This involves estimates based on knowledge of the operations of the stores involved, their strengths and weaknesses. Explains a fictional developer in a U.S. case study, "If I know that the department stores will have a lot of space devoted to shoes but are likely to do a poor job merchandising shoes for teenage boys or for children, then I'd try to fill those slots with satellite merchants. But it would be a hard thing to measure."[27]

What is left over after the department stores' market share has been estimated will be spent in the centre's smaller stores. Knowing that camera stores typically pay 5.5 percent of their sales in rent in Canadian shopping centres, the developer estimates whether there will be enough spending on cameras, film and so on after the department store has taken its portion to support a camera store that can pay the kind of rent the developer wants. If it looks likely, the developer looks for a camera store tenant. The prospective tenant will do his own estimate of sales in that location, and if the figures look encouraging the developer's own estimate will be confirmed.*

Lease negotiations between developers and tenants are tough. The developer needs the tenants to make his project work, and the tenants need the space if they want to do business in that part of the city. The bargaining power of the anchor tenants means that they usually get a better deal than mall tenants.

Shopping centre leases always provide for two kinds of rent. There is a basic rent, expressed in dollars per square foot, for the space a tenant occupies. A shopping centre mall tenant agrees to pay this figure as a minimum. Leases also provide for a percentage rent, ranging from 1 percent to as much as 17 percent of total sales.[28] The tenant pays *either* the basic square-foot rent *or* the percentage rent, *whichever is higher*. The industry calls rents paid over the basic square-foot figure "overage" rents.

Tenant merchants also agree by lease to pay the cost of maintaining the common areas of the shopping centre. They agree to a compulsory levy which goes to the centre's merchant association and is used for promoting sales and special events. The lease almost always specifies that the tenant's store will be kept open for the same hours that the mall itself is open. It may even specify the type of cash register the tenant must use, to ensure for the developer that the tenant's accounting system is reliable, total sales are honestly reported and full rents (based on sales) are paid.[29]

Shopping centre "competitors." A provision giving a shopping centre

---

* Retailers learn from experience what kinds of locations work for them, how large a store they should have, what sales to expect and what kinds of rents they can afford. Take, for instance, this summary set of rules of thumb from the president of Gamble's, a hardware store chain:

  There seems to be a place for us [in shopping centres] with stores we open of between 30,000 and 35,000 square feet. We can do quite well by specializing. In one mall we are between Sears and Woodward's and we find we attract people ourselves, while the other stores do help us. We don't go into any centre where there's not a good food market. It's a key from the point of view of traffic. (*Globe and Mail* 21 July 1972)

tenant an "exclusive" on their kind of store or on their line of goods may be inserted on the insistence of a powerful tenant. Just as a developer obtains a territorial monopoly in his primary market area, so mall merchants may try to obtain a monopoly on hardware, books, or women's shoes in a centre. Developers don't like tenant monopolies because they limit the developers' freedom to control a centre's tenant mix. Notes a U.S. authority: "Tenants insist on some assurances against competition, and there is considerable justification for their position. The shopping centre developer must, therefore, artfully word his exclusive use provision."[30]*

Indeed, shopping centre tenants and developers have discovered that there is a kind of competition which increases the sales and profits of all tenants and the developer as well as the kind of competition that sometimes goes on between rival merchants selling the same goods and competing on the basis of price. Usually, for instance, when a second department store is added to an existing regional centre the sales of the first department store and of the mall merchants all *increase*. The second store increases the

---

* Agreeing to monopolies for department store anchor tenants was one of the barriers that slowed the expansion of many shopping centres to include two or more such stores:

> In the early stages of development of regional shopping centres, department stores sought exclusives, and for some years thereafter they sought to be associated in shopping centres with other department stores not directly competitive with respect to price lines.

Given the devotion of most businessmen to the principles of free enterprise and competition, it may seem surprising to find retailers so eagerly joining with shopping centre developers in trying to ensure local monopolies for themselves, and to rule out competitors. Indeed the U.S. textbook authors who quoted a shopping centre authority saying baldly that tenants want "protection against competition" felt so awkward about citing this statement with approval (perhaps giving their students a bad impression) that they inserted a footnote about it: "From the context, one may conclude that the writer meant 'direct, duplicative competition'." (Applebaum and Kaylin, *Case Studies*, pp. 161-2)

number of people shopping in the centre, and increases the centre's success at capturing retail spending of people in both its primary and secondary trading areas. Of course only if an expansion is expected to have this effect on existing tenants' business will those tenants support (or permit, if their leases give them the power) the expansion. Merchants have also learned that they can do an increased level of business if they locate close to the other mall merchants selling the same type of goods, rather than trying to steer clear of the competition. A U.S. authority advises mall merchants, "Stay as close to your competitors as possible. Don't get stuck with stores that are completely alien to your operation or do not complement your operation."[31]

As well as calculating the best tenant mix for his centre, the developer has to keep in mind the credit ratings of his tenants. Mortgage lenders will undertake to finance a project only on the basis of commitments from tenants to take space in it. To ensure that the centre will generate a constant cash flow large enough to cover mortgage payments, lenders put much more weight on leases from retail chains than on independent store owners. Notes the U.S. textbook on shopping centre development: "The insurance companies historically required about 75 percent of the space in a shopping centre to be leased to triple-A tenants — highly rated national companies."[32] Not only has this requirement greatly assisted the expansion of national retail chains through shopping centre locations, but it has also given greater bargaining power to the chains in their negotiations with developers. The result is that mall developers usually demand higher rents from independent businessmen than from the national chains. "The well-rated tenants on the 'A' list not only usually pay lower minimum rents than do local merchants but also may receive additional considerations."[33]

Lobster-trap architecture. "Everything about the physical space in a shopping centre is geared to selling."[34] That straightforward comment from an official of Campeau Corp. sums up the approach of developers and their architects to shopping centre design.

In a way, the physical arrangement of a shopping centre is little more than a manifestation of the size and relative strength of its tenants. Indeed a shopping centre is designed only after the tenants are signed up and construction is almost ready to start. Design begins with the anchor tenants. In 1960 two U.S. shopping centre theorists explained the function of anchor tenants and their relationship to other mall tenants:

> By placing primary and secondary customer attractors [anchor tenants] in locations where they function as magnets, customers are pulled through the centre, from one magnet to another, past the doors of the tenants who fall into the category of traffic users. These latter cannot in themselves attract a sufficient number of customers to survive, and therefore are dependent upon the foot traffic generated by the primary and secondary traffic attractors.[35]

With two anchor tenants, the shopping centre is usually designed as a straight line; with three, as a triangle or a T-shape; with four, as a square or an X-shape. The basic design of the building established, next comes the tricky business of placing each tenant in the mall. This requires the developer to negotiate with everybody.* Every store must have mall frontage in order to attract customers, and the more mall frontage the architect can squeeze out of the

---

* Says a "fictional" leasing director in a U.S. case study:

> As the leasing director I have to contend with the ideas of the key department stores as well as with the problems of dealing with the prospective tenants. In the shopping centre business we must face the fact that the biggest cat swings the greatest weight. We are moving into a deal with two of the biggest cats around... If their views on tenant mix and merchant location conflict with ours, we'll try to effect compromises without trimming the tenant-mix balance out of the deal.

Department stores worry about who will be next to them, and merchants want to snuggle up to the department store whose customers are going to be most likely to buy their wares:

> The developer has a problem of providing "spheres of influence" for each of the department stores — that is, discrete areas in which each of the department stores will exert influence, with back-and-forth feeding of traffic among the satellites and the department stores.

(Applebaum and Kaylin, *Case Studies*, pp. 70-1, p. 81)

design the more accommodation the developer can provide. Explains the fictional architect in a U.S. case study:

> Merchandise planning calls for selecting stores and placing them to attract the greatest possible number of shoppers to a centre and funnelling them through it, thereby creating the maximum number of customer-exposures for the retailer...[36]

A real architect elaborates on this point:

> Centres do a large proportion of business in a relatively short period...Consequently it is important for each merchant... to be in direct contact with a maximum number of pedestrian customers...his kind of customers. It does a dress merchant little good to be located in a stream of food buyers.[37]

The design planning goes far beyond maximizing mall frontage to encourage people to spend. The blank, forbidding exterior walls of shopping centres, both downtown and in suburbs, are intended to make walking outside the building unpleasant in comparison with walking through the mall. A newspaper reporter noted that in one shopping mall, twenty different kinds of fluorescent bulbs were used, to enhance the attractiveness of displayed goods.[38] Shopping centre architects go to great lengths to avoid windows through which customers can see outside. If people are aware of changes in the weather, they tend to reduce their shopping time.

One architect summed up shopping centre design as the lobster trap approach: easy to get into, difficult to get out of. "A slight sense of confusion or disorientation also helps." James Hodges, general manager of a regional shopping centre, confirms that the approach works: "People wander around, they look at things, and they are going to start impulse buying."[39]

Profits: highly satisfactory. The financing of shopping centres is similar to that of other types of income properties, and developers possess the same advantages: operating profits now, appraisal surplus profits in the future as the value of the property increases, and the bonus of paper losses to use to avoid paying income tax on profits made in land development. There is, however, a special feature which gives shopping centres an attraction other types of income properties can't match: the guarantee of ever-increasing rental incomes thanks to the "overage" rents generated by the percentage which shopping centre tenants pay on every sales dollar.

The minimum rents set by shopping centre leases are high enough when the centre is virtually fully rented to generate enough cash to pay all the developers' operating expenses, plus interest on mortgages, leaving a cash surplus for operating profit from the beginning. If a cash surplus cannot be earned, it is unlikely that a developer will be able to borrow mortgage money to build the shopping centre. What this means, however, is that all "overage" rents collected by the developer are *certain to be pure profit*. Expenses have been more than covered by minimum rents. Most developers expect to earn "overage" rents on shopping centre projects, but usually pro forma financial statements on the basis of which mortgage lenders provide financing forecast no "overage" rents at all.

Data collected by the U.S. Urban Land Institute shows that the median basic rent in a sample of twenty Canadian regional shopping centres in 1975 was $4.75 a square foot.[40] Common area charges and other charges brought the median operating receipts to $5.76 per square foot. In a sample of twenty-nine community centres, median basic rents were $2.89, and total charges $3.75 a square foot. In twenty-six neighbourhood centres, median basic rents averaged $2.82, and total charges $3.06. But actual rents varied considerably between different tenants. The median total charges paid by supermarkets in regional centres in 1975, for instance, was $4.34 per square foot, somewhat less than the average overall figure of $5.76 for regional centres. Delicatessens, in contrast, paid a median rent of $10.54. Candy and nut shops paid $14.78. Fast food outlets were highest in the food category, paying $29.91 per square foot in rent and related charges.

In contrast, department stores in regional centres in 1975 paid a median rent of $2.84 per square foot. Bookstores paid a median rent of $8.16, with national chains showing a median of $8.74 and independent bookstores a median of $6.16. The chain bookstores sold an average of $96.30 for every square foot rented annually, while sales for the independent stores averaged $61.63, so rent as a percentage of sales was 10 percent for independents and slightly less for the national chains. Many types of retailers paid rents in excess of $10 a square foot, about four times what department stores paid.

Developers also reported on the expenses of their shopping centres to the U.S. organization that publishes shopping centre industry statistics. For a sample of twenty Canadian regional shopping centres in 1975, total revenues were $5.76 per square foot, and total expenses were $2.53 per square foot for the median shopping centre.[41] Operating profit after all expenses including mortgage, principal and interest was $2.84 per square foot — almost half the rent received! For community shopping centres, operating profit was $1.35 per square foot, about a third of total rents paid for the median centre. For neighbourhood centres, operating profit amounted to $1.40 out of the $3.06 paid on average for every square foot rented for the median centre. So profits are a larger component in shopping centre rents than any expense, even the interest paid by the developer on his mortgage. Shopping centre rents could be reduced by a third to almost a half for the average Canadian shopping centre tenant before developers would begin to lose money.*

Profits measured as a percentage return on developers' investment in shopping centres are equally high. Depending on the operating income projected by a developer's pro forma financial statements, a mortgage lender will lend from 75 to 100 percent (or even more) of the actual creation cost of a project. Lending is done, of course, not on the actual creation cost of the project but rather on its market value or its lending value as a completed pro-

---

* These amazing profit figures are confirmed by an analysis done by Ira Gluskin of Cadillac Fairview's shopping centre business. Rents for 1976 totalled $43.5 million. Allocating operating expenses, interest and general and administrative expenses on the basis of confidential information provided by the company, profits turn out to be $14.4 million on the company's total shopping centre operation, 37.5 percent of total rent income. Of every dollar paid in rent and other charges by shopping centre tenants to Cadillac Fairview in 1976, 37.5¢ was profit to the corporation. (Ira Gluskin, *The Cadillac Fairview Corporation Limited.* A corporate background report: study no. 3 [Ottawa: Royal Commission on Corporate Concentration, Supply and Services, 1977] p. 41, p. 44-9)

ject. Market value is a function of the income it generates. Developers generally can choose among a number of financing options for a shopping centre on the basis of how much of their own cash they want to invest in the project and the rate of profit they would earn on that cash.[42]

Assuming an investment by the developer of 25 percent of the capital cost of the typical Canadian regional shopping centre in 1975, the rate of return on that investment that year was 39.5 percent.[43] If the developer invested 10 percent of the capital cost of the centre, the rate of profit on his investment in 1975 was about 98 percent. These profit levels are not out of line with calculations done by investment analyst Ira Gluskin in his study for the Royal Commission on Corporate Concentration. Gluskin makes very conservative assumptions for hypothetical cases based on his analysis of Cadillac Fairview, and shows a first-year rate of profit on a shopping centre project ranging from 14.6 percent (if the developer puts up 20 percent of the cash cost) to infinity (if the developer finances 100 percent of the project cost from mortgage money). But Gluskin shows that 14.6 percent return grows to 40.2 percent after five years and 103.3 percent after ten years, assuming that the centre is successful and sales (and rental income, of course) increase at the rate they increased for successful Cadillac Fairview regional shopping centres in the last ten years.[44] Concludes Gluskin: "It is clear that the shopping centre business is highly profitable."[45] He is echoing Cadillac Fairview chairman A. E. Diamond's 1976 statement that he expected shopping centre profits for the year to be "highly satisfactory."[46]

Retailing goes corporate. The single most important effect of the shopping centre on Canadian retailing has been the enormous contribution it has made to strengthening the corporate chain retailers at the expense of small independent businesses. In spite of the weakening of downtown retail areas where department stores have traditionally been dominant, the Canadian department store chains have been able to maintain and even increase their share of retail spending by locating in shopping centres. National retail chains have expanded enormously since 1945 at the expense of small independent businessmen. The biggest factor in this gain has been their reliance on shopping centre developers to open up locations for them across the country.* Reitman's, a national ladies' wear retailing chain, "can or will locate a store in every shopping centre in Canada beyond a minimum size," reports Ira Gluskin.[47] One developer described his leasing approach for a small downtown mall this way: "We approached and won Laura Secord, Shoppers Drug Mart, United Cigar Stores, W. H. Smith and Agnew-Surpass Shoe Stores among others. These are more or less a family that seems to stick together and like to work out of the same complex."[48]

The importance of shopping centres to the corporate retailers is clear from the statistics. For department stores, shopping centres in 1968 accounted for 35 percent of their total $2.4 billion in retail sales.[49] By 1973, shopping centre sales for department stores had tripled in dollar terms, and now accounted for 52 percent of their total $4.3 billion sales. In 1956, shopping centre locations accounted for 9 percent of the sales of supermarket chains. In 1973, they accounted for 41 percent of the chains' sales.[50]

The prominence of corporate chain retailers in shopping centres increases with the size of the shopping centre. Independent merchants accounted for 22 percent of total sales at neighbourhood centres in 1973, 16 percent of community centre sales, and only 13 percent of regional shopping centre sales.[51] Summarized Statistics Canada: "Together with the department store outlets, the chain outlets captured over 87 percent of all retail dollars spent by consumers in regional centres. For the smaller merchant it was another story. Although almost half of the outlets in regional centres were operated by independent merchants, they received only 12.7 percent of the 'retail pie'."[52]

For the retail chains as for the department stores, shopping centres account for a very substantial portion of their total sales. Of the sales of women's clothing chains, 62 percent are in shopping

---

* The retail bookselling business is typical of how the national chains have rapidly gained a substantial position of power in the last two decades. The chains, Classics, Coles and W. H. Smith, did this mainly with shopping centre. "The renovation and enclosing of Bonnie Doon in Edmonton, for example, is drawing Coles Books...to Western Canada for the first time," reported the *Globe and Mail* in 1968. (*Globe and Mail* 14 May 1968)

centre locations; for men's clothing chains, 57 percent; for chain hardware stores, 53 percent; shoe stores 44 percent; jewellery stores, 34 percent. The only retail chains for whom shopping centres are not particularly important are those that do not generally locate in shopping centres. Service station chains, for instance, earn only 3 percent of their total sales in shopping centre locations.[53]

The picture is very different for independent retailers. Independently owned women's clothing stores, for example, make only 29 percent of their total retail sales in shopping centre locations. That is the highest figure for any of the major types of retail business. Independent drug stores have 21 percent of their sales in shopping centres, independent hardware stores 8 percent, independent grocery stores 4 percent. The average figure for all independent businessmen is 7.6 percent of sales in shopping centre locations, with the balance of 92.4 percent of their sales outside of shopping centres.[54] The share of total shopping centre sales made by independent merchants did rise from 12 percent in 1956 to a high of 20 percent in 1968, slumping back to 17 percent in 1973 as more large regional centres opened their doors.[55]

For independent retailers, shopping centres are a completely different phenomenon than they have been for the corporate chains. The independents have lower sales per outlet, pay more rent as an overall percentage of sales, and face lease terms that skim off a large portion of any potential profit they might make in a shopping centre location. The general manager of one large regional centre in suburban Toronto explained the difference between the position of independent businessmen and the chains:

> I have only one store in here that is a one-man operation. All the rest are corporations, large and small. I used to live on the Danforth and I love those little neighbourhood stores. But they can't operate here. They are aiming at $100,000 a year total sales and the places here are aiming at a quarter of a million. The people in those one-man operations want to make a living. The people here want to make a profit.[56]

Commented Donald McGiverin, managing director of retail stores for The Bay, as he wiped away his crocodile tears, "I don't like the thought, but as time goes on it's going to be very difficult for independents to prosper."[57]

Shopping centre cities. Shopping centres have had a major impact on the shape of Canadian cities since 1950.[58] Virtually from the beginning, they have been weakening the position of downtown retailers. As shopping centres absorbed a larger percentage of total retail spending, downtowns lost some of their multi-purpose functioning and became mainly office precincts.* In smaller towns, one or two shopping centres in the suburbs have also had a drastic effect on downtown businessmen.

Like suburban industrial parks and residential developments, shopping centres are built at very low densities and use large amounts of land. A Mississauga city politician, Mary Helen Spence, summed up her view of their impact this way:

> They are a tremendous waste of space. They are a colossal waste of good land. Three-quarters of them are under asphalt, no use except for a car, they are isolated from the community and they are destroying historic commercial centres, community shopping areas.[59]

Ironically the success of shopping centres in the suburbs and their weakening of downtown retailing also led to circumstances that later permitted the shopping centre developers to take over more and more downtown retailing as well. Land assemblies for downtown redevelopment projects were eased by the recognition of many downtown businessmen that their position was deteriorat-

---

* In a survey of the residents of Edmonton's Sherwood Park suburb which is just outside the city boundary, the nearby community and regional shopping centres outdrew downtown Edmonton for every kind of item except furniture shopping. Thus for instance 53 people said they regularly shopped in the local shopping centre for children's clothes and shoes, and 274 shopped at other Edmonton regional shopping centres. Only 69 shopped downtown. For large electrical appliances, 18 shopped locally and 248 in larger regional shopping centres. For these items 190 Sherwood Park residents went downtown. ("The Hamlet of Sherwood Park: A review of alternative forms of government" [Special projects and policy research, Municipal Affairs, Government of Alberta, January 1977] p. xvii)

ing. Through commercial redevelopment, downtown retailing has gained a new lease on life. Downtown shopping malls, however, are quite different from the old downtown. Just as in the suburban centres, downtown shopping malls are oriented towards the corporate retailers. Having triumphed in the suburbs, the chains are moving to take over the sizeable portion of the retail business which independent businessmen still control. As we saw in the last chapter, the developers and their retail chain associates are doing this with a full range of assistance from government at every level. In the suburbs, the granting of effective territorial monopolies to the shopping centre developers permitted this form of retailing to predominate. In the central city, government subsidies and assistance promote mall redevelopment projects.

Corporate shopping. With suburban shopping centres, virtually every aspect of shopping has been changed from the pattern which existed in Canadian cities until 1945. Daily and weekly shopping for food and other necessities was done in local stores, a short walk or transit ride away. Shopping trips to suburban centres are made mainly by car. Stores were run by owner-managers who, even if they didn't live in the community where they worked, were figures of local importance and had substantial ties to their community. Shopping centre outlets are run by employees, except for independent stores which do only 17 percent of total shopping centre business. Owner-managed stores were far from homogeneous; the range of goods offered was tailored by the owner's tastes and by the preferences of the community. The corporate chains offer much the same range of goods in every shopping centre across the country.

Shopping areas were public streets, just like the rest of the city, and they accommodated the whole host of activities that happen on public streets. In contrast the "public" spaces of shopping centres are controlled by the developers whose constant concern is increasing their sales volume. If a politician is glad-handing his way through the mall and the developer doesn't like it, out goes the politician. If teenagers are hanging around and being what the developer considers "a nuisance," out go the teenagers. If the Red Cross wants to hold a tag day, either they succeed in getting permission from the developer or they stay outside the shopping mall.

As one shopping centre manager explained to journalist Graham Fraser, when he wants to get someone out of his mall he can fall back on "a little something called the Petty Trespass Act."[60] That's legislation under which Ontario property owners, including shopping mall owners, have the right to decide who may use their property.

The most profound difference between traditional retailing and shopping centres is of course the status of businesses as tenants rather than owner-occupiers of their premises, combines with the lease provisions that give shopping centre developers a percentage of every dollar spent in their malls. The percentage varies somewhat, but for a sample of twenty Canadian regional shopping centres reporting for 1975 it averaged 2.5 percent of every dollar in sales for the median supermarket, about 5 percent of sales for department stores, and roughly 10 percent of sales for mall stores of all types.[61] As we've seen, a third to a half of the total rents paid by shopping centre tenants are profit to the developer. Given the way that shopping centre rents are structured, however, only a modest profit is earned on department store and supermarket rents. The bulk of the profit comes from rents paid by mall tenants.

Neither Statistics Canada nor the land development industry measures total shopping centre rents paid in Canada. Combining industry information about rents as a percentage of sales with information on total shopping centre sales from Statistics Canada and elsewhere, my own estimate for 1975 is that shopping centre sales were about $8.5 billion. Total rents paid by shopping centre tenants I estimate at about $500 million.[62] Of this, $166 to $250 million was profit to shopping centre developers.

There are two ways of looking at that total profit figure. It can be seen as the private tax assessed by shopping centre developers on shopping centre customers which would not be levied if, say, shopping centres were operated on a non-profit basis by their tenants. Seen that way, I estimate that shopping centres added $180 to $250 million to people's shopping bills in 1975 alone.

The other way of looking at that profit figure is to consider that retail prices are set by what the market will bear, and that retailers would charge the same prices in the same location even if their rents were lower. To the extent that this is the case, shopping centre developers are basically using their position to muscle in on the profits of retailers, mainly mall retailers. That $166 to $250 million is profit which in other circumstances would be made by the retailing chains and independent businessmen, and which the shopping centre developers have been able to capture through their market power.*

The role of government. Having put enormous support into the corporate suburbs, the federal government needed to play no direct role to assist the developers of shopping centres. The consumer market was there, thanks to the suburban housing; the mortgage lenders were happy to provide money for these buildings, thanks to federal-provincial regulation of the industry that permitted them to put their money into mortgages of this kind; the urban transportation systems, particularly the expressways, were being built by city and provincial governments; the basic principle of a limited territorial monopoly enshrined in the location of shopping centres and often in the leases between developers and their tenants was no violation of federal competition law, thanks to a very mild Anti-Combines Act. The only direct inducement offered by Ottawa to shopping centre developers was the usual capital cost allowance concession which applies to all developer-owned rental properties, and which is the cherry on the icing on the developer's cake.

Provincial governments had a more direct role. Through their involvement in regional planning and regional infrastructure, particularly expressways, their actions were often instrumental in creating potential locations for shopping centres, especially the larger regional centres. With their responsibility for property law, provincial governments might have looked askance at the concessionaire relationship between shopping mall tenant and developer,

---

* Consider the implications in terms of this book. People who bought it in a shopping centre bookstore paid the same price for it as most people who bought it elsewhere. The shopping centre bookstore pays 10 percent of the retail price of this book to the developer in rent. Of that 10 percent rent, roughly 5 percent is expenses for the developer and 5 percent is profit. In shopping centre bookstores, the developer takes that 5 percent profit. Elsewhere, the 5 percent is available for the bookstore owner to take as profit or to spend on expenses — or, if it makes competitive sense, to give as a discount to customers.

and at industry practices of charging different prices for the same commodity (physical space) to different customers. Provincial governments might also have insisted that the effective public property created by shopping centres, particularly the pedestrian malls themselves, be treated as public property. They could insist that merchants in shopping centres have the right to own their stores outright, to purchase them from shopping centre developers. Responses along these lines would have reduced the profitability of shopping centres generally, shifted profits from developers to merchants, and redirected the bias of shopping centres away from national chains toward local independent businessmen.

Municipal governments at the local and regional level have been vital in supporting the growth of the shopping centre. Their central contribution has been to create and enforce the limited territorial monopolies of the shopping centre developers, by respecting the industry's notions about the market area necessary to support a shopping centre and by ruling out competing merchants and would-be rival developers by refusing them development approvals. Equally valuable is the municipal role in providing the necessary infrastructure, particularly the road systems, that are so important for shopping centre developers. And while they have created the monopoly territories for the developers, municipalities in Canada have made no effort to collect through a system of franchise fees some portion of the enormous profits these monopolies permit the developers to make.

Next: regional town centres. Though governments at all levels have done everything that shopping centre developers might want in terms of supporting the industry so far, the industry's next wave of expansion calls for an even greater level of involvement and support from public agencies and local government. This is the essence of the industry's new goal of moving from mere regional *shopping centres* to regional *town centres.*

The wave of regional shopping centre development which peaked in the early 1970s had subsided by 1975-76. During the late 1970s, very few new large centres were constructed. The industry, however, was planning for the long term, and is now ready for the next round of expansion:

Developers of shopping centres are busy assembling land for future centres to be built in the 1980s while the current lull of building continues for the next three years, according to industry sources.

...In the meantime, strong developers with the foresight and know-how are picking sites five to ten years ahead of time. They will be in an excellent position when department stores are ready for another major expansion program.[63]

The corporate developers plan to move forward from their success in capturing the growth of retail space to include every type of central-city activity in new suburban downtowns built on land they own. The key to this goal is to combine shopping centres, high-rise office towers, high-rise hotels and high-rise apartments with a range of public and cultural facilities as has been done in large downtown commercial redevelopment projects. Building up to downtown densities in the suburbs, the developers will also be able to make the shift from virtually total reliance on car transportation to obtain public transit service to their centres.

The strategy of turning regional shopping centres into regional "town centres" is most fully developed in the 1975 Vancouver regional plan, which proposes four "regional town centres" for Vancouver by 1986.[64] Of course the details of this proposal produced tremendous rivalries among municipal politicians, and made downtown developers and property owners edgy because of the over-expansion of space in downtown Vancouver.*

---

* For the developers, regional town centres are a development technique which responds to public resistance to further expressway construction, emerging limitations on the use of cars because of high energy costs, and public opposition to continued high-density downtown development. While urban planners across Canada have been developing the arguments for promoting regional town centres, the developers have been practising building prototypes. One is the "City Centre" project by Bruce McLaughlin in Toronto's suburban Mississauga, which combines the Mississauga city hall with office buildings and McLaughlin's Square One regional shopping centre. A similar project is the Scarborough Town Centre, developed by Trizec on the east side of Toronto. It combines a shopping centre, office space, and the Scarborough city hall and board of education offices.

"Friendly competition." In every respect as far as the developers are concerned, shopping centres have been an enormous success. As a development technique, they have gone from strength to strength: from the smaller community and neighbourhood centres built around a supermarket to the large regional centres with two, three or even four department stores to anchor them. Triumphant in the suburbs, they have built on that base to launch an assault on the last stronghold of independent retail businessmen, with large suburban-scale projects being built in downtown areas in every large city.

They have successfully imposed a whole new way of shopping on suburban residents, and been crucial to the transformation of the retail trade in Canada from a field dominated by independent small businessmen to one where corporations are quickly taking over the bulk of every major line of business.

The essence of shopping centres is monopoly combined with what might be termed complementary relationships among businesses. Shopping centre merchants are not competitors in the real sense of the term, fighting with each other for business and profit. They are in a complementary relationship, in the sense that every merchant adds to the business of all the others instead of fighting to take some of it away. A Simpsons-Sears official at the opening of Saskatoon's Midtown Plaza had a nice phrase for it: he called it "friendly competition." Simpsons-Sears, he told the assembled mall merchants, was "very eager to be active but friendly competitors" with the other fifty businesses in the project "so that we can all prosper together."[65]

The real competition among shopping centre developers is over sites and effective territorial monopoly franchises from municipalities. The competition between department stores and retailers is over locations in shopping centres, giving them a slice of the developer's exclusive location. From then on, it is "friendly competition," meaning only policies that will add to total sales in the shopping centre. There is above all to be no serious price competition among mall merchants designed to lure away customers who would otherwise be paying higher prices. As G. Allan Burton, chairman of Simpsons, which owns its own department store chain as well as 50 percent of Simpsons-Sears, has noted, price-cutting by competing retailers is "the last act of an impoverished mind."[66]

"Friendly competition" among shopping centre developers means vicious fights over locations, but generally when one developer wins the others in the race give up.

Every year, Canada's shopping centre developers get together to gossip about the business. Asked at a convention of shopping centre developers by a puzzled reporter who evidently did not understand the rules of "friendly competition" and who wondered why the developers so readily shared trade secrets, Neil Wood, president of Cadillac Fairview, explained that the tradition had started in 1957 when the shopping centre development business in Canada was getting going. "Everyone was groping around trying to develop the industry," he said. "That built a special esprit de corps which continues."[67] Given the facts about how the shopping centre business works, it's perhaps not surprising that the developers have to tell each other their amazing success stories. Who else would believe what they've managed to do in less than thirty years with these astonishing money machines?

PART III

11

THE CONSEQUENCES OF THE CORPORATE CITY

The corporate city was created out of faith, not out of knowledge of what its consequences and benefits would be. It arose from the belief of Liberal governments in corporate business over small business and over publicly owned, non-profit or co-operative enterprise. It was helped by the trust of social planning and housing experts in the efficiencies and economies of large, rational organizations. It was assisted immeasurably by the conviction of senior economic planners in Ottawa that large amounts of new urban buildings were good in their own right and appropriate uses for the nation's wealth and resources.

The desirability of postwar policies leading to the emergence of the development industry and the corporate city is no longer a matter of abstract or futuristic debate. Most of us are now living with the consequences of these policies. All of us know more about their real implications than anyone did in 1945.

In this chapter we look at the impact of the developers and the corporate city on the way people live, on the cost of urban living, on the distribution of wealth in Canada both in the short term and the long term, and on the overall pattern of Canadian economic development. As we will see, the consequences of the developers' success go well beyond the kinds of issues which have traditionally been raised in urban politics. They touch on some fundamental questions about the structure of this country's economy, and about Canada's economic future.

How we live. Through the new building forms which it has built in every Canadian city, the development industry has had a dramatic impact on the daily lives of most urban Canadians. Most of us have some sense of how we are affected by high-rise apartments, shopping centres, and downtown office buildings. Users of these building types are influenced directly every day by their internal and external design.

In the corporate city people may *feel* free to make their own decisions about how they will live, but in fact they are restricted by the limited number choices offered by developers and planners. No one is forced to shop in shopping centres, but the developers know what share of the incomes of people living around a shopping centre they can count on capturing. No one is forced to live in high-rise apartments, but they fill up, even though most of the people who live there would rather live somewhere else. The developers collectively set out the options; and the only freedom people have left is to decide which of those options is best suited to their means and tastes. Often there is only one rational choice for most people. If you live in the suburbs, and if every shopping centre offers the same range of goods at the same prices, you can choose to shop anywhere you want, but the only rational choice is the centre nearest your home. If you are looking for accommodation and you have young children, you can choose a high-rise apartment or a detached single-family house. The apartment is far cheaper but only the house offers satisfactory family accommodation. Theoretically a range of alternatives between these two forms of new housing could exist, but in fact rarely does in most cities. The choice of the suburban house is really, therefore, not a choice at all.

The structure the corporate city imposes on urban living gives people little freedom to live their lives as they would choose. Surveys of suburban residents indicate substantial dissatisfaction with aspects of suburban life, for instance the absence of adequate public transit. Surveys of executives who run companies that operate out of downtown office buildings reveal considerable dissatisfaction with the concentration of large numbers of office workers in a tiny area of the city, even though proximity to related businesses is a key element in office location. Factory workers are often unhappy about having to relocate from a central location to a suburban plant because of the new expense and difficulty involved in travelling to work.

Clearly there are more subtle ways in which people's lives and experiences are affected by the types of development projects that have been built since 1945. Growing up in a postwar suburb is completely different from growing up in a central-city neighbourhood. Family life is bound to be more rigidly structured when the social and recreational life of the children depends heavily on the availability of a parent to drive them from place to place. Contact between a working parent and children is more limited than it would otherwise be when travel time to work adds an hour and a half or two hours onto the working day. The possibility of living in an extended family is narrowed by suburban house designs and zoning requirements that make it awkward and difficult for an aged parent or relative to live next door in a flat without having to be incorporated in family life. High-rise apartments, on the other hand, appear to discourage social contacts among neighbours and lead to people living a more isolated existence. Because of the unsuitability of this housing form for children, high-rise apartments tend to become "ghettos" for single or elderly people.

Profits and high prices. Unlike the complexities involved in assessing the impact of the corporate city on daily life, the effect of the developers' high profits on the cost of urban living in Canada can be estimated reasonably accurately.

No satisfactory information is published on the overall operating profits of the development industry. Adding up the figures for the public real estate corporations yields only a fraction of the total, because so much of the industry is accounted for by private companies that do not publish financial statements. Based on the information on operating profit levels in Part II, and using the estimates of the total holdings of land developers derived from figures published by analyst Ira Gluskin, I have estimated total annual operating profits for the industry.[1] This calculation does not include annual appraisal surplus profits.

Assuming that all 150 million square feet of rented office space in Canada are owned by developers (an over-estimate) and that operating profit on average is $1 per square foot (an under-estimate), annual profits in this field are $150 million. Using the figures presented in chapter 10 on shopping centres, I estimated a profit range for shopping centre developers of $166 to $250 million a year. Here I use a mid-range figure, $180 million.

There were 1,128,000 rental apartment units in Canadian cities in 1977. I assume that just a third of these were owned by developers, the balance being held by small property investors, owner-occupiers with flats to rent, doctors, lawyers and other landlords. Assuming an average operating profit per apartment of $40 per month, or $480 per year (a smaller margin than that reported for Cadillac Fairview by Ira Gluskin), total developer operating profits on apartment rentals amount to approximately $180 million a year. Assuming the same profit margin, other owners of rental apartments would be earning annual operating profits of $360 million.

For industrial space, Gluskin estimates a total supply in Canada of 400 million square feet. Assuming a third of this total is owned by developers, and that their profits average $0.25 per square foot per year, operating profits are $33 million. In suburban land development, a somewhat more accurate estimate of annual profits is possible. Assuming what would seem to be a relatively conservative profit margin of $10,000 per single-family lot built on in 1977 in high-priced cities only, and $5,000 per lot for semi-detached and row houses in the same cities, total profit made in suburban land development in these cities alone in 1977 would be $508 million. This is based on 34,500 single-family starts, 11,800 semi-detached and 20,900 row housing starts, a total of 67,200 of the 87,400 starts in all metropolitan centres in 1977.[2]

These estimates would suggest that the development industry is earning operating profits in the order of $1 billion annually. As we have seen, these profits have an immediate effect on prices and the cost of living. They have a dramatic impact on the price of new suburban housing, adding $8,000 to $25,000 to the price of houses that are already relatively expensive and making them unafford-able for all but very high-income families in the cities where the large developers dominate the supply of suburban lots. Apartment tenants pay rents that generate a high rate of return on developer investment in their buildings, and add an average of 15 to 25 percent to rents. Rents that are high enough in office buildings and industrial space to yield the profit levels which are standard in the development industry add to the costs of businesses and of government, and are ultimately paid mostly by consumers. Rents in shopping centres account for 2.5 cents of every dollar spent in the average shopping centre supermarket, 5 cents of every dollar in the average shopping centre department store, and 10 cents of every dollar in the average mall store. Of this portion of shopping centre spending that goes to the developers, a third to a half of the total is pure profit to the developer in the average Canadian centre.*

A certain portion of these profits would have been paid by tenants to landlords if there had not been a land development industry created in Canada after 1945, and if the traditional patterns of urban living and development had continued in the postwar city. The bulk of the development industry's profits, however, have been created by the industry's new development techniques.

Development industry profits also add indirectly to the high cost of urban living. High prices for new suburban houses, for instance, raise the prices of existing houses. This forces people to spend more money both on housing (in the form of higher house prices) and on interest (in the form of payments for mortgage money borrowed to finance the purchase of these expensive houses). For every developer who has made a million dollars in the residential field, there are several hundred urban Canadian families who are

---

* Though rates of profit are notoriously difficult to compare between different countries, the figures collected by the Urban Land Institute, an industry organization, report the profits of Canadian and U.S. shopping centres on an identical basis. Profits in Canada are consistently 50 percent higher than in the U.S. Thus for instance operating profit on regional shopping centres in the U.S. in 1975 was 32 percent of rents paid on the median centre in that country, 48 percent of rents paid in Canada. For community centres, operating profit was 22 percent of rents paid in the median U.S. centre, 36 percent in Canada. For neighbourhood shopping centres, operating profit was 32 percent of rents in the median centre in the U.S., 46 percent in Canada. (*Dollars and Cents of Shopping Centers: 1975* [Washington, D.C.: Urban Land Institute, 1975] calculated from data at p. 69, p. 121, p. 173, p. 208, p. 210, p. 212) "house-poor" because the high cost of housing is absorbing a larger portion of their total income than it needs to. So the industry's $1 billion in annual operating profits is only a fraction of the total amount added to the cost of living as a result of the industry's activities.

The new urban feudalism. High industry profits and higher prices for housing and many other items are short-term and immediately visible consequences of the development industry's success. As we have noted in our discussion of the financial structure of the developers' income properties, there is another long-term and even more dramatic consequence of the way the industry has operated.

The assets of all land developers in Canada are probably twice the total for the public companies and largest private firms, a total of about $17 billion at book value. Book values are considerably less than market values, and it would be reasonable to put the total market value of all urban property owned by all developers in Canada in 1978 at $30 to $35 billion. This is a fraction of total urban property in Canada, which runs in the low hundreds of billions, but it accounts for a major share of the new urban rental accommodation that has been built in postwar Canadian cities.

All the developers need do is hold those properties and collect rents and operating profits from them for twenty to twenty-five years. Then they will own $30 to $35 billion in urban property (at 1978 prices) outright. The concentration of such huge wealth in the hands of a relatively small number of investors will have dramatic implications for the country's economic, social and political structure. Since a sizeable percentage of land development corporations are foreign-owned, it will also have a major impact on Canada's international balance of payments as large amounts of rents that had previously been directed to paying off (mainly Canadian) mortgages go instead to foreign property owners.

The new urban feudalism created by the development industry has more aspects than just the long-term concentration of property wealth. There is, for instance, the change in status of many businesses from being owner-occupiers of the buildings they use to being tenants of the relatively small number of large urban landlords. Large national retail corporations have been given a substan-

ESTIMATED ANNUAL OPERATING PROFITS

of Canada's Urban Land Developers, 1977
— millions of dollars —

Office rentals	$150
Shopping centre rentals	180
Apartment rentals	180
Industrial space rentals	33
Total profits on rentals	543
Suburban land development	508
Total operating profits	$1,051

tial lead over their smaller rivals because of the structure of shopping centres, and the bias of the developers and their mortgage lenders in favour of the large department stores and national store chains over independent local businessmen.

Urban political life, as we have already noted, has also been substantially changed to support the developers' takeover of the process of urban growth. Decision-making has moved upwards, from small municipalities representing relatively compact geographic areas to larger city councils and regional bodies. The large developers are more successful at dealing with these remote bodies than small businessmen and citizens to whom they are often inaccessible and difficult to influence.

Distorted development. Though all the consequences of the corporate city are dramatic and far-reaching in their impact on Canadian society, none is so critical as the effect which the development industry has had on the use of Canadian investment capital. In the last few years, it has become clear that the Canadian economy has moved out of the era of general prosperity, relatively full employment and growth which characterized the postwar period up to the early 1970s. The economy appears to be in the midst of a state of continuing crisis. The symptoms of this crisis are high and persistent rates of unemployment, relatively high rates of inflation, and a balance of international trade which relies heavily on exports of largely unprocessed natural resources to pay for a rapidly growing influx of manufactured goods. The economy is over-developed in some areas, like the extraction of natural resources for export, but underdeveloped in others, like the manufacturing sector.

The land development industry has had a key though largely unrecognized role in this pattern of distorted development. It has absorbed huge and rapidly accelerating amounts of Canadian investment capital during a period when those resources should have been available for more productive investment purposes. Financial institutions have invested heavily in urban development. In 1946, Canada's institutional mortgage lenders had lent a total of $644 million in mortgages on real estate, most of it urban real estate. During the next fifteen years, mortgage lenders provided an additional $6.6 billion in investment capital for mortgages, so that mortgage loans outstanding in 1960 totalled $7.4 billion. During the 1960s, financial institutions provided a net increase of another $14.1 billion, double the amount that they had made available in the previous fifteen years, and total mortgage loans outstanding from financial institutions were $21.5 billion in 1970.[3] In the next seven years, Canadian financial institutions increased their mortgage lending by an astonishing $52.4 billion, so that as of 1977 the total value of real estate mortgages outstanding was an incredible $73.9 billion.

The amount of money lent on urban real estate by Canadian financial institutions increased more than one hundred times between 1945 and 1977, and the rate of increase was constantly accelerating. It took fifteen years to 1960 for mortgage lending to go up by about $7 billion, then ten years to go up by $14 billion, then seven years to increase by $52 billion. In 1977 alone, the mortgage lenders received about $4 billion in principal repayments from mortgage borrowers, but lent out new mortgages that year of $12.6 billion. On top of the mortgage funds provided by financial institutions, governments have themselves provided additional mortgage funds directly to finance new construction. The total of government mortgage lending in 1977 was $12.8 billion.

Where has all this money come from? In general terms, it has come from the savings of individuals deposited with the financial

CANADIAN LENDING INSTITUTIONS AND THEIR INVESTMENT IN REAL ESTATE

Mortgage Loans Outstanding, 1970 and 1977

— in millions of dollars —

	Life insurance companies	Chartered banks	Loan companies	Trust companies	Others	Corporate lenders	Credit unions	Pension funds	Estates trusts, admin. by trust companies	Total
Mortgage loans outstanding 1970	$ 7,723	$ 1,481	$2,868	$ 3,829	$382	$2,052	$ 1,353	$1,022	$ 2,714	$23,424
Mortgage loans outstanding 1977	12,800	12,100	8,000	17,000	760	3,900	8,300	4,200	8,800	75,860
Increase 1970-1977 (rounded)	5,100	10,600	5,100	13,200	400	1,800	6,900	3,200	6,100	52,400
Total assets 1977	29,500	150,500	9,600	23,800	*	*	23,700	*	49,600	
Mortgages as a percentage of total assets—1977	43%	8%	83%	71%	*	*	35%	*	18%	

Source: *Canadian Housing Statistics 1977*, pp. 67, 68. Figures for 1977 are preliminary.
* Information unavailable

institutions. The lending institutions have chosen, to an increasing degree, to make this investment capital available for real estate mortgages. Between 1970 and 1977, life insurance companies provided an additional $5.1 billion for mortgage lending, loan companies an additional $5.1 billion, corporate lenders $1.8 billion, credit unions $6.9 billion, pension funds $3.2 billion and trust company-administered funds $6.1 billion. Trust companies themselves lent an additional $13.2 billion in mortgage money during that period. But the biggest percentage increase, and the second-biggest dollar increase, was recorded by the chartered banks who had $1.4 billion in mortgages outstanding in 1970. By 1977 they increased that figure by $10.8 billion, to $12.2 billion.

Canadian financial institutions have several incentives to make investment capital available for mortgage loans. First, government programs have removed most or all of the risks involved in mortgage lending on new housing. Housing mortgages are long-term loans, attractive to institutions looking for long-term investments for their funds. Mortgage interest rates are relatively high compared with other long-term, equally safe investments and give a better "spread" between what financial institutions pay for their money and what they receive when they lend it out. Noted the *Globe and Mail* Report on Business in an analysis of Canadian trust companies, which have 71 percent of their total assets in real estate mortgages, this field is "traditionally the most important and profitable financial service offered by trust companies."[4]

Second, mortgage lending permits the financial institutions to participate in a profitable and successful new industry without themselves having to get involved directly in the business, unless they decide it is in their interest to do so.*

With government economic policy supporting rather than resisting this tendency of Canadian financial institutions to direct invest-

---

* Generally, they prefer to have the developer on the front line dealing with the problems that are involved in most land development projects. On the rare occasion where mortgage lenders find themselves embroiled in difficult projects, they don't seem to enjoy the experience. Halliwell Soule, president of Hamilton Trust and Savings Company, unexpectedly found himself involved in problems of condominium owners after a Toronto developer, Kuhl Construc-

ment capital into urban property, far more money than was needed has been used in urban real estate and land development in Canada. Investment capital has been wasted by this sector in three major ways. First, the dramatic increases generated by the developers' activities that have occurred in urban land prices ranging from suburban lots priced at $30,000 instead of $10,000 to downtown land at $200 or $300 per square foot have increased the value — on paper — of all urban land in Canada. Had government policies promoted low rather than high urban land prices, considerably less investment capital would have been required to finance the construction of every form of new urban accommodation from suburban houses in high-priced cities to downtown office towers. More significant, however, is the effect of these high land prices in urban land development on the price of existing urban properties. New suburban house lots at $30,000 pull up the prices of the land existing houses are built on, and the average house sells for $20,000 more than it would if suburban lots cost $10,000. Considerably greater amounts of investment capital are then required to finance the purchase and sale of existing urban property.

Without better information on the urban real estate market, it is difficult to estimate the unnecessary demand for Canadian investment capital which has been generated directly and indirectly because of high urban land prices. With the rapid rise in house lot prices of most other types of urban land, it might be reasonable to estimate that a third of the $52.4 billion in investment capital absorbed by real estate in Canada in the first seven years of the 1970s was used to finance the excess of the price of new suburban lots over their production costs and the increases in the value of all other urban land which occurred during that period. That would suggest that about $35 billion in investment capital was used from 1970-1977 to add new buildings to the stock of urban accommodation in Canadian cities. The other $17.4 billion absorbed by the real

---

tion, ran into financial problems. Soule told reporters he was fed up having to deal with all the problems of the project and its residents, and that he was refusing to attend any further meetings with residents. "I'm sick and tired of being bothered by nutsy people, the press and other communications media," he said. (*Globe and Mail* 9 August 1975)

estate market added nothing productive to the economy.*

A second way in which investment capital has been wasted by the development industry has been in financing the construction of new buildings that simply replace the accommodation provided by existing buildings that have been demolished before their useful life was over. A third major waste of investment capital has come from a pattern of public infrastructure which is far more expensive than would be required by a more economic and compact pattern of urban development. An illuminating indication of how much more than was necessary has been invested in sewers, schools, water services, roads, and other facilities to support urban growth comes from an analysis done by Vancouver's regional planners. They calculated the costs of infrastructure for the expected growth of Vancouver's population from 1.1 million in 1976 to 1.5 million in 1986. This growth would require infrastructure capital spending of $2.5 billion, mostly on transportation facilities,

---

* Published housing statistics do not provide much detail on the use to which the financial institutions' mortgage funds are put. *Canadian Housing Statistics* reports that the value of new housing created in Canada in the seven years from 1971 to 1977 inclusive was $52.4 billion. Funds to finance this came from the lending institutions ($26.4 billion), from owners' equity cash ($7.1 billion), from sources categorized as "other" ($13.3 billion), from federal funds to private owners ($5.3 billion), and from federal direct spending on housing ($0.4 billion). A portion of the lending institutions' $26.4 billion was of course advanced against the high prices which were generating high profits on suburban lots and on land assemblies for apartments.

I have found no statistical reports on the amount of land *profit* included in this $52.4 billion in housing at market value created from 1971-1977. Using statistics for house completions in that period across Canada and using very crude average profit figures for each major type of unit (for single-family units, a low of $3,000 per unit, a high of $10,000; for semi-detached $3,000 and $8,000, for row housing $3,000 and $8,000, and for apartments $2,000 and $4,000) the total estimated land profit component in new housing would lie in the range between a low of $4.3 billion and a high of $12.3 billion.

Statistics for housing construction value include the cost of the labour and materials which go into the construction, plus normal construction profits, *plus profits on developed land.* Land profit is considered to be the difference between what the land cost the builder-

if current growth patterns were followed. Yet a modestly modified pattern of growth which the planners worked out would have required infrastructure spending of only $1.6 billion to support the same population increase. All but $226-$242 million of this spending would have been incurred by government.[5] The $900 million saving (36 percent of projected spending) in infrastructure investment for one city for one ten-year period indicates the substantially excessive amount of spending on these services which has been part of the corporate city pattern of urban growth.

Decisions about the use of investment capital are key ones for any economy. An investment of $1 million in new urban buildings creates a modest number of jobs, temporarily, while the $1 million building is constructed. The job-creating effect of the investment is one-time, since buildings once they are erected do not on their own create jobs. An investment of $1 million in mortgage money lent against a parcel of land which this year was worth $1 million more than last year generates absolutely no new jobs whatsoever.

---

developer and what it was worth after the new building was erected on it. The reported value of new housing construction in Canada in 1977 was $8.2 billion. Costs of the labour and materials used to produce this housing are not given separately. Using reported per square foot construction cost figures (including normal builders' profit) of $28 for single-family housing and $24 for semi-detached, row and apartment construction, average unit sizes, and reasonable servicing cost estimates, my calculation of the cost of producing this new housing is $6.9 billion. With its construction value reported at $8.2 billion, that leaves a residual of $1.3 billion between costs and value representing developers' administrative and other costs (a small figure) and profit on land (evidently a large figure).

Since lending institution mortgage funds are used to finance existing housing and all other forms of urban property as well as new housing, it is difficult to estimate very closely what portion of new institutional mortgage lending between 1971 and 1977 would have been unnecessary if urban land prices had remained moderate during the period, and if suburban lots had been priced across Canada at the level they sold at in Montreal and elsewhere in Quebec. My best estimate would be that the figure lies between $10 billion and $25 billion of the total increase of $52 billion, and in the text I have used the figure of one-third of the total additional lending, $17.4 billion. (*Canadian Housing Statistics* 1977, p. 21; Statistics Canada, *National Income and Expenditure Accounts*, fourth quarter 1977, pp. 36-7; Statistics Canada, *Construction in Canada* 1975-1977).

It adds nothing at all to the productive capacity of the economy. In contrast, an investment of $1 million in a manufacturing industry adds new production capacity to the economy and generates, on average for Canada, 61 permanent jobs.[6]

In the postwar period in Canada, and particularly in the 1960s and 1970s, Canadian investment funds were flowing very heavily into urban property. At the same time, investment in manufacturing was relatively low and that sector of the economy was in a state of decline. Excessive and wasteful use of Canadian investment capital in urban land development and real estate, perhaps as much as $17.4 billion in the first seven years of the 1970s alone, has been accompanied by an insufficient supply of investment capital to other vital sectors of the economy. Canada has gone abroad in the search for more investment capital, particularly for resource development projects. Other sectors have gone without needed capital investment funds. Overdevelopment of the real estate and land development sector of the Canadian economy goes hand in hand with underdevelopment of other sectors, particularly manufacturing.

It has taken the crisis conditions of the last several years to draw attention to the extent of this distorted pattern of economic development in Canada, and the need for a new national economic strategy. It is clear that urban real estate's enormous appetite for new investment capital, increasing rapidly every year since 1970, cannot continue when that investment capital is clearly needed for other much more urgent uses. The fact that this flow of investment to urban real estate cannot be sustained is the Achilles' heel of the Canadian land development industry.

The European connection. There is a further element of distortion in the pattern of Canadian economic development which results from foreign ownership in the development industry. Foreign property investors, mainly British, Swiss, Italian and Belgian, have played a major role in urban land development here through Canadian subsidiaries. Firms of foreign parentage like Genstar, Trizec, Costain, Fidinam and British Properties have strengthened their position in the industry through the 1960s and 1970s. Some, like Genstar and Trizec, have grown mainly by takeovers of independent entrepreneur-owned Canadian firms. Foreign ownership of individual urban properties is also substantial in at least some Canadian cities, though no one really knows its full extent. The impact of the Foreign Investment Review Act was, as we've seen, to produce some restructuring of foreign-controlled developers, as with Trizec and Genstar. These companies may argue that they are no longer foreign-controlled, and FIRA may rule that Trizec and Genstar are Canadian-controlled, but foreign shareholders still exercise a major role in their ownership.

Government policies in Canada (and to some extent abroad) have been important in promoting this feature of the Canadian development industry. Foreign ownership of urban land has been permitted by provincial legislation, and many obvious and effective legislative measures used to limit and discourage foreign ownership of urban property in other countries are neglected in Canada. Foreign-controlled developers, for instance, are able to borrow Canadian investment capital from mortgage lenders in this country on exactly the same terms as Canadian borrowers, and most of course choose to use this form of financing. Other countries have required foreign property owners to bring all the capital they require for land development with them from abroad, meaning that their activities supplement the total supply of domestic investment capital.

Foreign ownership of Canadian urban property adds to the difficulty of regulating and controlling property investors in Canada, as tenants of foreign-owned buildings have often learned as they have attempted to bring pressure to bear on their landlords to deal with management questions. Foreign developers have speeded the process of corporate concentration in the industry, and have helped push urban land prices even higher. The most severe distortion caused by foreign ownership in the urban property sector, however, is its current and long-term impact on the Canadian balance of payments. Even now, foreign owners of urban property can collect operating profits annually on their investments, adding to the outflow of royalties, interest and profits from this country which have to be paid for with Canadian natural resources or other real exports of goods. In the long term, however, this outflow of rents and profits will increased by hundreds of millions of dollars, perhaps even in the low billions, as operating profits jump dramatically when mortgages on buildings are paid off.

The perpetual and growing burden on the Canadian balance of payments generated by foreign ownership of urban property could perhaps be justified if foreign capital had demonstrably added to the wealth of the country by providing badly needed housing or office space that we could not finance ourselves. This clearly has not happened. The Canadian-owned developers have been perfectly capable of supplying more than enough urban accommodation through the entire postwar period, as we have seen, and the supply of Canadian investment capital to finance this growth has been more than adequate. What makes the impact of foreign ownership of urban property insupportable is that the foreign developers have been able to buy and develop Canadian urban land using mostly Canadian investment funds. So Canada has permitted foreign investors to create a situation that places a permanent drain on our balance of payments *using mainly Canadian investment capital, and doing things Canadians could and would have done equally well.* It is difficult to imagine the combination of wilful bias in favour of any and all foreign ownership plus failure to analyse the real conditions in the development industry required in order to find a rationale for this particular policy of the federal government and of most provincial governments in Canada.

More of the same? When the developers talk about the future of Canadian cities and the prospects for their industry, they foresee the patterns which have emerged since 1945 extending indefinitely into the future. They consider that the role of suburban land assemblies will increase in the growth of cities; the scale of corporate suburb developments will grow; high-rise apartments will continue to be built; industrial parks will provide an even greater portion of total industrial space; downtown developments will become even larger and more inclusive by incorporating housing; and shopping centres will expand to embrace every type of public and cultural facility.

Bruce McLaughlin, for instance, has said that he has two unrealized ambitions he hopes to see achieved in his lifetime: "The first of these is the completion of a city free from the transportation, servicing, pollution and technological problems of older cities, and the second is the redevelopment of Canada for an eventual population of 100 million."[7]

Urban planners and politicians share much the same vision of the future, though their aspirations are expressed in terms of advancing the public interest through the further extension of the corporate city. Consider, however, this very succinct summary of the basic assumptions made by the planners who developed a new regional plan for Toronto. It spells out the overall economic and political context the planners assumed in setting out their detailed plans for the city's growth:

> The major considerations [for the future] are:
> — The national economy is expanding and becoming increasingly integrated.
> — Canada is increasingly involved in international commerce and finance.
> — Toronto's role as the primary financial and administrative centre for Canada, and Canadian international finance, is increasingly important.
> — Regional centres in other parts of Canada are simultaneously growing in importance.
> — The Toronto region remains the primary manufacturing area for the Canadian market.[8]

The planners' view of the future amounts to a continuation of the same pattern of economic development that has existed in Canada since 1945. Rephrasing their projection in less guarded and neutral language, it amounts to the continuing expansion of the role of the large national and multinational corporations in the Canadian economy, further integration of Canada into the continental U.S. economy, even greater dominance by Toronto over the rest of Canada, expansion of the dominance of the major regional cities over their regions, concentration of economic growth in major cities only, and continuation of a weak U.S.-controlled manufacturing sector concentrating what industrial jobs there are in southern Ontario. On the basis of this vision of the future, it is not hard to understand why the planners confidently project that the corporate city will continue to develop in much the same direction it has followed in the last three decades.

The consequences of the pattern of urban growth generated by the development industry, as we have seen in this chapter, pose many problems for Canadian cities and their residents. One of the major ways in which residents of Canadian cities are taking concrete steps to oppose this undesirable pattern of growth is by organizing and opposing the development industry and its projects. The developers have been involved in a struggle which is far from over about whose vision of the city and its possibilities will prevail. The outcome of this conflict is not yet certain, but it is far from clear that the future is going to be more of the same corporate city the developers have been building for the last three decades.

12

RIVAL URBAN FUTURES

The development industry's success in carrying out its projects in cities across the country and in obtaining the necessary support from government has been the force which has created an alternative to the industry. The developers have produced their own rival.

Canada's urban future is in no way settled. For each of the major development types pioneered and perfected by the developers, there are alternative ways of meeting the same basic accommodation needs. Though the development industry has brought with it new structures for urban government, there are now obvious alternative models of how our cities could be governed. Though the development industry has gained enormous political power in the past three decades, it is now being effectively opposed by well-organized anti-development groups at the municipal level.

The developer's rival for power is the urban citizen movement. In this chapter we look at how the citizen movement arose out of the developers' impact on cities, the breakdown in the consensus that the development industry's activities are in the interests of urban residents, what it is that people want to see happen to their cities, what alternatives have been generated to implement this new urban vision, how the question of the way our cities develop relates to the country's economic and political future, and what the developers' prospects seem to be.

Standing in the way of progress? In the postwar period while the federal government's overall strategy for economic development was being implemented and while the development industry was being brought into existence, few people had fundamental objections to these policies. The economy was delivering the goods; people were better off every year, and the signs of increasing prosperity were clear in most parts of the country. The developers too were delivering the goods: houses were going up, apartments were being built, and people were able to find adequate urban accommodation even if the price was often relatively high.

The first serious resistance encountered by the developers was from individuals who found themselves standing directly in the path of progress, and who were expected to suffer dislocation, disruption, even financial loss in the name of growth and development. Publicly funded urban renewal projects which involved the expropriation and demolition of large central-city residential areas were often the first to produce citizen opposition.* For a long time citizen groups protesting the harmful impact of development projects were portrayed as extremists, malcontents, or selfish minorities trying to make money at the expense of the public or the developer. They had relatively little success in winning their issues, and little impact on urban politics.[1]

In the decade between the mid-sixties and the mid-seventies, however, particularly in those cities where the pressures of urban growth were most intensely felt, political life changed dramatically.[2] More and more citizen groups organized in response to an ever-increasing number of disruptive development projects. Circumstances varied widely from city to city, and of course so did the local citizen movement. Everywhere, however, it had the same key characteristics: it cut across social class lines; it had no recognized national leaders but many able local ones; and its participants represented a wide range of basic political convictions but shared the view that at least some of the projects which were imposed on cities by city hall and the developers were undesirable and should be halted. The groups gained political skills and learned successful strategies to implement their resistance. They had some victories,

---

* The first such project in Canada, Regent Park North in 1949 had residents protesting that the plans called for the demolition of sound houses, forced homeowners to become tenants if they wanted to stay in their neighbourhood, and paid expropriated owners less than it would cost to replace their house with a similar house in a similar neighbourhood. (Albert Rose: *Regent Park* [Toronto: University of Toronto Press, 1958, pp. 84-5])

holding up and blocking some projects. As more people had direct personal experiences with urban growth they came to share the objections expressed by organized citizen groups.

The success of the citizen movement varied enormously. In some cities, notably Vancouver and Toronto in their 1972 elections, citizen reform candidates plus moderates who looked sympathetic to the movement dislodged the "old guard" majorities who were linked to the development industry. In others, like Edmonton, Calgary, Winnipeg, London and Ottawa, local politicians whose organizations and funds came from citizen groups led a newly invigorated opposition at city hall and in some cases went on to hold a majority of votes on local city councils.

The political successes of the citizen movement in 1972-76 combined with the slump in the development industry resulting from over-building in most cities led to a decline in the direct industry-citizen confrontations which had been common in the late 1960s and early 1970s. Some observers have suggested that the citizen movement has dissolved as an urban political force. Another interpretation is that, with the immediate pressures generated by the developers reduced, citizen movement activists and politicians have been occupied with creating an alternative to the development industry and its corporate city.

Breakdown of the corporate city consensus. Whatever view one takes of the present state of the urban citizen movement, it is clear that there has been a substantial shift in public opinion in most Canadian cities away from the consensus of earlier years which unquestioningly supported the developers and their projects. The critique of the developers and their projects which was first articulated by the citizen movement has become more widely shared than it was when it was first formulated. More and more people have come to the opinion that the development industry is not "delivering the goods." It is not producing the kind of city people want, and the prices which people have to pay for what the industry does produce are excessive and unaffordable.

People have become conscious of a whole range of problems created by the corporate city. The public facilities which have to be built to support the corporate city, the expressways, the new bridges, the subway systems, are too often disruptive of existing patterns of urban life. Worse, they are very expensive and add to the costs of city living through property taxes.

People are also concerned about larger planning issues raised by the developers' pattern of urban growth. There is, for instance, a nagging concern about the consumption of valuable farmland for urban development. Residents of rural areas and small towns who live in the shadow of large cities have faced and opposed spillover impact: gravel pits, garbage dumps, new hydro plants and high-tension lines. Urban residents see familiar landmarks being demolished to make way for progress, and often share the protesters' view that old buildings should be preserved and protected.

One indication of the shift in public opinion is provided by the electoral success of the politicians who have emerged from the citizen reform movement. Reform politicians have attracted many votes, and moderates who express some sympathy for the reform position have had even more success in many cities. The old-guard position of uncritical support for growth and the developers has lost much of its credibility in most of urban Canada.*

A rare instance of the depth of public scepticism about developers and their projects was given in an opinion survey of a randomly selected sample of business and professional people from middle and senior levels across Canada conducted in 1974 by the *Financial Times*, a weekly business newspaper. The *Financial Times*

---

* One impressionistic but quite striking indication of the shift in public opinion that has undoubtedly occurred on a wide range of urban issues since about 1965 in many cities comes from comparing newspaper clippings dealing with local controversies from earlier and later periods, and from the cities where this shift has occurred to the few (Halifax, for instance) where it has not. Newspapers generally have had a vested interest in supporting the development industry, but their writers and editors cannot build into their writing general assumptions which are not widely shared. In most cities, the tone has shifted away from uncritical boosterism for everything the developers do to a more sceptical tone which, while usually favouring the developers and their city hall supporters, is less enthusiastic. In cities that have experienced rapid urban growth, no newspaper would now talk of "spanking new buildings," the *Winnipeg Tribune*'s 1963 description of a series of life insurance office buildings in the city's Broadway area, or "luxury living" being offered by an ordinary high-rise apartment.

is editorially friendly to the development industry, and the people whom it surveyed are also from a segment of the population where support for the industry would be expected to be greater than elsewhere. The results of the survey were startling. For instance:

☐ On the question of whether developers should be able to operate without strict controls imposed by government, 9 percent of the sample said they should, 3 percent didn't know — 88 percent said they should not.

☐ On the question of whether there should be limits on high-rise development in Canadian cities, 72 percent said there should and 22 percent said there should not. 68 percent of the sample were in favour of height restrictions on high-rise buildings.

☐ On the issue of demolition of old buildings to make way for new developments, 29 percent said that stronger laws were not needed to protect old buildings, but 60 percent said stronger laws were required.

☐ Finally, asked a general question about whether they agreed with the objectives of environmental and citizen groups, 62 percent said they agreed with the groups' objectives; 27 percent disagreed; and 11 percent didn't know.[3]

What people want for their cities. As the consensus of support for the developers and the corporate city has been breaking down, people have been developing other views about how cities should grow. Often the sense that there should be some alternative to the corporate city and to continued rapid urban growth in the forms which the developers have established is expressed in rather vague and inarticulate ways; for instance, in the notion that unlimited growth is not necessarily desirable, or that growth should not be at the expense of existing city neighbourhoods.

There have been few attempts to determine the views of urban Canadians about how their cities should grow. Urban planners, whose work involves setting out what are supposed to be generally held objectives about a city's future, usually operate on the assumption that they already know what the public thinks on this matter. They are generally reluctant to get involved in the messy and politically difficult business of public debate on the basic issues involved in urban planning.

There has, however, been one exercise in planning for the future of one large Canadian city where the planners involved did attempt to probe public opinion. This was done by a group headed by senior planner Harry Lash working for the Greater Vancouver Regional District and developing a regional plan for Vancouver in the early 1970s. Though many criticisms can be made about the extent of the public consultation undertaken by the planners and their success in soliciting the views of all segments of the population, their effort came far closer than any similar exercise in giving urban residents an opportunity to formulate a comprehensive view of Vancouver's future. The planners were reasonably careful not to predetermine the outcome of this exercise in the way they structured it.*

Evidence that they did not predetermine the outcome of their attempts is given by Lash's frank account of what happened and how surprised the planners were by what people thought:

---

* Lash has since explained how this happened only after a full year's attempts by the planners to decide how they would go about their job of producing a regional plan. He writes, "We ended 1971 having thrashed around in the bush all year exploring many paths, without discovering a landmark by which to set our course." Then suddenly in early 1972 the planners did discover how to go about their task. The idea they settled on was remarkably simple, and it is the sort of thing that would be a revelation only to people who were used to working in isolation from the public:

> Quite suddenly, early in 1972, we did discover the signpost: find out from the public what livability means; abandon the idea that planners must know the goals first and define the problem; ask the people what they see as the issues, problems and opportunities of the Region.
>
> ... This was a hard-fought decision. There were furious debates within the Planning Department and among the politicians on our Committee. How, asked the dissenters, could we intelligently discuss with the public the questions they might ask if we did not anticipate the issues they might raise? We might look like fools... We weren't likely to hear anything worthwhile. (Harry Lash, *Planning in a Human Way:* Personal reflections on the regional planning experience in Greater Vancouver [Toronto: Macmillan, 1976] ms. p. 61-2)

... The meetings began. Thank God we had decided not to trot out our own little list of issues to open the meetings. Although we had guessed rightly about many of the specific issues the people raised, the mood of the Region and the overriding issues were quite beyond anything we had expected... The hard kernel of public opinion was, "A *resistance to further rapid growth*, a concern for *personal livability*, a desire to *participate in community decisions*, and a wish to see *action*."[4]

The planners were startled by their discovery that people were not unanimously and enthusiastically in favour of as much urban growth as the developers were prepared to undertake, and that they were concerned about the ultimate impact of regional growth. Says Lash:

> The growth issue was a stunner: it struck at the planner's long-accustomed view that his job is to plan for growth, and it showed up our ignorance of the real causes and components of growth. Could we indeed plan for limiting growth?[5]

The final planning document, titled *The Livable Region 1976/ 1986*, published by the regional planners, summarizes the major concerns which emerged from the public consultation process and set out the ideas that people had about how the city should grow.[6] This is a particularly interesting document, because it sets out for the first time a reasonably comprehensive view of the future of a city which is substantially different from the developers' corporate city.

The full list of major concerns is:

> □ Control the impact of growth. "People want to avoid the disruption to their lives which often accompanies rapid population growth — crowded schools, overloaded community services, and the complete lack of services, such as public transit, in some fast-growing areas."
> □ Protection of the environment. "People do not want pollution to ruin the clean air and clean water or shatter the quiet which has attracted so many of them here." People also want to preserve the natural assets of the region.
> □ Improved community services. "People want a broader

range of community services near their homes... in addition to the usual shopping centres..."

☐ Transportation. "People want to reduce the time and effort involved in travelling..."

☐ High housing costs and unsuitable housing forms. "People are worried about the high cost of housing. Many are worried about whether they can afford to buy any type of home, while others are concerned they may be forced to choose housing which does not have the qualities they want."

☐ Transit versus cars. "People are willing to rely less on their cars, but they want fast, frequent and convenient public transit..."

☐ Public involvement in government. "People want to participate in government decisions which affect their lives."

This list of widely felt issues and concerns is to a large extent a response to the impact of the developers and their projects on Vancouver. It is effectively a devastating critique of the corporate city and of the achievements of the development industry. It is clear that major changes would have to be made in the policy context in which the developers operate, in the practices of mortgage lenders who finance the industry, in the role of the development industry and in the urban forms which are being built in order to change the pattern of urban growth to respond to these concerns.*

A more complete account of the concerns urban residents have and their notion of how cities should develop would probably now include all the items identified in Vancouver plus some others. Protection of old buildings and conservation of energy resources (as well as land resources mentioned in the Vancouver summary)

---

* Harry Lash and his staff of planners identified these concerns, but they did not manage successfully the far more difficult task of formulating and then having accepted a regional plan which effectively expressed them. In fact the eventual Vancouver document proposes some planning strategies — like regional town centres — which are in direct conflict with these public concerns. And on the key question of high housing costs, the planners ended up making no recommendations at all that would have any substantial impact in bringing down house prices. There is more, the Vancouver planners must have realized, to producing a whole new range of urban development policies than knowing that this is what most people want.

are certainly widely shared concerns not included in the Vancouver list.

Alternatives to the corporate city. Public dissatisfaction with some aspects of the corporate city has been a major factor leading to the implementation by some city and provincial governments of policies and projects which offer alternatives to the developers and their standard development types. City residents, often fresh from the frustrating experience of opposing the developers and their projects, have in many instances taken the initiative in coming up with alternative projects through non-profit and co-operative development companies which provide more satisfactory urban acommodation than the standard developers' schemes. Just as the corporate city is tightly tied to an urban government structure where citizens have little influence and politicians are friendly to the development industry's interests, so these innovations and alternatives have been produced (indeed, have been required) by different local government structures and by politicians not so inclined towards the developers.

One major and rather traditional alternative to the development industry is the public land bank approach to producing serviced lots in the suburbs. Public land banks are generating house lots in many cities across Canada. The public land bankers have generally developed suburbs that are identical in their forms to those of the private developers.[7] The only difference — and of course it is a key one — is that public land bankers can control the price of suburban lots in a city, if they supply a substantial portion of the total lots being developed in that city.[8] If lots are sold for $2,000 to $3,000 plus services charged as a local improvement tax, the effect would be not just to bring down the price of new suburban houses to an affordable level but indirectly to keep all house prices in that city reasonably low. Following a low-price policy, a public land bank can eliminate the "economic surplus" profits made in suburban land development completely. Alternatively, a public land bank can charge the same high prices now charged by the developers. The only difference is that the profits would go 100 percent to the public instead of 0 percent or close to that, as at present.

Public land banks across Canada, from Halifax to Vancouver, demonstrate the viability of this alternative to the suburban land developers. If public land banks had the power to purchase the private land banks of the corporate developers from the developers at the historic book value cost of buying plus operating costs plus some reasonable mark-up — say 10 or 20 percent — new house prices in cities like Vancouver, Victoria, Edmonton, Calgary, Toronto and Ottawa could be brought down by $15,000 to $25,000 in a matter of months.

A second alternative to the present pattern of urban development arises from the policy of an agricultural land freeze, which rules out the use of all agricultural land for urban development and forces all new development onto already urbanized land or land unsuitable for agricultural uses. A measure of this kind by B.C.'s NDP government reduced the consumption of valuable farmland for urban purposes, and led public and private land developers to seek non-agricultural land.

A third alternative, also tried for the first time in B.C., is a public takeover of ownership of land development companies whose shares are publicly listed. Dunhill Development Corp., a B.C. developer, was acquired by the provincial government which purchased the firm's shares on the market from shareholders. Through this approach, public owners get ownership of the companies' income properties and land banks and acquire the management talents of the corporation's employees. Dunhill carried on with development projects after the takeover, but the aims of its activities were modified by the fact that its shareholder was no longer interested simply in maximizing profits.*

A fourth alternative, this time to high-rise residential redevelopment, has been developed by a municipally owned non-profit development corporation in Toronto. This developer, organized

---

* After the defeat of the Barrett government in 1975, the Socreds in B.C. eventually moved to sell Dunhill (under its new name, B.C. Housing Corporation) back to private industry.

It is intriguing to note that takeovers of the corporate developers by purchase of their shares at or somewhat above the present stock market price for these shares would be a much cheaper way of acquiring the properties of these firms than expropriation or purchase of these properties at their market (and perhaps even their book) value. This is because the so-called break-up share value of these companies is far higher than the market price of these shares.

from scratch by former CMHC policy analyst Michael Dennis, has worked with land whose value reflects high-rise densities and has built projects whose densities are similar to those achieved by high-rise apartments. The design of these projects is, however, substantially different from high-rise towers. Heights are lower overall; many more units have ground-related access; gardens and private outdoor spaces are more common; and old houses and other buildings on the site are renovated and incorporated in the projects rather than demolished. This alternative medium- to high-density residential redevelopment pattern has some problems of its own, but the accommodation it offers is generally far better suited to people's needs than standard high-rise buildings.

In looking for prototypes for alternative patterns of urban development, there is no lack of additional precedents and examples in contemporary Canadian cities. If government policies and subsidies were changed to favour other patterns of urban development, if mortgage lenders were required to lend to other kinds of developers and to conserve their funds for other uses, there would be no shortage of examples close at hand for alternatives to the corporate city.

Alternatives at city hall. One result of the urban citizen movement was that in many cities starting in the mid-1960s a new kind of city politician began to run for office. These citizen candidates had come into contact with city politics through the citizen movement. They shared the perspective of citizen groups and the critique of the corporate city developed from that experience.

Most Canadian cities have a history of a battle for power at city hall between politicians friendly to the local business community

---

Break-up value involves taking the market value of a developer's assets less outstanding debts, and dividing that surplus of assets over debts by the number of shares outstanding. Appraisal surplus profits of course add substantially to the break-up value of the public development corporations. The break-up value is what the company would receive if their properties were purchased or expropriated by government at their current market value. Buying up these companies' shares at their current market price would effectively give a city or a province ownership of those properties for only a fraction of that amount.

and those whose base of support is with working-class organizations and labour unions. Up through the 1930s and early 1940s, labour candidates were a real challenge to the dominance of business-oriented city politicians. During the postwar period, the rivalry between these groups persisted but the consensus which developed around the desirability of what the developers were doing resulted in many of the old labour politicians becoming effective supporters of the policies the developers wanted from city hall. The first real challenge to the "old guard" majorities that governed Canadian cities through the 1950s and early 1960s came from citizen candidates working out of the citizen reform movement. As an opposition minority, reform politicians have had considerable impact on the policies of city councils in many centres. The developers are no longer able to obtain exactly the policies and action they want from city governments when there is a conflict between the industry's interests and those of city residents.

More has changed in city politics than just the make-up of city councils. There have also been some major innovations in city government structure which have successfully given citizens a measure of real power and influence in decisions that affect them directly. This happened first in the area of city planning. In some cities residents' organizations in neighbourhoods for which a plan was being drawn up gained the right to play a major role in determining the content of that plan. Developers found that in order to get approval for their projects they had to negotiate with local citizen groups, rather than being able to count on a city council majority to approve a development project over local objections. Citizen organizations have also gained a certain measure of power in the planning of development projects, particularly when these are being done not by the corporate developers but by government bodies like CMHC or a municipal non-profit housing company, or by a non-profit or co-operative developer organized by citizens themselves.

The new style of municipal government involves a much broader range of political activity on the part of citizens than just working in election campaigns and voting. It does not so much lead to a complex reorganization of city government as to an effective change in the way decisions are arrived at so that citizens are involved in low-level policy-making and decision-making that have until now often been the preserve of bureaucrats. Instead of leading to a breakdown in city government, as the opponents of the citizen movement suggested, this alternative structure produces policies, plans, developments and city services that are successfully responsive to people's interests and needs.

Another vision of the urban future. The story of what has happened to Canada's cities since 1945 is an integral part of the overall postwar pattern of economic and political development. As we have noted, though the developers have gone from strength to strength, though the corporate city has clearly triumphed as the dominant form of urban growth, difficulties with this pattern of growth have been emerging and the resistance and opposition to it have been increasing.

Much the same thing is true about the overall pattern of economic development which Canada has followed since 1945. The major orthodoxies that have been the foundation of the country's history for the past three decades are now being questioned. It is evident to most people that Canada has run into serious economic and political difficulty. The postwar economic era, based on prosperity founded on the exploitation and export of our natural resources, has come to an end, and a new national consensus is required to deal with Canada's major structural problems in both the economic and political spheres. It seems likely that this will involve the development of a more independent Canadian economy with substantially greater strength in manufacturing industry. It will involve the creation of new jobs for unemployed workers, jobs that are less subject to the vagaries of international demand and the multinational corporations. This new strategy for the country's economic future will have to create a more even pattern of economic growth and prosperity across Canada, instead of concentrating growth in a few cities and in southern Ontario.

These objectives could be achieved by a new industrial development strategy for Canada which led to the creation of a major secondary manufacturing capacity in the Canadian economy, well distributed across the country. In view of the experience of the last three decades, it seems unreasonable to rely on the multinational corporations to generate a more independent and self-reliant Canadian economy. An alternative to this would be the creation of conditions in which Canadian entrepreneurs would find opportunities opened up in centres across the country for the development of Canadian industry, parallel in a way to the federal policies which created opportunities for land development entrepreneurs after 1945. Another option would be the strategy employed by the Canadian government during the Second World War, when the urgent need for new industries led to the formation of Crown corporations and an astonishing display of aggressive public enterprise.

Whatever the new strategy is for the Canadian economy, it is clear that settling the question of the development industry's future and determining the path which Canada's cities are going to take is a key element in this strategy. To achieve a pattern of economic development which stressed the equalization of growth, wealth and jobs among all regions of Canada would require quite a different pattern of urban development than the developers and urban planners now foresee. Urban growth would have to be distributed over a far wider range of medium and smaller cities, instead of being concentrated in a few large ones. The investment capital used by urban growth would have to be minimized, so that additional resources were available to finance industrial development. The pace of new construction would have to be adjusted to actual requirements, so that vast amounts of investment capital and resources are not consumed in putting up buildings for which there is no immediate need or demand. Foreign ownership of urban property would have to be severely restricted, because of the long-term and damaging implications which the resulting outflows of profits and rents have on the Canadian balance of payments.

A key issue in overall economic development policy is the price of urban land and housing, and the disposition of the profits which are earned from urban land. Lower urban land prices would greatly help to minimize the demands of the development sector for investment capital, and indeed reductions in the supply of investment capital available for mortgage purposes would lead to a decline in urban property values. The size of the profits earned from urban land development every year, and the proportion of those profits going to government, is also a major policy question given the huge amounts of money involved.

The alternative to the developers' view of how Canada's cities should grow which has been emerging from the urban citizen movement coincides very closely to the urban policy implications of a new Canadian industrial development strategy. The citizen movement is in general sceptical about the advantages of substantial further urban growth, particularly in the cities that have been growing rapidly. It is hostile to the over-building generated by the developers, and critical of the excessive use of resources involved in the corporate city pattern of development. Citizen groups have opposed foreign ownership of urban land, partly because it adds to the pace of development and partly because foreign developers are far less accessible to the political pressure citizen groups can mount. There is a continuing critique of the high profits earned by the developers from urban land development, and the high prices they charge.

The citizen movement has the potential to generate tremendous political pressure for changes in urban policy in directions that would support a new industrial development strategy. The only obstacle in the way of this arises from the fact that until now citizen groups have responded to the developers and their projects on an *ad hoc* basis, arising from their experience with the immediate consequences of these projects. The citizen movement has not always seen the connections and interrelationships between the various elements of the corporate city. There can be no piecemeal alternative to the developers and the corporate city; as we have seen, all parts interlock both in their function and in their financing. A more complete appreciation of how the corporate city works, however, is certain to lead the citizen movement to decide that it must opt for a completely different structure for urban development in order to achieve the kind of city it envisages.

Other interest groups also have a stake in finding a satisfactory alternative to the corporate city. Doing so is essential in the implementation of a new approach to economic and industrial development in Canada. A wide range of established interest groups, from the Canadian Federation of Independent Businessmen to labour unions concerned about the need to protect and increase the number of jobs, professionals and managers who would like to see the manufacturing sector of the economy expanded, and regional economic elites who have seen their areas downgraded in favour of central Canada all share an interest in a new Canadian industrial strategy. They too have a stake in replacing the developers' vision of Canada's urban future.

Urban land and natural resources policy. The development industry and the corporate city were created out of two ideas: first, that urban land and buildings are private property, and should be used, owned and developed by the private sector; and second, that corporate business is preferable to small business or public enterprise.

With hindsight, it is easy to see that urban land has always been and should have been recognized as more than private property, and as one of Canada's natural resources. It is of course a permanent natural resource, like the rivers that have been harnessed for hydro-electric development, not a non-renewable resource like oil or nickel ore. Though the supply of all land is fixed, the supply of urban land can and has been vastly increased, though only at the expense of reducing the supply of rural farmland.

As we have seen, government policy decisions about the use and exploitation of urban land have had far-reaching implications for social, political and economic life in Canada. One major issue of natural resources policy is the timing and the pace of development, and a consideration in this is of course the capital requirements of development. A second major issue has to do with the distribution of the "economic surplus" or "economic rent" or "monopoly profit" which is earned in the exploitation of natural resources. This is the profit over and above the normal profits earned in business.

Neither of these issues was explicitly faced in developing the urban land policy which has been followed in postwar Canada. Implicitly, however, both issues have of course been resolved. As we have already seen, the pace of the development of urban land has been rapid and accelerating and has absorbed huge amounts of investment capital directly and indirectly. The "economic surplus" generated in the use of urban land has been substantially increased by the development techniques of the developers, and $1 billion a year of it is now flowing annually to the development industry and is subject to a low effective rate of taxation. In other natural resource fields, such as oil, provincial and federal governments have fought enormous battles in the last few years over the distribution of the spoils of taxation of this economic surplus, and the notion that these profits should be subject to special taxation is generally accepted.

The rationale for the need for a fundamentally different approach to urban land in Canada might well start from the idea that urban land is a natural resource, and all the usual issues of natural resource development policy should be addressed in connection with urban land. It is clear, for instance, that the pace of development of urban land could and should be moderated in order to reduce the investment capital requirements of this sector to free up funds for more productive use in other areas of the economy.

It is also clear that the high price of urban land, and particularly of suburban house lots, which gives rise to very sizeable economic surplus profits in the urban land field is inappropriate for two reasons. First, these high prices are transmitted through the urban housing market and affect all urban property prices. High prices increase directly the demand for investment capital to finance new housing and indirectly add even more to investment capital demand because of the need for mortgage funds to finance the new high paper values of existing houses and other forms of urban property. Lower prices would reduce the need for investment capital in this sector, and free it up for more productive uses. Second, lower prices for new house lots would have the effect of improving the real standard of living of urban Canadians by making housing more affordable. This would also reduce substantially the cost to governments of the expensive housing subsidy programs which are attempting to bridge the gap between people's incomes and excessive house prices and rents. These subsidies now cost Ottawa and the provinces of hundreds of millions of dollars annually.

Even with policies which reduce the price of suburban house lots and moderate urban land values generally, some economic surplus will be earned from urban land. It would seem reasonable to tax these profits at a rate greater than the ordinary rate for corporate profits of about 50 percent but lower than a 100 percent rate which would discourage any transactions on the market in the hope of the tax's being later removed.

Once government began to capture a reasonable portion of the profits earned from urban land, it might make sense to follow the example of the Alberta and Saskatchewan governments, and place these revenues in a special heritage fund. They could then be devoted to capital investment projects designed to make the economy more productive.

The key elements in a new approach to urban land policy coordinated with an overall strategy to strengthen the Canadian economy and to even out the pattern of growth and wealth by ensuring that the bulk of new industrial development was not concentrated in a single region would be these:

☐ Encouragement of new industrial development in all regions of the country and in small and medium-sized centres to manufacture goods now imported into Canada, thus evening out the pattern of economic growth regionally and between larger and smaller cities by sharply reducing the focus of new job creation in the largest cities.

☐ New regulations on the lending of financial institutions, sharply reducing the flow of new investment capital into urban land and redirecting it to finance needed industrial development.

☐ Major reductions in the price of new suburban house lots so that these are sold at or near the cost of production, making new houses more affordable and reducing the amount of mortgage lending needed to support house construction and housing resales.

☐ New tax measures to capture a substantial share of the "economic surplus" profit generated by urban land, and use of this tax revenue for a heritage fund to assist in the long-term development of the country.

☐ Substantial changes in the pattern of urban development, to make more efficient use of existing urban land and to minimize the costs and capital requirements of growth.

☐ Encouragement of new urban forms in place of those built by the corporate developers, to produce a more efficient and livable city and to provide housing that is better suited to people's interests and needs.

☐ A reversal of the process of concentration of political power by larger municipal governments, and development of new urban decision-making structures that give people a real say in the government of their city and their neighbourhood.

☐ Takeovers by public bodies of some of the large corporate

developers, to ensure that their appraisal surplus profits are never realized and to give public bodies access to the managerial and entrepreneurial skills of the development corporations.

□ Gradual replacement of the corporate developers as the major source of new rental space by a range of non-profit, co-op and public developers that are structured to respond to users' needs and interests instead of profit maximization.

Taken together, and listed in such an abbreviated way, these changes may sound radical and far-reaching. They are, however, far less radical and far-reaching than the changes which have been made in the course of the last three decades to permit the developers to dominate the process of urban growth.

The developers' uncertain future. It is clear that such an alternative approach to urban land policy in Canada would change the prospects for Canada's cities and would directly affect every urban resident. It would also have a substantial effect on the development industry. The industry's profit potential would be reduced, its prospects of realizing its appraisal surplus profits substantially eliminated, and its opportunities for future activity would be concentrated in construction rather than land development itself. As long as they retained ownership of their income properties, the developers would continue to function as real estate investment companies. Their declared after-tax profits from their income property operations would not change from current levels, though their actual operating profits would be reduced if they were required to pay tax even at the standard corporate tax rate.

The kind of policy measures which might be implemented as part of a new economic development strategy for Canada would substantially reduce the future profits of developers. This might be expected to have a very dramatic impact on the stock market prices of the shares of the public real estate corporations, since these prices are directly tied to the market's expectations of future profits of these companies. This, however, would not happen for a simple, and quite astonishing reason: the stock market and the financial community *already expect* that steps along these lines will be taken by government. The stock market expects that urban land values will fall, that the appraisal surplus profits which the developers appear to have earned will never in fact be realized. The result of these expectations is that the shares of the large developers already sell for prices substantially below the value of the developers' interest in the property they own, at prices much closer to the historic book value of those assets.

The fact that real estate corporations' shares sell for relatively low prices on the stock market is one which is often noted in the business press by stock analysts and developers themselves. Usually this fact is recorded as a complaint, but no explanation is offered for it. If there is some effort to explain it, it is put in innocuous terms; for instance, that the market has yet to realize the enormous profit potential of the developers. Given the general reluctance of the industry and of the financial community to discuss this fact in public, it is particularly significant that the matter has been addressed by financial analyst Ira Gluskin in his analysis of Cadillac Fairview for the Royal Commission on Corporate Concentration. Gluskin's views are not in the main text of his report, but rather tucked away in an obscurely titled appendix:

□ The market notes the collapse in real estate and real estate values in the United Kingdom and the United States and believes that Canada is to undergo a similar experience in the near future.

□   The market is very concerned about overbuilding in all of the principal areas of real estate; i.e., office buildings, hotels, shopping centres and industrial.

□   ... The market believes that residential land values are overstated. They believe that house prices are beyond the earning power of most consumers. Thus it is felt that a collapse in both housing and land is imminent.[9]

It is, in a way, a remarkable situation. The business community has seen the developers take hold of an opportunity created by the federal government and supported by the financial institutions to build a new industry in thirty short years. The developers did so by transforming the way that Canadian cities grow, and by finding ways of making unimagined profits out of urban development land. Though the developers encountered political opposition on the way, they seemed to go from success to success. Yet, watching them do it, the financial community has come to a conclusion similar to that of ordinary city residents: it has decided that the industry cannot sustain its rate of growth and success. Its fortunes are expected to collapse, and the financial community has already taken that collapse into account through stock market prices on real estate shares. No one is sure what the future of the developer is, or how Canada's cities will grow. But almost everybody agrees that the time for drastic change is at hand.

13

TOO CANADIAN
A SUCCESS STORY

The story of the land developers contradicts two widely held beliefs about Canada and Canadians. We are often said to live in a country where very few people are willing to gamble, to take risks, to try out new ideas and to pursue these ideas until they succeed. We lack native entrepreneurs. Yet, when the federal government took the lead in creating opportunities for entrepreneurs in house-building and apartment development and related areas, literally hundreds of people across the country took them up. There has been no shortage of entrepreneurs in land development in Canada.

We are also said to live in a country that suffers from a serious and long-standing shortage of investment capital. For Canada to grow and develop, it is thought that we have to attract not just foreign entrepreneurs to undertake risky projects but also foreign investors with the necessary capital. Yet in the last three decades, starting from a base of a mere $600 million in real estate mortgages of all kinds, Canadian financial institutions have been able to mobilize a total of $75 billion in Canadian investment funds to finance the development of real estate, mainly urban real estate, in this country. That's about $3,000 to every person in the country. Fully $50 billion of that total was generated in the first seven years of the 1970s alone, when most people thought we had to borrow abroad to finance projects like the $16 billion James Bay Hydro-electric project or the $10 billion Alcan pipeline from Alaska to the U.S.

As far as the developers are concerned, they have done everything that could be expected of them. There is no question that they set out to do something useful for the country. Of course they hoped to make lots of money in the process, though they have

258

exceeded even their own expectations. But in the 1940s, 1950s and the early 1960s, there was no argument that what the developers wanted to do was valuable and useful to people. Building new houses, providing apartment buildings to rent, putting up office space for burgeoning businesses and governments, providing shopping facilities: all of this was needed, sometimes desperately needed, by Canada's expanding economy.

But the industry's story is not quite as simple as that. It is now clear that, without noticing it at the time, the industry went beyond the point at which its activities were unquestionably in the public interest. Just where that point is, and when it was passed in different development activities in different cities, would be very difficult to define. My own view is that in some fields it came very early. In the shopping centre business, for instance, I think it happened the moment that shopping centre landlords began to demand percentage rents from their tenants instead of ordinary rents based on the amount of space occupied. In the suburban land development business, however, I think it occurred at the imperceptible moment when the number of land developers with small holdings in a local land market declined to the point where suddenly a handful of developers had effective market control and were operating not like small competitive firms in a large marketplace but like oligopolists.

It would, however, be very misleading to hold the developers solely responsible for the direction their industry has taken, and for the excess that has followed success. The structure of the industry, as we've seen, was created not by the developers but by governments operating in partnership with the financial institutions. Moreover the over-development of this sector of the economy has clearly been the result of activities by these two outside partners. The financial institutions have happily invested billions of dollars in mortgage financing, particularly since 1970. They have never stopped to consider the overall implications of this practice and the long-term effect on the Canadian economy of forcing other borrowers to look for investment funds outside the country or abandon their projects. Nor has Ottawa's responsibility for the structure and health of the Canadian economy led it to recognize the harm done by over-investment and high prices in the land development and urban real estate sector.

With hindsight it is obvious that Ottawa could have followed a different path in its policies towards the land development industry. Recognizing that the combination of real opportunities for entrepreneurial activity and readily available investment capital had been a success in the land development industry, Ottawa might have decided to pursue this same approach in other sectors of the economy where independent Canadian business enterprise is required. It could simultaneously have dampened down the expansion of the urban land development industry beginning in the early 1960s, avoiding the excesses of the later 1960s and 1970s. This would have freed up a substantial supply of Canadian investment capital for alternative uses, and encouraged Canadian entrepreneurs to look not to land development but to other fields of activity.

The most obvious sector of the Canadian economy which requires strengthening is manufacturing. With imports of manufactured goods running at an annual level of $11 billion over exports, there is both an urgent need and an obvious opportunity to encourage new manufacturing industries to produce goods to replace these imports.[1] Expansion of the manufacturing sector would have the crucial additional benefit of producing new, stable, reasonably well-paid jobs in Canada.

There is an intriguing aspect to this alternative government strategy. If opportunities had begun to decline in the land development business in the period from 1960 to 1965, the developer entrepreneurs would have looked around for other profitable activities. If Ottawa had simultaneously been taking aggressive steps to encourage entrepreneurs in the manufacturing sector, the brightest and the toughest of the land developers would have been quick to take advantage of these new openings. Many developers have, in fact, explored other opportunities. When Robert Keenan began to run out of things to do in land development in Thunder Bay, he became involved in two new businesses only vaguely related to his previous activities: the retail gasoline field, with a chain of gas bars, and the building supply retailing business. Had there been attractive opportunities in manufacturing industry in Thunder Bay, Keenan would have been likely to take them up. Robert Campeau already has a side interest in the manufacture of a unique Canadian-designed dishwasher which is more economical and energy-efficient than larger dishwashers. It is sometimes used in restaurants and bars for washing glasses. Government policies promoting the growth of independent Canadian manufacturing industries could easily have encouraged Campeau to go much further into this and related kinds of business.

All this rather fanciful speculation is intended to underline two related facts: first, the developers had the talent and interest to involve themselves in other fields; second, the developers got into the business they're in and stayed there as a result of explicit government policies combined with support for those policies from the financial institutions.

It is Edmonton's Charles Allard who clinches this argument. Allard has followed the standard pattern of successful developers: he put together a large suburban land assembly, accumulated a portfolio of rental apartments, offices, shopping centres and other income properties. Unlike his colleagues, however, Allard has also got into a whole range of financial and commercial activities not closely related to land development, like car dealerships, life insurance, a trust company and so on. When opportunities came along for major industrial development in Alberta, with the usual support of government policies and subsidies, Allard was quick to respond. He has developed a $50 million petrochemical complex in Medicine Hat in partnership with Alberta Gas Trunk Line Co. Ltd. It has been, of course, the Alberta government that has worked out the industrial development strategy that makes this an attractive entrepreneurial opportunity. There is also a very strong argument that the kind of enterprise Allard has undertaken would be far better mounted by entrepreneurs working in the public sector instead of in the private sector. Nevertheless the example stands: Allard was encouraged to get involved in large-scale industrial development because he received aggressive government support.

Since the recent collapse of the market for most kinds of new development projects in most cities, many Canadian developers have decided to expand their development activities into the United States. The scale and significance of the Canadian developers' move into the U.S. is not yet clear. One worrisome possibility is that large amounts of Canadian investment capital might be exported by Canadian banks and other financial institutions to the U.S. to finance the projects of Canadian developers there. This would be in marked contrast to the operations of foreign-controlled developers in Canada, who were able to obtain the bulk of the investment capital they needed from Canadian sources. It would of course be the height of economic folly for Canadian investment capital to be exported to the U.S. to finance the expansion of the real estate sector there instead of being directed into those sectors in Canada where it is badly needed.*

The other recent response of the developers to stagnation in their industry has been to use the cash that in better times would go to new development projects to buy up shares in their companies owned by outside shareholders. Generally the buy-back offers are for a price that is higher than the shares are currently selling for on the stock market, but lower than the company originally sold them for. It is an understandable move for the developers to make because it increases their personal holdings in their own companies at what may well be bargain prices, but it is a completely unproductive use of capital.

In many ways, the story of the development industry is a very Canadian one. It involves the familiar pattern of partnership be-

---

* Industry estimates are that projects totalling $2 billion were undertaken in the U.S. in 1978 by Canadian developers. *Financial Times* writer Susan Goldenberg reported that most of the financing for these projects was by Canadian chartered banks, both from their U.S. subsidiaries and from their Canadian head offices:

> The successful foray of most Canadian developers into the U.S. is being aided both by money from Canadian banks' head offices or U.S. branches and by Canadian managerial skills. "Because the Canadian banks know us well, we get quick response to our credit requirements," says Cadillac Fairview's A. E. Diamond.

The developers' explanations of this diversification are tailored for Canadian consumption. They sometimes claim higher rates of profit for their U.S. ventures, but generally the stress is on the absence of red tape and government restriction. Understandably, industry spokesmen are not hasty about pointing out that profit levels are usually lower in the U.S. and the attractive thing about the American market was that it offered opportunities for new projects whereas most Canadian cities were overbuilt and offered insufficient opportunities to use up the developers' available cash. (*Financial Times* 3 July 1978)

tween the federal government and the Canadian banks and financial institutions to create a pattern of economic development that is comfortable and convenient for them, and which encourages Canadian business in the finance-real estate-commercial sector of the economy. As some historians have recently pointed out, the banks and financial institutions are and always have been the major centre of economic power in Canada. With their command over much of the country's savings and their ability to mobilize investment capital, the financial institutions have the power to direct the pattern of growth of the Canadian economy and they have not hesitated to use it. Their policy always has been that Canadian business should be supported mainly in the fields of commerce, finance and real estate. Other sectors, particularly resources development and manufacturing, are left to foreign investors and foreign initiative, and there it is foreign owners and not independent Canadian entrepreneurs whom the Canadian financial establishment supports. There is nothing unusual about the enormous assistance the Royal Bank has provided to Genstar, since Genstar started out as a foreign-controlled resources corporation and in many ways has remained that.[2]

Corporate businessmen, some (as we've seen) in successive cabinets in Ottawa, others in the boardrooms of Canadian financial institutions, decided after 1945 that they would indeed support and promote the land development industry. This suited their own business interests and their overall strategy for Canadian economic development. Until recently these policies were accepted by most people. Now, however, it is clear that the industry the developers have built on the basis of this support can no longer be sustained. On the one hand, its success has given it a voracious appetite for both government subsidies and valuable Canadian investment capital, and has convinced the investment community that the urban land development boom will soon turn into a bust. On the other hand, the industry's impact on Canadian cities has created a new political force in the urban citizen movement that poses a political threat to the industry's monopoly on urban growth patterns. The eventual collapse of the industry is more likely to come, I think, from economic rather than political pressures. Either way, it will illustrate how the very policies which supported the development industry are also responsible for its demise, as people realize that its consumption of both land and capital have been to the detriment of Canada as a whole.

The land development industry has so far been an amazing and impressive success story. It demonstrates the potential for vigorous business enterprise in this country, proving that reserves of entrepreneurial ability and investment capital exist and can be mobilized in Canada. It establishes what can be done when government policy encourages the development of the kinds of productive enterprise that are needed to set Canada on a path to balanced industrial growth and long-term prosperity. Yet at the same time the development industry itself is now a threat to the prosperity and wealth of the country. It has got out of hand. Its success cannot — and should not — last.

APPENDICES

CANADA'S MAJOR PUBLIC REAL ESTATE

Company (All figures $000,000)	Assets	Share-holders' equity	Declared pre-tax profit	Return on equity[1]
Abacus Cities	244	27	18	66%
Allarco Developments	134	33	4.7	14%
Alliance Building	75	6	(4.2)	-70%
Bramalea	347	34	13.1	38%
Cadillac Fairview (1978)	1,405	168	41.1	24%
Campeau Corp.	625	34	3.6	10%
Carma Developers	179	48	21.3	44%
Consolidated Building	109	20	6.5	32%
Costain Ltd.	148	22	11.9	54%
Daon Development	464	34	21.5	63%
Genstar[3]	1,249	368	121	33%
Halifax Developments	48	9	.5	5%
Headway Corp.	115	14	4.8	34%
Markborough Properties	205	50	6.9	14%
S. B. McLaughlin	253	36	.9	2%
Melcor Developments	68	21	7.5	36%
Nu-West Development	482	75	25.8	34%
Oxford Development (1978)	852	77	8.5	11%
Revenue Properties	114	21	(4.6)	-22%
Sifton Properties	113	9	5.6	62%
Trizec	931	178	10.5	6%
Y&R	95	26	3.7	14%
Totals	8,880	1,310	328.6	25%
20 company totals	6,226	774	166.5	21%
Cadillac Fairview/ Genstar	2,654	536	162.1	30%

CORPORATIONS: PROFITS AND TAXES, 1977

Tax paid	Effective tax rate	Deferred tax[2]	Total deferred tax	Deferred tax as % of shareholder equity
—	0%	8.9	16	59%
—	0%	2.1	8.6	26%
—	—	(3.2)	3.7	61%
.8	6%	5.8	26.8	79%
1.0	2%	17.6	94.4	56%
(.8)	22%	(1.8)	33.6	99%
4.4	21%	5.6	14.0	66%
.01	.1%	3.2	10.7	165%
2.2	18%	3.6	13.5	61%
—	0%	11.0	34.2	100%
45.7	37%	10.9	88.6	24%
—	0%	.2	.9	10%
.007	0%	2.1	6.7	48%
3.7	54%	(.6)	15.3	31%
(.5)	-55%	(.8)	6.9	19%
2.4	32%	1.1	3.6	17%
5.3	20%	8.1	22.1	29%
—	0%	4.3	37.1	48%
(1.6)	-34%	—	3.6	17%
1.3	23%	1.3	10.8	120%
.1	1%	5.6	39.8	22%
—	0%	1.8	10.9	42%
64	19%	87	502	38%
17	10%	58	319	41%
46.7	29%	28.5	183	34%

Sources: Company annual reports for fiscal year 1977 except where noted; *The Real Estate Development Annual 1978.*

Notes to table

1. This is calculated using pre-tax declared profits and computing them as a percentage of shareholders' equity. The method used in chapter 3 is somewhat different; there, consistent with the argument that deferred taxes are a fictitious deduction and should in fact be included in operating profit, the figures for rate of return in terms of operating profit as a percentage of shareholders' equity are computed using as shareholders' equity the total of the amount reported by the companies in their annual reports plus the total deferred taxes to date.
2. In some cases, companies do not in their published financial statements distinguish clearly between the paid and deferred portions of their corporate tax. In those cases, an estimate of the total tax deferred has been made on the basis of other information in financial statements.
3. Genstar is exceptional among this group in terms of the substantial share of its revenues and assets which comes from activities other than land development. This accounts for most of the differences between the financial results reported by Genstar compared to those reported by the other companies.

EYEWITNESS TO A DEAL

In Saskatoon in 1962, the CNR entered into negotiations with city officials and politicians over a scheme to vacate the railway's downtown lands and move their operations to the outskirts. Minutes were kept of the meetings between city and railway representatives, and of the private sessions where city negotiators discussed their strategy and tactics. The minutes sometimes summarize what was said, but on key matters they are verbatim accounts. They offer a fascinating glimpse of the way negotiations of this kind work, and demonstrate how the developers determine the rules of the game accepted by politicians and planners, resulting in the outcome described in chapter 9.[1]

The main characters involved were, for the City of Saskatoon, Mayor Sid Buckwold, chief city commissioner McAskill, and two city aldermen. The CNR's main negotiator was Bob Park, assistant to the vice-president and chairman of the CNR's negotiating committee for Saskatoon.

The negotiations began with the CNR saying that they were interested in working jointly with the city on a scheme to "relocate" the railway station and yards from Saskatoon's downtown to the suburbs. On the face of it, this was the CNR's main interest. For the first two meetings, virtually the only subjects discussed were the practical and technical details of how such an arrangement would be accomplished. It was not until the third meeting that the CNR's negotiators got down to brass tacks. They read a letter which stated that the cost to the CNR of this relocation would be $6.8 million. The replacement facilities would, however, be more modern so CN would be somewhat better off with the new yards than the old ones. Then CN presented its pitch: the railway wanted a subsidy of $3.9 million from the City of Saskatoon towards its relocation costs.

The city's negotiators had never heard a figure from CN before, and they were shocked that the railway would be asking for a $3.9 million subsidy to move their yards. The mayor, Sid Buckwold, repeated CN's proposal, almost as if he was ensuring that he'd heard correctly.

Saskatoon's chief commissioner McAskill immediately put his finger on the factor the CNR had left out of their calculations. Relocating their railway yards would leave them with a thirty-acre vacant site adjoining downtown Saskatoon ready for redevelopment. CN had calculated the cost side only of the relocation, and had left out the profit to be made out of developing their downtown land. "What," the commissioner asked immediately, "is the value of the land?"[2]

"We have no appraisal on that," was the CNR's astonishing reply.

Assuming that the downtown thirty acres would be worth $4 million, the commissioner went on immediately, the railway could relocate their yards at no net cost to themselves without any subsidy. But that wasn't what the CNR was after; they wanted the city to cover the cost of relocation, and they wanted the entire profit on their downtown land, which they intended to rent to a developer.

The mayor was nonplussed. "It has always been my early understanding from Mr. Gondor that the CNR would not want to be out of pocket on the deal. I don't think it ever entered our minds that the city would be asked to underwrite a very expensive move and leave the CNR to capitalize on land rights."[3] But Mayor Buckwold chose not to stick to this position. Instead he said, "From now on we will have to try and reconcile our positions." A moment later, he asked if the CNR would give the city time to pay the requested subsidy.

"We would certainly entertain such a request," said Bob Park, chairman of the CNR's development committee, probably noting that the mayor was thinking of how the city could come up with the cash instead of continuing to object to the idea that it should.[4]

Commissioner McAskill did not give up nearly so easily. "I

think the next important thing from our point of view is what is taken out for roads and what is the actual value of the land."[5] But the CNR wasn't going to sell the land; it was going to lease it to a developer for ninety-nine years. And when the mayor came back again to the $3.9 subsidy request, Bob Park lost no time in sliding downwards a bit. "We realized we had to start at some talking figure," he said.[6]

A city alderman came back to the question of the future of the downtown land. He wanted to know how much the CNR would want if the city bought the land. Asked by the mayor if they'd given consideration to that kind of deal, the CNR's Bob Park said they had not. And he added that even though the railway didn't expect to make much money in the short term, over the long run they were hoping to share with the developer the profit from re-use of the land.

Asked for a breakdown of the $3.9 million figure, the CNR came up with an analysis which the city's negotiators reviewed on their own a week later. They did not challenge any of CN's estimated moving costs, but they noted that the railway was valuing six acres of downtown land it was going to sell to the city for roads at $425,000 and an old railway bridge the city was going to take over at $1 million, so they knocked those items down and came up with a revised cost to CN of $2,367,000. They went on immediately to decide that, yes, Saskatoon should offer the CNR a subsidy of $2,367,000 towards relocating their facilities and redeveloping their downtown land. The question of the CNR's remaining downtown land that wouldn't be used for roads didn't even come up in the city's meeting, according to the minutes.

The next day the two groups got together and the CN officials made a long and complicated speech which boiled down to saying they would take $3,020,000. The statement was long on technical details, and short on the matter of the downtown land. On that point, the city was told that if it wanted to it could submit a developer proposal to the CNR in competition with private developers.

Hearing the railway's statement, Mayor Buckwold was caught: he wanted to be co-operative, but he saw the political problem of giving the CNR a subsidy to help them relocate to the suburbs without the city's getting anything in return for its money. Said Buckwold:

> I want to make it quite clear. We are trying to do the best we can. We have to come up with a figure we think the city can afford. I want to emphasize that you have to look at this from our point of view. We are spending $2.4 million for assets that are largely intangible. We have to come up with a figure which we think is realistic. We have to sell it to our council and the people of Saskatoon.[7]

Then the city officials made their offer: $2.4 million, paid over five years. The two parties separated to discuss the offer, and while the city officials were on their own they decided for no recorded reason to up their offer from $2.4 million to $2.6 million.

At this point the CN team knew they'd won. Their strategy of presenting the proposal as "rail relocation," not "redevelopment of downtown rail yards" had succeeded in focussing the city officials on the question of the railway's relocation costs. The potential profits arising from redevelopment had come up, but the city wasn't pressing the point. Evidently they had accepted CN's argument that both the railway and the city would benefit from downtown redevelopment: the railway from their land rentals and profits, the city from the increased assessment. CN's representatives lost no time in coming to terms. When the city said it would go from $2.4 million to $2.6 million, the CN group retired briefly and returned to accept the offer before anyone again brought up the question of the value of the vacated lands.

CN's Bob Park took the deal, though he was careful to leave himself an out: "We are prepared to recommend your offer to our management and hope that they will accept."[8]

As these negotiations turned out, the developer's success in getting the city to subsidize the Midtown Centre project rested on the city accepting the role for itself that the developer defined. The CN looked for some element in their scheme for which they could plausibly request city assistance, and came up with their moving costs. In other projects, other developers talk about land assembly or parking garages. The developer says, "We will develop this project if you give us a subsidy." Then he names the price.

The response of the Saskatoon negotiators showed that, in spite of CN's careful strategy to distract them from thinking about the value of the vacant downtown yard land, they instantly realized the real nature of the proposition they were faced with.

What Saskatoon's team didn't know was what kind of a bluff CN was mounting. What they needed to know was what CN certainly knew: the real value of those vacated lands, the prospects for redevelopment, and the profits that the redevelopment would generate. Armed with that information, they would have known whether the project required any city subsidy at all. And they could have explored seriously the alternative that came up in the key session for a moment, public development of the site by the city.

These negotiations followed the standard rules and procedures followed by developers and city officials across the country. In this case, it appears that the city subsidy was a windfall gain to CN. The sale of two acres of the downtown land for use by the city as an auditorium site at $125,000 an acre indicates a value of about $3.75 million for the site. This is about the same as the amount CN claimed as its net cost of moving its facilities. If so, CN would have covered its costs through the redevelopment use of its lands. That makes the city subsidy pure profit to CN, a windfall gain which was their reward for following the rules of the downtown land redevelopment game.

NOTES

Preface

1. There is no satisfactory up-to-date bibliography of the rapidly growing literature on Canadian cities and the land development industry. For a selected list of the most interesting and important books published before 1976 which come to grips with Canadian cities on their own terms rather than trying to filter the data through the theories of American social science, see Kent Gerecke's annotated bibliography in James Lorimer and Evelyn Ross eds., *The City Book* (Toronto: James Lorimer, 1976), pp. 220-2.
2. John Whitelaw began pursuing the two subjects of organized crime and land development in 1978 in an intriguing newsletter, "Bimonthly Reports" (P.O. Box 731, Postal Station "A", Toronto).
3. For representative examples see Donald Gutstein, *Vancouver Ltd.* (Toronto: James Lorimer, 1975) p. 102-10 and John Sewell, *Up Against City Hall* (Toronto: James Lorimer, 1972).
4. This report was later published as Peter Spurr, *Land and Urban Development: A preliminary study* (Toronto: James Lorimer, 1976).

Chapter 1

1. Headway Corporation Limited, *Annual Report* 1974 through 1976.
2. Peter Spurr, *Land and Urban Development: A preliminary study* (Toronto: James Lorimer, 1976), p. 204.
3. Ira Gluskin, *The Cadillac Fairview Corporation Limited.* A corporate background report: study no. 3 (Ottawa: Royal Commission on Corporate Concentration, Supply and Services, 1977), p. 55-65.
4. *Globe Magazine* 4 April 1970.
5. The details of the company's history are recorded in S. B. McLaughlin Associates Limited, *Prospectus* dated 14 March 1972 and *Prospectus* dated 27 November 1975.
6. 1972 *Prospectus*, p. 4.

7. See Desmond Morton, ''Mississauga: An inquiry that never happened,'' in James Lorimer and Evelyn Ross eds., *The Second City Book* (Toronto: James Lorimer, 1977).

8. *Financial Post* 11 December 1976.

9. Ibid.

10. S. B. McLaughlin, *100 Million Canadians: A development policy for Canada* (Mississauga: McLaughlin Planning and Research Institute, 1973).

11. *Globe and Mail* 3 August 1973.

12. For a brief account of postwar housing policy see Michael Dennis and Susan Fish, *Programs in Search of a Policy* (Toronto: Hakkert, 1972), chapter 4.

13. Quoted in John Sewell, ''Where the suburbs come from,'' *The Second City Book*, p. 11.

14. Frank Lewinberg, ''Towards a political economy of urban land and housing: The Canadian situation'' (M.A. thesis, Massachusetts Institute of Technology, June 1973), p. 84.

15. Quoted by Sewell, *The Second City Book*, p. 12-3.

16. *City Magazine* vol. 2 no. 6 p. 18.

17. *Financial Post* 22 May 1976.

18. For Campeau Corporation history see the *Prospectus* dated 14 February 1969 and *Annual Reports* of the company, particularly 1971.

19. *Ottawa Citizen* 10 February 1967.

20. 1969 *Prospectus*, p. 10.

21. *Canadian Real Estate Annual*, entries for Campeau Corp. for 1973 through 1976.

22. *Ottawa Journal* 1 December 1975.

23. *City Magazine* vol. 3 no. 6 p. 32ff.

24. James Lorimer, *A Citizen's Guide to City Politics* (Toronto: James Lorimer, 1972) p. 100-1.

25. This account is based on Ruben Bellan, ''Report and Recommendations of the Winnipeg Land Prices Inquiry Commission,'' (Winnipeg: Queen's Printer, 1977). Bellan does not actually name Simkin or any of the other Winnipeg entrepreneurs in his histories of their companies.

26. For details on this project, see *London Free Press* 6, 14, 15, 16 July 1974, 10 September 1974, 21 July 1976, 24 March 1977.

27. Henry Aubin, *City for Sale* (Montreal, L'Etincelle/Lorimer, 1977).

28. Robert Collier, *Contemporary Cathedrals* (Montreal: Harvest House, 1975).

29. *Globe and Mail* 21 September 1976.

Chapter 2

1. Oliver Marriott, *The Property Boom* (London: Pan Books, 1969), p. 223ff.

2. *Globe and Mail* 3 August 1973.

3.   See the fascinating history of this project in William Zeckendorf, *The Autobiography of William Zeckendorf* (New York: Holt, Rinehart and Winston, 1970), chapters 14 and 15.

4.   Trizec Corporation Ltd., *Annual Report* 1975.

5.   Robert Collier, *Contemporary Cathedrals* (Montreal: Harvest House, 1975) p. 193n., p. 13.

6.   Marriott, *The Property Boom*, p. 234-5.

7.   Ibid.

8.   *Toronto Telegram* 16 June 1970.

9.   Ibid.

10.   *Globe and Mail* 27 December 1975.

11.   *Halifax Mail-Star* 24 August 1960.

12.   Collier, *Contemporary Cathedrals*, p. 9ff.

13.   *Financial Post* 10 August 1971.

14.   *Financial Post* 26 October 1974.

15.   *Toronto Telegram* 16 June 1970.

16.   Ibid.

17.   *Financial Post* 21 November 1970.

18.   *Toronto Telegram* 1 March 1971.

19.   *Globe and Mail* 22 July 1972.

20.   *Globe and Mail* 9 June 1974.

21.   *Executive* magazine June 1976.

22.   *Toronto Star* 6 December 1975.

23.   *Globe and Mail*, 9 December 1975.

24.   *Globe and Mail* 27 April 1976 and 9 June 1976.

25.   Ibid.

26.   James Lorimer and Evelyn Ross eds., *The Second City Book* (Toronto: James Lorimer, 1977) p. 106ff.

27.   Cadillac Fairview Corporation Limited, *Annual Report* 1977.

28.   Cadillac Development Corporation Limited, *Prospectus* dated 19 January 1971.

29.   *Globe and Mail* 5 January 1972.

30.   *Globe and Mail* 14 May 1968.

31.   For a description of Fairview as of 1974, see press release "Statement from the Fairview Corporation of Canada Limited, Canadian Equity & Development Company Limited and Cadillac Development Corporation Limited" datelined Toronto, 22 February 1974.

32.   This assembly has been described by Brian Magee who took part in it and who is now president of A. E. LePage Ltd., Canada's largest real estate broking firm.

33.   "Statement" dated 22 February 1974.

34.   Cadillac 1971 *Prospectus*, p. 6.

35.   *Financial Post* 2 March 1974, 25 May 1974; *Globe and Mail* 24 May 1974, 31 May 1974; *Toronto Star* 23 May 1974, 1 June 1974.

36.   Ira Gluskin, *The Cadillac Fairview Corporation Limited. A corporate background report: study no. 3* (Ottawa: Royal Commission on Corporate

Concentration, Supply and Services, 1977), pp. 25-7. This study of Cadillac Fairview is written by an investment analyst who professes undisguised admiration for Cadillac Fairview and its senior executives, and it has to be read with a thorough knowledge of industry terminology in order to understand fully what it is saying. Gluskin had access to information about Cadillac Fairview not usually available to outsiders, and his analysis brings to light a number of interesting aspects of the company. It is not uncritical, and Gluskin's viewpoint is quite an independent one. Extensive use of some of the information provided by Gluskin is made in Part II of this book.

37. Cadillac Fairview, *Annual Report* 1977.
38. *City Magazine* vol. 3 no. 2 p. 10.
39. *Globe and Mail* 26 October 1976.
40. On Genstar's history in Canada see Henry Aubin, *City for Sale* (Montreal: L'Etincelle/Lorimer, 1977), chapter 7 p. 179ff.; "Report of the Preliminary Investigation on Activities of Genstar Limited," prepared by the City of Calgary by Burnet Duckworth Palmer Tomblin & O'Donoghue and Laventhol Krekstein Horwath & Horwath (Calgary: City of Calgary, December 1973); Donald Gutstein, "Genstar: Portrait of a conglomerate developer," in *The Second City Book* pp. 122-30; and Frank and Libbie Park, *Anatomy of Big Business* (Toronto: James Lorimer, 1973), p. 155-9. The Calgary document, referred to in these notes as the Calgary Genstar Report, was public for a time in 1974-5, as the text explains but was later withdrawn from publication by the City of Calgary. The Parks deal with the early history of Genstar in Canada when it operated under the name of Sogemines.
41. Calgary Genstar Report, p. III-11..
42. Aubin, *City for Sale*, p. 181.
43. "Offer to the holders of shares of McAllister Towing Ltd. by Sogemines Limited, April 16, 1968," p. 12, quoted in Calgary Genstar Report, p. III-7.
44. Aubin, *City for Sale*, pp. 213-7.
45. Calgary Genstar Report, p. III-7.
46. Donald Gutstein and Bill Henderson, "Verbal presentation to the Royal Commission on Corporate Concentration concerning the activities and operations of Genstar Ltd.," 13 November 1975, p. 7, p. 11. Gutstein's testimony and the response of the commissioners are available in transcripts of the commission's hearings for November 13, 1975.
47. Gutstein, "Verbal presentation," p. 8.
48. Aubin, *City for Sale*, p. 200.
49. Genstar Ltd., *Prospectus* dated 15 March 1976.
50. Calgary Genstar Report, p. III-10.
51. Calgary Genstar Report, p. III-12-3.
52. Genstar Ltd., 1976 *Prospectus*, p. 10; Calgary Genstar Report p. III-
53. Aubin, *City for Sale*, p. 185.

54. Calgary Genstar Report, p. III-16.
55. Calgary Genstar Report, p. IV-10ff., Genstar Ltd., 1976 *Prospectus*, p. 10.
56. Genstar Ltd., "A submission to the Royal Commission on Corporate Concentration," 3 November 1975, p. 21.
57. Genstar, "Submission," p. 25.
58. Genstar, "Submission," p. 4.
59. Genstar, "Submission," p. 13.
60. Genstar Ltd., *Form 10-K* 1976; Calgary Genstar Report, Exhibit A. Form 10-K is an annual publication by Genstar required under U.S. securities legislation.
61. Genstar Ltd., *Form 10-K* 1976, p. 17.
62. Calgary Genstar Report, p. IV-18.
63. Donald Gutstein, *The Second City Book*, pp. 124-5.
64. Alan Christie, "Cement companies target for criticism about bids," *Winnipeg Free Press* no date 1976.
65. *Financial Post* 13 November 1976.
66. Genstar, "Submission," p. 34.
67. Calgary Genstar Report, p. II-1.
68. *Calgary Herald* and *Calgary Albertan* 1-8 October 1974; *Calgary Albertan* 28 February 1975.
69. This was done, for instance, when Donald Gutstein presented his brief to the Royal Commission on Corporate Concentration dealing with Genstar Ltd., 13 November 1975. The commission had a copy of Calgary's apology but, apparently, no copy of the Genstar letter detailing the alleged inaccuracies in the Calgary Genstar Report.
70. *Calgary Herald* 17 June 1976.
71. Donald Gutstein and Bill Henderson, "Submission to the Royal Commission on Corporate Concentration concerning the activities and operations of Genstar Ltd.," undated; Gutstein and Henderson, "Verbal presentation"; Genstar, "Submission."
72. Gutstein, "Verbal presentation."
73. Aubin, *City for Sale*, p. 196ff.
74. Genstar Ltd., *Form 10-K* 1976, p. 6.
75. Genstar Ltd., *Form 10-K* 1976, p. 12.
76. *Financial Post* 17 April 1976.
77. *Globe and Mail* 15 July 1976.
78. *Globe and Mail* 15 September 1976; Genstar Ltd., *Form 10-K* 1976, p. 6.

Chapter 3

1. Cadillac Fairview Corporation Limited, *Annual Report* 1977. All information on Cadillac Fairview and other developers in this chapter is taken from their annual reports unless otherwise noted. Dates used are the dates of fiscal year-ends, so as of 1978 for Cadillac Fairview means as of 28 February 1978.

2. Daon Development Corporation, *Annual Report* 1977.
3. Peter Spurr, *Land and Urban Development: A preliminary study* (Toronto: James Lorimer, 1976), p. 214.
4. Daon *Annual Report* 1974, p. 2. This explanation is repeated with minor variations in wording in every Daon annual report.
5. Trizec Corporation Ltd., *Annual Report* 1976.
6. The average rate for all corporations in 1976 was about 33 percent. The standard rates for large corporations are 40-50 percent. Statistics Canada, *National Income and Expenditure Accounts*, Fourth quarter 1977, p. 58.
7. *Globe and Mail* 9 December 1975.
8. Ira Gluskin, *The Cadillac Fairview Corporation Limited* A corporate background report: study no. 3 (Ottawa: Royal Commission on Corporate Concentration, Supply and Services, 1977), p. 184.
9. *City Magazine* vol. 3 no. 3 p. 32.
10. Gluskin, *Cadillac Fairview*, p. 43.
11. *Globe and Mail* 5 May 1972.
12. Gluskin, *Cadillac Fairview*, p. 17.
13. Lafferty, Harwood & Partners Ltd., "Investing in Real Estate Companies in Canada" (Montreal: Lafferty, Harwood, 1972). This report prepared for the firm's investment clients contains acerbic and in many instances highly revealing comments on every major land development firm in Canada. It is the best single analysis of the industry I have encountered.

Chapter 4

1. George Nader, *Cities of Canada* Vol. II (Toronto: Macmillan, 1976), p. 430.
2. Humphrey Carver, *Cities in the Suburbs* (Toronto: University of Toronto Press, 1962), p. 36ff.
3. Nader, *Cities of Canada* II, pp. 393-4.
4. John Sewell, "Don Mills: E. P. Taylor and Canada's first corporate suburb," in James Lorimer and Evelyn Ross, eds., *The Second City Book* (Toronto: James Lorimer, 1977), p. 18ff.
5. Ruben Bellan, "Report and Recommendations of the Winnipeg Land Prices Inquiry Commission," (Winnipeg: Queen's Printer, 1977), chapter 3.
6. Peter Homenuck, "Housing preference and perception study" (Toronto: Institute of Environmental Research, Inc., July 1973), p. 44. This study was prepared for Deltan Realty Company.
7. L. I. Bell and Jan Constantinescu, "The Housing Game: A study of consumer preferences in medium-density housing in the Greater Vancouver Region" (Vancouver: United Way of Vancouver, July 1974), p. 12.

8.   Bell, "The Housing Game," p. 20ff.

9.   Price emerged as a far more important consideration than a whole range of other factors in the decision by residents of a typical Edmonton suburb to buy there rather than elsewhere. See "A Review of Alternative Forms of Government" (Edmonton: Government of Alberta, 1977) appendix pp. viii-ix.

10.   Genstar Ltd., *Form 10-K* 1975, p. 6, p. 55.

11.   Abbey Glen Property Corp., *Annual Report* 1976, p. 24.

12.   Daon Development Corporation, *Annual Report* 1977, p. 11.

13.   Peter Spurr, *Land and Urban Development: A preliminary study* (Toronto: James Lorimer, 1976), p. 211.

14.   For parallel Ottawa data, see *City Magazine* preview issue.

15.   *Calgary Albertan* 27 April 1976.

16.   Between 1976 and 1978 CMHC undertook a land mapping project to show ownership of all vacant land around about twenty major Canadian cities. As of mid-1978, these maps were available for inspection in the local office of CMHC in the city concerned. Some analysts have suggested that they are not particularly useful because CMHC did not go beyond the first-order ownership information provided on assessment rolls to look for intercorporate linkages in order to arrive at a complete list of holdings of any single large firm. The Calgary Genstar Report discussed in chapter 2 contains a model map of land ownership carefully drawn to illustrate not only intercorporate linkages but less direct corporate relationships.

17.   Bellan, "Land Prices Inquiry Commission Report," p. 35.

18.   BACM, "Castle Downs Annexation Request" (on file at the Government Information Centre, Edmonton, no date).

19.   Bellan, "Land Prices Inquiry Commission Report," p. 37.

20.   *Canadian Building* October 1975 p. 15.

21.   Bellan, "Land Prices Inquiry Commission Report," p. 39.

22.   Planning department, "Housing in Calgary" Background paper no. 4 (Calgary: City of Calgary, April 1976), p. 23.

Chapter 5

1.   *Edmonton Journal* 4 September 1974.

2.   9 January 1973

3.   Ira Gluskin, *The Cadillac Fairview Corporation Limited.* A corporate background report: study no. 3 (Ottawa: Royal Commission on Corporate Concentration, Supply and Services, 1977), p. 157.

4.   Rhys Smith, "Director's report, Calgary Regional Planning Commission meeting, 7 June 1976 for meeting 11 June 1976," p. 2.

5.   There have been very few studies published of costs, profits and prices in suburban land development. One dealing with a number of Canadian cities is Andrzej Derkowski, *Costs in the Land Development Process* (Toronto: Housing and Urban Development Association of Canada, 1975). Some of Derkowski's data seems reasonable, but some of it is not.

For a discussion of this report, see my article "Housing and land: two sides of the story," in James Lorimer and Evelyn Ross, eds., *The Second City Book* (Toronto: James Lorimer, 1977), p. 48ff. Some preliminary cost, profit and price estimates are included in Peter Spurr, *Land and Urban Development: A preliminary study* (Toronto: James Lorimer, 1976). The cost and price information reported in the text I collected in the cities concerned in 1976.

6.   As of mid-1978 this study was still being kept under wraps by Peel chief planner Peter Allen. It was prepared by housing task force planners of the Regional Municipality of Peel in 1975-76 as part of the preparatory work for the Peel regional plan. In 1978 the planners were saying the study was incomplete.

7.   Sources for these servicing cost estimates are: Winnipeg, Templeton Engineering Co., "On the Costs of Land and Land Development," (Brief submitted to the Winnipeg Land Prices Inquiry Commission, 1976); Edmonton, costs for servicing the City of Edmonton's Mill Woods project; Toronto, the Peel regional planners' study mentioned in footnote 6; Halifax, costs incurred by the Nova Scotia Housing Commission on their Halifax-Dartmouth land bank projects; Thunder Bay, costs to the city in servicing its small subdivision underway in 1976; Vancouver, costs in Port Moody's Barber Street subdivision project. Servicing standards vary from city to city, and that accounts for much of the variation in the figures.

8.   Based on new houses offered for sale by Qualico in the Mill Woods area on privately developed land and by Genstar subsidiaries in the Castle Downs area, summer 1976.

9.   River Terrace development data from interview with M. A. Stewart, City of Thunder Bay.

10.   Data from price lists for Forest Hills project of Nova Scotia Housing Commission.

11.   Advertisement by Ontario Housing Corporation, *Globe and Mail* 21 October 1975.

12.   Central Mortgage and Housing Corporation, *Canadian Housing Statistics* 1971, 1976.

13.   *Canadian Housing Statistics* 1976, pp. 88-9.

14.   Templeton Engineering, "Costs of Land," appendix 1, newsletter dated 25 June 1976.

15.   Bellan, "Land Prices Inquiry Commission Report," pp. 27-8.

16.   Ibid.

17.   Ibid.

18.   The RHOSP is effectively a subsidy to first-time home buyers, and it has offered many opportunities for individuals in high-tax brackets to obtain housing subsidies equal to as much as 50 to 60 percent of their RHOSP contributions depending on their effective marginal income tax rate.

19.   17 June 1973.

20. *Calgary Herald* 8 June 1973.

21. *Executive* magazine July-August 1976.

22. Templeton Engineering, "Costs of Land," pp. 54-5.

23. *Calgary Herald* 7 July 1973.

24. Planning Department, "Residential lot inventory" (Compiled quarterly, City of Calgary, June 1973).

25. See for instance *London Free Press* 24 August 1974 quoting city report showing inventory of 1,676 approved lots; City of Winnipeg, "Brief to the Winnipeg land prices inquiry commission," p. 6, noting an inventory of 3,768 serviced and approved single-family lots as of 31 December 1976.

26. Templeton Engineering, "Costs of Land," p. 55.

27. Interview, 10 September 1976.

28. *Canadian Housing Statistics* 1977, pp. 12-3.

29. *Canadian Housing Statistics* 1976, p. 81.

30. Steve Jacobs, "Single-family housing no bargain in Winnipeg" (Unpublished article, 21 July 1976).

31. Michael Dennis and Susan Fish, *Programs in Search of a Policy* (Toronto: Hakkert, 1972), p. 125ff.

32. Paul Hellyer, "Why they killed public land banking: A political memoir," *City Magazine* vol. 3 no. 2 p. 31ff.

33. For details, see *Globe and Mail* 27 August 1976; for confirmation of non-impact of AIB on Cadillac Fairview, see *Globe and Mail* 19 August 1976.

34. *Calgary Herald* 17 June 1976.

35. George Nader, *Cities of Canada* Vol. II (Toronto: Macmillan, 1976), p. 160.

36. Calgary August 1975.

37. *Globe and Mail* 27 June 1974.

38. Interview, summer 1976.

39. *Executive* magazine July-August 1976 p. 43.

40. Rhys Smith, "Director's report," p. 2-3.

Chapter 6

1. Humphrey Carver, *Cities in the Suburbs* (Toronto: University of Toronto Press, 1962), p. 45.

2. Central Mortgage and Housing Corporation, *Canadian Housing Statistics* 1977, p. 19. CMHC does not report on the number of units in highrise buildings *per se*. The figure of 450,000 is certainly an underestimate, and is based on the assumption that most apartments in buildings of 50-199 and all apartments in buildings of 200 units or more are high-rise. There were altogether 1,128,127 apartment units in Canadian urban centres as of 1977. The maximum number which could have been highrise is about 650,000.

3. Carver, *Cities in the Suburbs*, p. 45.

4.   General manager, Metropolitan Toronto Housing Company Limited, "Cost comparison," 9 February 1977.
5.   High-rise construction in Toronto in January 1976 cost $22 per square foot. *Globe and Mail* 16 April 1976.
6.   Statistics Canada, *Perspective 1975* (Ottawa: Supply and Services, 1976), p. 256.
7.   Maurice Yeates, *Main Street* (Toronto: Macmillan, 1975), p. 125.
8.   *Canadian Housing Statistics* 1977, p. 19.
9.   Ibid.
10.   Michael Dennis and Susan Fish, *Programs in Search of a Policy* (Toronto: Hakkert, 1972), p. 183.
11.   Donald Gutstein, *Vancouver Ltd.* (Toronto: James Lorimer, 1975), p. 99.
12.   John Sewell, *Up Against City Hall* (Toronto: James Lorimer, 1972), p. 140ff; Gutstein, *Vancouver Ltd.*, p. 106.
13.   George Nader, *Cities of Canada* Vol. II (Toronto: Macmillan, 1976), p. 221.
14.   L. I. Bell and Jan Constantinescu, "The Housing Game: A survey of consumer preferences in medium-density housing in the Greater Vancouver Region" (Vancouver: United Way of Vancouver, 1974), p. 13.
15.   Bell, "The Housing Game," p. ii., pp. 20-34.
16.   Peter Homenuck, "Housing Preference and Perception Study" (Toronto: Institute of Environmental Research Inc., 1973).
17.   Homenuck, "Housing Preferences," pp. 20-34.
18.   Homenuck, "Housing Preferences," p. 43.
19.   Homenuck, "Housing Preferences," p. 35.
20.   Homenuck, "Housing Preferences," p. 68ff.
21.   Homenuck, "Housing Preferences," p. 26.
22.   Homenuck, "Housing Preferences," pp. 20-34.
23.   *Vancouver Province* August 1971.
24.   Yeates, *Main Street*, p. 33.
25.   Experience with condominiums as provinces gradually increased the amount of regulation of this aspect of the development business in the light of scandals and sleazy practices by developers clinches any argument about the necessity for detailed regulation of the development industry in order to protect the public interest. A random selection of horror stories for Toronto alone is provided in the following clippings: *Toronto Star* 20 February 1971, 9 December 1971, 30 October 1971, 15 January 1972; 7 July 1973; 17 June 1974; 22 January 1976; *Globe and Mail* 5 June 1974, 12 September 1974, 6 June 1975, 9 August 1975; *Toronto Sun* 11 August 1973.
26.   *Globe and Mail* 24 September 1976.
27.   Ibid.
28.   *Globe and Mail* August 1976.
29.   Burns, Fry Ltd., "Confidential memorandum, Victoria Wood Scarborough Brandywine," no date, schedule 4. In this typical project devel-

oped by Victoria Wood in suburban Toronto, investor returns are shown (in this memorandum which supplements the official prospectus for the project) to be at least this high.

30. *Edmonton Journal* 15 June 1977.
31. H. B. Mayo, *Report of the Ottawa-Carleton Review Commission* (Toronto: Government of Ontario, October 1976), p. 225.
32. *Calgary Herald* 29 January 1977.

Chapter 7

1. Oliver Marriott, *The Property Boom* (London: Pan Books, 1969), p. 224.
2. Service de l'Habitation et de l'Urbanisme, "Le Centre ville de Montréal" (Montréal: Ville de Montréal, 1974), p. 23.
3. George Nader, *Cities of Canada* Vol. II (Toronto: Macmillan, 1976), p. 214.
4. Planning Department, "Downtown development in Calgary: Inventory and prospect" (Calgary: City of Calgary, December 1973).
5. David M. Smith, *Industrial Location: An economic geographical analysis* (New York: John Wiley, 1971), p. 489.
6. Jack Oldham, "Don Mills: 'Today's new town'", *Urban Land* January 1960.
7. Nader, *Cities of Canada* II, p. 346.
8. *Guide to Industrial Parks and Area Development* 1970-71, Princeton, N.J.
9. W. N. Kinnard and S. D. Messner, *Industrial Real Estate* (Washington: Society of Industrial Realtors, 1971), p. 534.
10. Y. S. Cohen and B. J. Berry, "Spatial components of manufacturing change" (Chicago: Department of Geography, University of Chicago, 1975), p. 42.
11. Robert E. Boley, *Technical Bulletin* #41, Urban Land Institute.
12. Cohen, "Spatial components," p. 38.
13. For a brief summary of Ray's views see Paul Phillips, *Regional Disparities* (Toronto: James Lorimer, 1978).
14. For more details on this matter see Phillips, *Regional Disparities*, chapter 1.
15. S. P. Walsh, "Twelve common mistakes in industrial land development" *Urban Land* June 1963, p. 1.
16. *Guide to Industrial Parks* 1970-71, p. 10.
17. *Industrial Development and Manufacturers Record*, March/April 1970, p. 10.
18. Kinnard, *Industrial Real Estate*, p. 572.
19. A. E. LePage, "Real estate market survey: Toronto 1976," p. 17-9.
20. Greater Vancouver Regional District, *The Livable Region 1976/1986* (Vancouver, 1975), p. 16.
21. Matthew Lawson, *Jobs and the Economy* (Toronto: Metropolitan To-

ronto Planning Department, May 1975), p. 96, p. 99.
22.   Planning Department, "Housing in Calgary" Background paper no.
4 (Calgary: City of Calgary, April 1976), p. 19.
23.   *London Free Press* February 1976.
24.   Lawson, *Jobs and the Economy*, p. 20.
25.   Department of Development, "Halifax Metropolitan Area Survey
and Inventory of Commercial Space (Halifax: Government of Nova Scotia, March 1976)
26.   Lawson, *Jobs and the Economy*, p. 69.

Chapter 8

1.   *Financial Post* 20 September 1975 advertising supplement
2.   J. Dent Pigott, "Real estate" (Toronto: Burns, Fry Ltd. investment
newsletter, February 1977), p. 8.
3.   *Winnipeg Tribune* 10 December 1963.
4.   *Vancouver Province* 23 May 1968.
5.   Planning department, "Downtown development in Calgary: Inventory and prospects" (Calgary: City of Calgary, December 1973), p. 16.
6.   Donald Gutstein, *Vancouver Ltd.* (Toronto: James Lorimer, 1975),
p. 61ff.
7.   George Nader, *Cities of Canada* Vol. II (Toronto: Macmillan, 1976),
p. 138.
8.   Robert Collier, *Contemporary Cathedrals* (Montreal: Harvest House,
1975), p. 101.
9.   Economic research bureau, "Economic Montreal #8 Office buildings" (Montreal: City of Montreal, 1970).
10.   Development Department, "The downtown area — major development projects completed 1960-1969" (Toronto: City of Toronto, 20 May
1970). The figures are apparently for gross floor area.
11.   Nader, *Cities of Canada* II, p. 216; A. E. LePage, "Real estate market survey: Toronto 1976," p. 8.
12.   "Halifax Metropolitan Area Survey," p. 2-3.
13.   J. D. Spaeth, "Regional town centres: a policy report" Background
report for *The Livable Region 1976/1986* (Vancouver: Greater Vancouver
Regional District, November 1975), p. 52.
14.   William Zeckendorf, *The Autobiography of William Zeckendorf*,
(New York: Holt, Rinehart and Winston, 1970), p. 175ff.
15.   A. E. LePage, "Real estate market survey: Montreal 1976."
16.   *Zeckendorf*, p. 178.
17.   Maurice Yeates, *Main Street* (Toronto: Macmillan, 1975), p. 172.
18.   Spaeth, "Regional town centres," p. 7ff.
19.   *Canadian Building* August 1975.
20.   *Office Equipment and Methods* November 1975.

Chapter 9

1. Robert Collier, *Contemporary Cathedrals* (Montreal: Harvest House, 1976).
2. Collier, *Contemporary Cathedrals*, p. 26.
3. *Vancouver Sun* 10 August 1966.
4. Ibid.
5. *Vancouver Province* 28 October 1971.
6. *Vancouver Sun* 5 November 1963.
7. *Journal of Commerce Weekly* 28 May 1968.
8. *Globe and Mail* 21 May 1968.
9. *Vancouver Sun* n.d. 1973.
10. *Vancouver Sun* 15 January 1972.
11. *Vancouver Sun* 10 August 1966.
12. "Draft agreement approved at joint meeting 13 February, 1963," City of Saskatoon.
13. *Saskatoon Star-Phoenix* 30 July 1970.
14. *Saskatoon Star-Phoenix* 8 December 1971.
15. "Winnipeg and Trizec: Giving it all away," in James Lorimer and Evelyn Ross, eds., *The Second City Book* (Toronto: James Lorimer, 1977), p. 106ff.
16. Ibid., p. 113.
17. This account is based on an excellent three-part series of articles by Don Gibb and Dave Scott, *London Free Press* 20-22 September 1975.
18. *London Free Press* 28 October 1976.
19. *Globe and Mail* 10 December 1975.
20. Collier, *Contemporary Cathedrals*, p. 24.
21. *Vancouver Sun* 29 October 1971.

Chapter 10

1. *Vancouver Sun* 12 January 1977.
2. Statistics Canada, "Shopping Centres in Canada 1951-1973" (Ottawa: Statistics Canada, Catalogue 63-527, 1976). Industry analysts do not consider the Statistics Canada data very reliable, and where there are alternative industry sources I have used them. Statistics Canada's publication has nothing to say about a key subject: rent paid by shopping centre tenants.
3. *Globe and Mail* 27 December 1975. I have made extensive use of this excellent long article on shopping centres by Graham Fraser in this chapter.
4. *Globe and Mail* 21 July 1972.
5. *Globe and Mail* 5 May 1972.
6. "Shopping Centres in Canada," p. 9.
7. "Shopping Centres in Canada," p. 46.

8. *Ottawa Citizen* 21 November 1972, 12 February 1977.
9. *Winnipeg Tribune* 6 November 1975.
10. George Nader, *Cities of Canada* Vol. II (Toronto: Macmillan, 1976), p. 216.
11. "Shopping Centres in Canada," p. 50.
12. "Shopping Centres in Canada," p. 52, p. 55.
13. "Shopping Centres in Canada," p. 55, p. 57.
14. "Shopping Centres in Canada," p. 24.
15. *Canadian Directory of Shopping Centres* 1975 (Toronto: Monday Report on Retailers, Maclean-Hunter, 1976).
16. J. Dent Pigott, "Real Estate" (Toronto: Burns, Fry Ltd. investment newsletter, February 1977), p. 8.
17. *Ottawa Citizen* 27 May 1973.
18. Matthew Lawson, *Jobs and the Economy.* (Toronto: Metropolitan Toronto Planning Board, 1975), p. 416.
19. *Globe and Mail* 24 May 1974.
20. *Globe and Mail* 27 December 1975.
21. "Report 1/6 of the Executive Committee of the Ottawa-Carleton Regional Council to the Council" (Ottawa: Regional Municipality of Ottawa-Carleton, 12 January 1977, with attachments); *Ottawa Citizen* 13 January 1977.
22. *Ottawa Citizen* 13 January 1977.
23. William Applebaum and S. O. Kaylin, *Case Studies in Shopping Centre Development and Operation* (New York: International Council of Shopping Centres, 1974), p. 39-40.
24. *Canadian Building* October 1975.
25. *Dollars and Cents of Shopping Centres* 1975 (Washington: Urban Land Institute, 1975) p. 216-221. Canada is treated as a separate region from the regions of the U.S. reported on in this document.
26. *Volume Retail Merchandising*, October/November 1975.
27. Applebaum, *Case Studies*, p. 78.
28. *Dollars and Cents* 1975, analyzing median rent figures reported for Canadian regional shopping centre mall stores by type of store.
29. Arthur E. Lasker, "Shopping Centre Leases are not non-negotiable," *Real Estate Review* Spring 1976 p. 116ff.
30. Applebaum, *Case Studies*, p. 88.
31. Applebaum, *Case Studies*, p. 87.
32. Applebaum, *Case Studies*, p. 32.
33. Applebaum, *Case Studies*, p. 42.
34. *Ottawa Citizen* 12 February 1977.
35. Victor Gruen and Larry Smith quoted in Applebaum, *Case Studies*, p. 84.
36. Applebaum, *Case Studies*, p. 80.
37. Applebaum, *Case Studies*, pp. 86-7.
38. *Toronto Star* 8 September 1972.
39. *Globe and Mail* 27 December 1975.

40.   Rents are reported in great detail for Canadian shopping centres in *Dollars and Cents* 1975, p. 214ff.
41.   *Dollars and Cents* 1975, pp. 207-12.
42.   *Dollars and Cents* 1975, pp. 109-10.
43.   *Dollars and Cents* 1975, p. 286 (capital cost information), pp. 207-8 (profit information).
44.   Ira Gluskin, *The Cadillac Fairview Corporation Limited.* A corporate background report: study no. 3 (Ottawa: Royal Commission on Corporate Concentration, Supply and Services, 1977), p. 110-2.
45.   Gluskin, *Cadillac Fairview*, p. 113.
46.   *Financial Post* 22 May 1976.
47.   Gluskin, *Cadillac Fairview*, p. 103.
48.   *Canadian Building* August 1976.
49.   "Shopping Centres in Canada," p. 42.
50.   "Shopping Centres in Canada," p. 13.
51.   "Shopping Centres in Canada," p. 50, p. 54, p. 58.
52.   "Shopping Centres in Canada," p. 25.
53.   "Shopping Centres in Canada," p. 38.
54.   "Shopping Centres in Canada," p. 45.
55.   "Shopping Centres in Canada," p. 42.
56.   *Globe and Mail* 27 December 1975.
57.   *Globe and Mail* 21 July 1972.
58.   "Shopping Centres in Canada," pp. 8-20.
59.   *Globe and Mail* 27 December 1975.
60.   *Globe and Mail* 27 December 1975.
61.   *Dollars and Cents* 1975, pp. 214-239.
62.   This calculation assumes that shopping centres captured the same percentage of total retail sales in 1975 as in 1973, a conservative assumption. The rent figure is calculated on the basis of 2.5 percent of estimated supermarket sales in shopping centres, 5 percent of estimated department store sales, and 10 percent of estimated sales of mall merchants.
63.   *Globe and Mail* 30 October 1976.
64.   *The Livable Region 1976/1986* (Vancouver: Greater Vancouver Regional District, 1975), p. 18-20.
65.   *Saskatoon Star-Phoenix* 30 July 1970.
66.   *Toronto Star* 8 September 1972.
67.   *Toronto Star* 22 May 1974.

Chapter 11

1.   Ira Gluskin, *The Cadillac Fairview Corporation Limited.* A corporate background report: study no. 3 (Ottawa: Royal Commission on Corporate Concentration, Supply and Services, 1977) pp. 55-70. I have not analyzed the financial structure of hotels as a separate development form, and developer profits on hotels which they own as income properties and (usually) lease to hotel operators are omitted.

2. This calculation is based on 1977 housing starts in the following cities categorized as high-price for the purposes of this analysis: Calgary, Edmonton, Hamilton, Kitchener, London, Oshawa, Ottawa, Regina, St. Catharines, Sudbury, Thunder Bay, Toronto, Vancouver, Victoria, Windsor and Winnipeg.
3. Central Mortgage and Housing Corporation, *Canadian Housing Statistics* 1977 pp. 67-8.
4. *Globe and Mail* 24 September 1976.
5. IBI Group with GVRD finance department, "Dollar burden of growth" (Vancouver: Greater Vancouver Regional District, December 1976) p. 2, p. 6.
6. Richard Starks, *Industry in Decline* (Toronto: James Lorimer, 1978).
7. *Globe and Mail* 3 August 1973.
8. Matthew Lawson, *Jobs and the Economy* (Toronto: Metropolitan Toronto Planning Board, 1975), p. 78.

Chapter 12

1. A number of issues which were fought in Toronto at this transition point in that city are recorded in *The Real World of City Politics* (Toronto: James Lorimer, 1972).
2. The selected bibliography by Kent Gerecke in James Lorimer and Evelyn Ross, eds., *The City Book* (Toronto: James Lorimer, 1976) identifies the most useful accounts of citizen group engagements with city hall.
3. *Financial Times* 5 August 1974.
4. Harry N. Lash, *Planning in a Human Way*. Personal reflections on the regional planning experience in Greater Vancouver. (Toronto: Macmillan, Urban Prospects series, 1976), p. 61. All references here are to the manuscript of this work.
5. Lash, *Planning*, p. 64.
6. *The Livable Region 1976/1986* (Vancouver: Greater Vancouver Regional District, 1975), especially p. 7.
7. For instance public land banks in Charlottetown, Halifax, Toronto, Thunder Bay, Edmonton, and Vancouver. For a comprehensive survey of public land banking in Canada, see Peter Spurr, *Land and Urban Development: A preliminary study* (Toronto: James Lorimer, 1976), pp. 244-361.
8. Very few Canadian public land banks supply a sufficiently large percentage of their local market to have this effect. Spurr suggests that Red Deer's land bank has done so. Whether Saskatoon's has done so is a controversial issue. See John Piper, "Saskatoon robs the bank," James Lorimer and Evelyn Ross, eds., *The City Book* (Toronto: James Lorimer, 1976) p. 192ff. and subsequent coverage of Saskatoon in *City Magazine*.
9. Ira Gluskin, *The Cadillac Fairview Corporation Limited*. A corporate background report: study no. 3 (Ottawa: Royal Commission on Corporate Concentration, Supply and Services, 1977) in an appendix entitled "Why the stock market does not like public real estate stocks," pp. 210-1.

Chapter 13

1. On the state of Canadian manufacturing see Richard Starks, *Industry in Decline* (Toronto: James Lorimer, 1978) and The Science Council of Canada, *Uncertain Prospects* (Ottawa: Science Council of Canada, 1978).
2. This thesis has been developed by Tom Naylor, particularly in his *History of Canadian Business* 2 vol. (Toronto: James Lorimer, 1976) and has been the subject of a controversy which has been carried on amongst economic historians and others. On the role of the banks and other financial institutions in Canada, the pioneering work is Frank and Libbie Park, *Anatomy of Big Business* (Toronto: James Lorimer, 1973). Much more information is found in Wallace Clement, *The Canadian Corporate Elite* (Toronto: McClelland and Stewart, 1975). For a more detailed discussion of the Naylor thesis in relation to the land development industry, see also Frank Lewinberg, "Towards a political economy of urban land and housing: The Canadian situation" (M.A. thesis, Massachusetts Institute of Technology, 1973).

Appendix

1. The documents are titled "Minutes. Committee re: removal of CNR downtown yards." Dates of the meetings of the city committee, sometimes on their own and sometimes with CN officials, are 1 August, 14 August, 12 September, 11 October, 12 October, 19 December 1962; 10 January, 29 January, 5 February, 7 February, 13 February, 21 February, 27 February, 23 May 1963.
2. "Minutes" 3 October p. 3.
3. Ibid.
4. "Minutes" 3 October p. 4.
5. Ibid.
6. "Minutes" 3 October p. 5.
7. "Minutes" 12 October p. 5.
8. "Minutes" 12 October p. 6.

INDEX

Abbey Glen 50,51; Calgary land assembly 90n; failed takeover by Cadillac Fairview 46; land assembly 89; takeover by Genstar 56
Accounting practices 67-8
Adams, Thomas 84
Affleck, Ray 184
Agnew-Surpass Shoe Stores 206
AHOP. *See* Assisted Home Ownership Program
Allarco Developments 25-6
Allard, Charles 25-6,261
Anchor tenants 170,187,196; and shopping centre design 201-202
Annacis Island 147,149
Anti-Combines Act 53n, 122,211
Anti-inflation Board 122
Apartments; annual profits 222. *See also* High-rise
Appraisal surplus 69,256; Abbey Glen holdings 56; Campeau 1968 21; Campeau 1978 23; Daon Development 25n,71; Erin Mills 45; McLaughlin 1971 12; McLaughlin 1977 sale 14; realization 70,70n; relationship to company break-up values 247n
Approval process: for suburban land development 91-2

Assisted Home Ownership Program (AHOP) 111,118n,120
Assisted Rental Program (ARP) 145
Associated Portland Cement Manufacturers Ltd. 48,55
Aubin, Henry 28,48,55
Automobiles: increase in numbers 188; key role in suburbs 85; public attitudes 244; suburban industrial location and car commuting 156

BACM: early history 26-7; Genstar takeover 26,49. *See also* Genstar
Balance of payments 225-6,233-4
Bank of Commerce 164
Bank of Montreal 184n
Bank of Nova Scotia 166,179; Calgary Scotia Square project 168n-69n
Banks: *See* Chartered banks; Financial institutions
Barber Street subdivision 106n
Baxter, Richard 192
Bay, The 33n,190,194n
B. C. Housing Corp. 246n
Bellan, Ruben 95n. *See also* Winnipeg land inquiry
Berman, Joe 41
Bird, Hugh 160n

291

By the same author

The Real World of City Politics (1971)
Working People: Life in a Downtown City Neighbourhood (with
    Myfanwy Phillips, 1972)
The Ex: A Picture History of the Canadian National Exhibition (1973)
The City Book (ed. with Evelyn Ross, 1976)
The Second City Book (ed. with Evelyn Ross, 1977)